HEAD & HEART

A Woman's Guide to Financial Independence

HEAD & HEART

A Woman's Guide to Financial Independence

Susan Weidman Schneider

and

Arthur B.C. Drache

with

Helene Brezinsky

Trilogy Books

Pasadena, California

PUBLISHER'S NOTE: This publication is designed to provide accurate and authoritative information in regard to the subject matter covered. It is sold with the understanding that the publisher is not engaged in rendering legal, accounting, or other professional service. If legal advice or other expert assistance is required, the service of a competent professional person should be sought.

Publisher's Cataloging in Publication

Schneider, Susan Weidman.
    Head & heart: a woman's guide to financial independence   / Susan
    Weidman Schneider and Arthur B.C. Drache. —
    p. cm.
    Includes bibliographical references and index.
    ISBN 0-9623879-0-8

    1. Women—Finance, Personal. I. Drache, Arthur B.C. II.
    Title.   III. Title: Head and heart.

HG179   332.024'042
                                               QBI91-315

Library of Congress Catalog Card Number: 91-65302

ISBN 0-9623879-0-8

For our mothers and our daughters

S.W.S.
A.B.C.D.

Contents

Introduction

Head & Heart: A Woman's Guide to Financial Independence

The premise of this book is that much financial advice for women must be, in fact, different from advice for men. Almost all money books take male experience as the norm— "Nothing is as Masculine as Money," reads one book review headline— without considering that women have different money attitudes and different financial needs.

Objectively, of course, money doesn't perform in different ways based on the sex of its owner. A hundred dollar bill doesn't know whether it's in the wallet of a man or a woman. But women often do different things with their money (and usually have less of it to begin with) than men do.

Being a woman has meant lower wages and the experience of what, at the lowest end of the economic scale, has come to be called "the feminization of poverty." In addition to generally earning less than their male counterparts, women have larger expenses for medical care, and they make up the overwhelming majority of single-parent families with dependent children. Also, because they live longer than men, women must anticipate the economic problems of old age.

In addition to these objective differences between women's and men's financial needs, women have been limited by simple ignorance and uneasiness. How many women were ever taught by their parents to balance a checkbook compared to how many were taught to measure ingredients when baking? And how many women, believing correctly that being moneywise equals being independent, have been uncertain how this new independence might affect their relationships with those around them—particularly with men. So, this book is about purse strings and heart strings.

Head & Heart attempts to show the ways in which you can learn to make wise money decisions sensibly, safely and self-protectively—without sacrificing your feelings in the life situations you face.

Some women in the 1990's are struggling, as many career woman are, to reconcile new roles with old attitudes; and many homemakers are trying to bring their new attitudes into old roles. Some women straddle both identities. It's tough for all. All of us today—women and men—are part of a generation in transition as we reshape our lives to take into account the new opportunities for women that have opened up in the past twenty years. The outer realities (more and different kinds of work opportunities; more and different kinds of reproductive options) are often both more visible and easier to bring about than the subtler changes in inner reality—that is, how we adjust to all this changes as daughters, wives, mothers and simply as self- respecting individuals.

How to use this book

As you can see from the Table of Contents, *Head & Heart* moves along two tracks. We've structured the book around the predictable life-cycle events which shape or alter women's lives: moving out of your parents' home, getting a job, marrying, having and raising children, coping with divorce, widowhood, and the care of one's own aging parents. In discussing the financial dimensions of these life choices, we identify certain essential tasks of self-recognition a woman goes through in taking control of her emotions and her money.

Woven through the fabric of the book are chapters that present the hard-headed financial information you want and need in order to use money in your life competently and successfully: buying insurance, negotiating a salary and benefits from your employer, renting an apartment, talking to your mate about a premarital contract, investing your earnings, dealing with the tax system, planning for your retirement, selling a home after your partner dies and more.

You can read the individual chapters or sections of *Head & Heart* that seem applicable to your present circumstances, and we believe that you'll derive fair benefit from the advice in each section. Or you can read the book through from start to finish—which we'd advise you to do at some point—because even scenarios which don't seem to affect your own life right now may come into play in the future, and forewarned is just about always forearmed.

How we came to write this book

Clearly, the two authors bring different areas of expertise to *Head & Heart*. Susan Weidman Schneider is a writer, magazine editor and lecturer whose special interests are women's issues, money among them. Arthur Drache is a lawyer and tax specialist who writes about personal finance; he is called upon both for expert testimony and to interpret money matters to lay audiences.

Head & Heart, which appeared in an earlier version in Canada in 1987, evolved over several years' discussion between two lifelong friends. The dialogue itself brought to the fore some of the solutions to women's particular financial challenges that this book addresses. Thus, our first thanks are really due one another. For the U.S. edition, our thanks go to Victoria Pryor, our agent, for her patience, persistence and tender mercies, to Thea Convissar for her invaluable help in preparing the manuscript for publication, and to Helene Brezinsky, who is responsible for helping to familiarize readers with the technicalities of current law and practice.

PART I

BUILDING YOUR
FINANCIAL WORLD

1

Single and Solvent

Music by Mendelssohn, orange blossoms scenting the air, admiring relatives on both sides of the aisle—the fantasy scene is the same regardless of class, race, religion or economic status. Men might anticipate careers or life patterns based on occupation or background or interest, but all women's adult lives are to be traced from the same pattern: marriage.

Despite this model for female adulthood presented to generations of women—that the main event would be a wedding, starring you in a long white gown, followed by a lifetime of partnership (if not bliss)—real life hasn't always followed the fantasy. While most women do eventually marry, they are marrying later than ever before. For example, the longer a woman stays in school the older she will be when she finally does marry; thus women's increasing commitment to higher education correlates strongly with delayed marriage. As of 1988, women under 24 were twice as likely never to have been married as their counterparts in 1960. All this is preamble to the news that even if they do marry somewhere along the way, more women are single for longer at the beginning of their adult lives than ever before.

Between women's own freely-chosen career tracks and what demographers have called the "marriage squeeze," realism would suggest that all women, despite the wedding music promised in the fairy tales, should plan on—and plan for — singlehood. Still, many single women have to deal with the often unacknowledged fear that if they actually plan for their own futures as single people this means that they are sealing their fate, and that they will stay single for life. While this is an attitude more common among younger single women, it's also true for a thirty-six year old woman we know who—despite an income of fifty thousand dollars a year— still lives with her parents' castoff furniture in a studio apartment and has never made a will or thought of herself as a financial entity simply because she isn't yet part of a marriage partnership.

Even if Mr. Right does come along, every index for a happy marriage predicts that a couple linked on an egalitarian basis— one in which she is not totally dependent on him for her support—will create the most satisfying marriage. So, taking your own work life and your financial future seriously does not necessarily mean that you are foreclosing the option of getting married. It just means you really understand that, contrary to popular mythology, economic dependency on a man can weaken your relationship with him, and that your own economic strength will buy you a measure of confidence and self-esteem if and when you do marry or remarry.

Some single women are not so much afraid that acquiring financial savvy would put the curse on any future marriage; they fear instead that developing a financial "consciousness" would be the equivalent of becoming stodgy and bourgeois and would somehow be inimical to the development of the appropriate carefree singles' lifestyle. But no one needs good financial planning as much as someone without a partner (or a large trust fund) to provide her with a safety net. In fact, such financial planning is *crucial* for single women, because they usually have no one to fall back on in case of emergency — for example, a robbery or fire that necessitates sudden major expenses, or a disability that eliminates any income for six months.

For those women who grew up believing that there would always be someone to share in life's major decisions, financial and otherwise, the biggest task of adult life is to separate themselves from those who have helped make decisions for them in the past (usually their parents). Women then have to learn both how to take charge of their own economic lives, and to treat the venture seriously as a permanent part of the equipment for facing life. And just as many single women are realizing that they don't have to put off buying a food processor or a gorgeous set of table linens until they have a wedding date to legitimize the purchase, so too are they coming to understand that they are entitled to do their own, independent financial planning as soon as they are self-supporting. This usually happens right after high school or college, although for some women (those whose lengthy postgraduate careers may be underwritten by their parents), financial planning won't start until they're in their mid-twenties.

In some families, the loosening of economic bonds comes as soon as a child earns more than just pin money; she is then expected to pay for part of all of her education. Other families are offended if a child offers to pay room and board, taking this as an attack on the family's solidarity or the parents' ability to provide adequately for their offspring. In still other families, as one woman put it, "they expect to be scrimping and paying for my education even if I decide to stay in graduate school forever!" We present these situations to remind you that money—especially money you earn yourself—has meaning beyond its simple buying power. It carries with it also the power to make you see yourself and to have others see you in a newly strong and independent way. (For information on earning what you're worth, see Chapter 2, "Women in the Workplace.")

Regardless of the age at which you actually establish relative financial independence, the financial "tasks" faced by single women are essentially the same: outlining attitudes toward work and money; seeing even your first job as part of a financial continuum; negotiating in the workplace; planning for benefits, savings, retirement; how to raise cash quickly; how to decide who pays for a date. Despite the breadth of this list, there are of course specific issues for never- married mothers, widows or divorcees with dependent children. Remember to turn to the chapters "Modern Problems," "When a Wife Becomes a Widow," and "Divorce: Coaching in Battlefront Tactics and Strategies" for information on these situations. If you are a single parent, please see also "Motherhood: Financial Strategies for Women with Children"; if you are caring for a parent, please turn also to "Parent Care: The Child as Adult."

The Single Woman as a Consenting Adult

"It is in vain to talk of the rights of women as long as they are obliged to confess the supremacy of the other sex in so many ways. What spinster is there who has a few thousands, that is not obliged to call upon some kind brother, nephew or friends, to transact her affairs? It matters not what the capacity of her mind may be for business; her education, or rather her want of business education, makes her a child in these affairs."

—Hannah Farnham Lee, *Elinor Fulton, 1837*

In the century and a half since those words were written women have certainly taken more control over their own economic destiny. But especially for young single women, wresting that control from parents or others is, in part, a matter of educating oneself about money matters and, in part, a matter of proving oneself as a competent adult. In the move from young and foolish to single and solvent, women experience a shift both in self- image and in the way others see them.

Because parents sometimes believe that their daughters need them more than their sons do, or that their daughters are more helpless, a daughter's first steps toward financial independence may be read by her parents as a signal that their family roles are changing drastically—and what equals independence more than earning money of one's own? A first full-time job carries with it certain messages to the family group: that the daughter is now self-sufficient as an adult, that her relationship to her parents is now based on voluntary emotional ties rather than on the necessity of economic dependency, and that she can make certain decisions about that relationship— will she seek her parents' advice and use their advisers? Will she heed this advice? Should she?

This book is entitled *Head & Heart* simply because for most women financial and emotional issues are linked. In this case, what happens if you earn more than a brother or a boyfriend? Or more than your father? Many men are proud to tell of their sons' successes, but are embarrassed and "unmanned" when their daughters' achievements exceed their own. One father, at the head of a multigenerational manufacturing company to which he had devoted his whole working life, had stifled his disappointment when his only son, who had worked summers in the plant, decided in his teens that he wanted to become a doctor. (The mother, typically, was not involved in the running of the business at all.) When this father reached retirement age, he prepared with some sadness to put the business on the selling block.

But wait! This man also had a daughter—a highly intelligent, single woman—a very resourceful grade-school teacher with terrific "people" skills and a good head for everything she'd ever done. "Let me have a crack at the business, Daddy," she said somewhat lightly. Had his son evinced such interest, though he was not temperamentally suited to run the business, the father would have leaped at the offer. But his daughter's plea became a family joke—with no unkindness intended. The father sold the business to a stranger. The daughter continued to teach and now, five years later, looking about for a career change, regrets that she didn't make her bid more forcefully, that she hadn't had more confidence in her own ability to get the business management skills she'd needed to take over.

Another woman tells a remarkably similar tale. After taking a business degree in college, she went into her father's business and was extremely successful in running his complex network of retail stores almost single-handedly after her dad fell ill. He was delighted with her performance, and showed her off to his colleagues and competitors at every opportunity. But as soon as she approached, as she put it, "marriageable age"—in her family that meant twenty-five— her father became panicky that her business interests would interfere with her dating time or her marriage prospects, so he sold the business! How did she feel? "I would never have said anything to him. His intentions were good, and even though I was disappointed, I had to face the fact that it was his business, not mine."

One money dilemma applies almost exclusively to single women; that is parents who need to still feel wanted and necessary in their daughters' lives, give, or offer to give, more assistance than the daughter feels comfortable with. Sons are usually allowed more leeway; parents want them to grow up appropriately macho or self-sufficient and avoid "babying" them.

A particularly doting father tried to convince his daughter, who was moving away to another town to take her first job, that she should maintain her bank accounts in her home town so he could manage them for her, depositing her paychecks and sending her packets of cash by mail, since "she always had so much trouble balancing her checkbook anyway when she was in college." This parent had to be told "no," kindly but forcefully, several times, and in the end still could not quite see that what was to him merely punctiliousness about keeping bank records perfectly reconciled was, for his daughter, a sign that he didn't trust her with financial matters, and that he was trying to infantilize her. (In fact, this father had never even taught his daughter how to write a check, balance a checkbook, or any of the other simple but relevant skills that every junior high school student should learn—far more practical than the classic girls' home economics curriculum focusing on so-called family skills.)

Some parents simply don't recognize their daughters' money skills. One woman, for example, felt torn about her parents' insistence that she let her father or the family accountant prepare her income tax return. She wanted to do it herself so that she would have a real feel for what her earnings and deductions mean. Her parents were afraid she'd goof up, forget to take deductions she was entitled to, and complicate their own returns, which included reports on a gift of money the mother gave to her daughter. The solution: they agreed that she would prepare her own return a month before the filing deadline and allow her parents to show it to the accountant they share.

In fact, it's not such a strange idea for the young woman to use an accountant recommended by family or friends if she feels comfortable with him or her. Since it is never too early to begin to build up your own support system—accountant, friendly banker, etc.—talk to the accountant in question before rejecting him or her just because of the family connection. The task for any woman at this stage is to make sure she's being treated as a consenting adult, not as a child, both by her parents and by her financial advisers. If you feel that the good old family retainers treat you like a bumbling twelve-year-old, it's time to find your own counselors. But remember to keep open the lines of communication with your parents, if that's relevant, to make sure that you're working in concert with each other and not at cross purposes in your financial planning.

Many women (and men too) are the beneficiaries of family tax and financial planning which can complicate life for the younger generation. In one scenario Daddy has created a small company in which the children are shareholders but which he continues to control. Often the children must pay taxes because of this plan, but the income from their shares is reinvested in the business. They usually refuse to confront Daddy with the problem which has resulted as a consequence of his generosity. If you're an adult child in this or a similar situation, one way of dealing with it is to ask your accountant (if you don't have one, this may be the moment) to talk to your parents' accountant so that the difficulty you face as a result of the older generation's tax planning is spelled out, understood by all parties, and its difficulties alleviated.

The trick is to assert one's desire for independence gently but convincingly so that you neither hurt the doting parents nor cut off all possibility of ever going to them if you really do need their help. Sometimes you can have it both ways by saying, as one tactful woman did, "I am tremendously touched and grateful that you want to help me. I really don't need your help right now, and in fact I'm really getting a lot of pleasure from learning that I'm capable of supporting myself, at least modestly, on my own. Please don't ever take this as any kind of rejection. I still feel as close to you as I ever did. And I promise you, on my word of honor, that if I'm ever in need, or if something comes up that I think I'll need extra money for, I'll let you know right away." The parents knew that their generosity was appreciated, admired their daughter's "spunk" as they put it, and were glad to be reminded that she still saw them as "significant others" to whom she had promised to turn in event of need.

In the early stages of defining one's new financial relationship with one's parents, there's also the risk of a false or foolish independence. If you find yourself in desperate financial straits because of unexpected expenses, you don't have to live on rice and beans for months rather than ask your family for funds to tide you over a hard time.

Take the case of a woman who has not yet built up any financial cushion of her own, but who is presented with an opportunity to make a significant investment or to buy her apartment when the rental goes co-op. Should she turn to her parents and offer them a piece of the action in exchange for their bankrolling her? A parent could buy the apartment, for example, as an investment, and the daughter could pay rent on it. They could draw up an agreement where the daughter might share in the profits if they all agree to resell the apartment after a certain period of time, or they could agree that she had the right to live there as long as she wanted to without being forced out, or they could build in whatever provisions suited their particular situation (emotional as well as economic). The family as a whole thus gains from being able to purchase some valuable real estate at the "insider's" price, the daughter is relieved to know she won't be evicted when the apartment becomes a co-op, and each party would seem to be satisfied.

But all of the above presupposes a civilized and cordial relationship between daughter and parent(s). Often what looks good on paper is difficult to create in real life, because people bring to their financial transactions (especially those with close relatives) a good deal of emotional baggage. Only you know how much financial strain or input your relationships can tolerate.

Putting a Roof Over Your Head

For young adult women one of the most immediate and ambivalent issues can be the decision to move out of one's parents' home (or out of a college dorm or student apartment, a kind of extension of the postadolescent dependent phase) and into a room of one's own (or a house or an apartment—don't take Virginia Woolf's phrase too literally).

Living with your parents

With a modicum of financial self-sufficiency, some women choose not to leave the family nest, but to stay on, sometimes paying a part of the household expenses out of their salaries. This choice is made on the basis of cultural expectation (for example, in certain ethnic groups and in certain locales single women are still expected to live with protective relatives), financial need, lack of suitable and convenient alternative housing, or a need to be present for certain care-giving tasks—say to help care for an aging or ailing parent.

If you choose to live in the home of what the sociologists call your "family of origin" after you are reasonably self-supporting, try to talk out the new arrangements or alignments that might be brought on by your change in economic status. One woman made it clear that she would be installing her own telephone line in her bedroom and adding a sofa for guests, and expected some freedom to keep her own hours and her own company. She wanted to put her relationship with her parents on a slightly more formal, boarderlike arrangement, so that she would herself appreciate her new status, and not continue as the dependent child she had been. Any change in family dynamics is stressful at first, even a change for the better, and it took this woman a while to convince herself that she could talk to her parents in a businesslike way without offending them or rupturing the closeness she felt for them.

Our own backgrounds play a significant role in how we (and our parents) perceive these changes. Historically, for example, live-at-home working daughters of Italian descent would turn over their paychecks to their parents and be given spending money. In Jewish families, daughters in the 1920s and 1930s would be more likely to keep their own accounts, contributing a portion of their earnings to the household maintenance, but making their own decisions about the rest.

The key to making the transition from dependency to a more mature adulthood is to remember that you will remain your parents' child throughout your life (or theirs), and it makes sense at this juncture not to tear yourself away from them in any fashion that will leave ugly scar tissue. You will need them in many ways in the near future—for counsel, financial backup, and, if you are a minor, for their signatures on documents. Moral support from your parents might prove invaluable; if possible, don't leave home without it.

Renting an apartment

You're no dummy and don't need to be told to read the fine print on a lease. What you might need to be reminded of is the fact that many things are *negotiable* in that lease, as in many other contracts. Some people (mostly male) know this. Others (mostly female) do not. It can be so distressing to sign a legally binding document obliging you to cough up a substantial amount of money each month for two or three years when you're just beginning to feel comfortable with your own earning power, that just signing the standard lease can itself be unsettling. (One lawyer tells us that "there is no contract on earth that cannot be broken"—it's just that most women, trained to be good girls and play by the rules, haven't found this out yet.)

But listen to this true-life story to give you some idea of what you can accomplish financially if you can practice not getting butterflies in your stomach when you sign documents obligating you to make regular payments: A woman living in a fifth-floor apartment was shocked to learn, when she became friendly in the laundry room with a man living six floors above her (and hence in a more desirable apartment), that he was paying $50 per month less than she, though they'd moved in at about the same time. The difference? Her neighbor knew that apartments in that city weren't much in demand and that he therefore had a pretty good chance of making the deal if he seemed lukewarm about signing the lease at the stated price. He also mentioned that he'd be willing to forego a new paint job since he'd noticed that the walls were in very good shape, and figured he would be entitled to one in two years' time anyway under the terms of the lease. Such tactics won't always work, and be prepared to back down if you are willing to rent the apartment even at the asking price, but try to keep in mind that certain trade-offs are possible if you are bold enough to ask for them.

One popular and financially more reasonable way to have a room of your own under a roof that isn't your parents' is to share accommodations with a roommate. This becomes necessary especially in cities with high-priced and/or scarce rental housing. Despite the advantages, some problems do exist over and above deciding who gets which bedroom and who will do the grocery shopping when.

• If you rent the apartment jointly, make sure all names appear on the lease, if possible. That way, if one person defaults the other is not left holding the bag. This also means that if there's a roommates' dispute that can't be patched up, each party has an equal chance to keep the apartment legally, with no huge escalation in rent as might be the case if a completely new name were to appear on the lease. In cities where apartments are scarce, the person holding the lease is at a distinct advantage if the partnership dissolves.

• If you must give a security deposit (usually at least one month's rent in advance), it's obviously to your advantage if the landlord places it in an interest-bearing account. Try to convince the landlord to let you apply the deposit, or part of it, toward your last month's rent on the lease if you're moving out afterward. This will save you from being financially strapped when you take your next apartment and must pay security there also while waiting what may be months before your first security deposit is returned to you. Laws on apartment rentals vary depending on where you live, with considerable local twists. Check with the local real estate board or other sources close to where you live to find out about the fine tuning that will apply in your case.

• Whatever financial agreements exist between or among your roommates, spell them out in writing—not because you would necessarily go to court over any violation, but because writing down your mutual expectations and obligations will clarify them for all of you. Make sure to include an understanding about who will get left with the apartment in the event of default, bitter dispute, a move, marriage, etc. If your roommate is also your lover, all the more reason to make sure that emotional and financial matters are sorted out as best they can be at the outset of the living arrangement. (For more details on this situation, see Chapter 6, "Living Together.")

A useful, though mundane, example of money tangles we tend not to anticipate is the case of roommates and telephones. The classic irritant among roommates is that one ties up the phone for long periods of time. Annoyance aside, there are financial consequences. Remember that if your roommate runs up big long distance calls and the phone is in your name too, the phone company will hold you equally liable, and may hold you responsible for the entire bill if your roommate reneges on her or his obligation. While it may at first seem sybaritic or an absurd expense, consider a separate telephone in your name.

• Make sure that you agree on the necessity for insurance and adequate security measures to protect your property, your safety, and your earnings (for example, protection against a lawsuit from the window washer who tripped on that stack of books on the floor and broke his arm and was disabled for sixty days). For everyone, but especially for women at the start of their earning trajectories, it is important to purchase replacement value insurance for everything you own. If your two-year old television set, which cost $350 new, is stolen, you may be insured only for its depreciated value—what it would be worth today— that is, about $125. If you have replacement value coverage, you will be reimbursed the amount that replacing the television set would be today—that is, about $425.

And in this and many other circumstances, remember the word entitlement. You are entitled to ask questions, to be satisfied in every way possible with the financial arrangements you are making. Nobody is doing you a favor by leasing you an apartment, selling you insurance, or renting you money (which is basically what banks do when they make a loan or a mortgage).

Buying your own home

Buying—actually buying, paying for, owning a piece of real estate in your very own name—is something you do when you have a ring on your finger, a man on your arm and, usually, a baby "on the way," according to all the advertising. However, since owning the place you live in may be the smartest financial move you'll ever make, the choice should obviously be totally independent of marital status. It's usually a great investment, a method of enforced savings, and it can provide you with tax benefits.

Many tax advisers say buying your own home is the best possible investment. When you buy stocks or bonds, you receive your return in the form of dividends or interest, both of which would usually be taxable. When you own a house, your return is in the form of rent-free accommodation, which is not taxable. There are additional tax benefits to you because the interest on any mortgage you take out to buy the house is tax deductible, plus you gain the advantage of a "home equity credit line" at many banks—essentially a loan secured by your house or co-op with interest tax deductible. (See "Borrowing with Skill and Savvy," to learn how borrowing to buy a house via a mortgage can be a smart strategy for investment.)

Over the long haul, the value of houses in urban areas has been spiraling upward for decades. While there may be a few downturns along the way, so long as you are living in it and are holding it for an extended period of time (three to five years at a minimum), you can figure that you'll never be able to make a better investment than a house. Many sagacious women, in fact, are buying houses for investment purposes only (see "Investing,"). The only real danger here (aside from the risks entailed in any venture when the whole economy shifts down, as happened after the October 1987 stock market debacle) is that the kind of housing a single person might be willing to pay "top dollar" to purchase—an upscale condominium townhouse, for example—may not be as easy to resell as a more traditional "family" dwelling.

Home ownership by singles is becoming so commonplace now that in some cities whole blocks of condominiums and areas of townhouse developments, plus "gentrified" down-town areas, have become magnets for single people—and not just for affluent singles, either. The phenomenon holds true even in older city neighborhoods that might not have great or accessible schools, for example, and hence aren't so appealing to people with young children. But this very situation, which is likely to depress real estate values, can work beautifully for single women with no dependents, because they may find in these neighborhoods terrific housing stock at bargain prices.

Some cities hold auctions in which city-owned or repos-sessed residential properties are offered to the general public. We know a woman who purchased a wonderful old central city house at auction, in a somewhat seedy neighborhood that was "coming up," for about one-fifth of what she would have had to pay on the open market. (Remember, you don't have to live in the house just yet—you can rent it out, use the rental income to help offset the house's costs, and move in when you are ready, or when they close down the meat-packing plant up the street.) Not everyone will find such bargains, of course, but just being aware of the fact that home ownership is a possibility in your own life will cause your ears to perk up when the topic is discussed. This may put you in line for bargains, but it will certainly also make you a better-informed prospective pur-chaser when you go out to look.

Many real estate companies and banks are anxious to lend on the security of a house or apartment. You should bear in mind that normally they will lend you only a percentage of the purchase price—usually 75 percent—which means you still have to come up with 25 percent as a down payment. Most such companies, however, will be quite willing to talk to you about the amount they'd lend, based on the amount of your down payment and the amount you can afford to meet in monthly payments, even if you don't yet have a particular house (or price) in mind.

In some cases, especially where the sellers of the house don't need a lump sum payment (an older couple moving into a rental apartment, for example), the seller may be prepared to "give back" a mortgage at better rates than a bank would offer. This means that the seller would lend you the money to buy his or her house, in essence drawing up a private mortgage agreement between you.

Normally, if there is already a mortgage on a house, a buyer has the right either to adopt the existing mortgage or require the seller to get rid of it. Your strategy will depend upon the terms of the existing mortgage compared to what you can negotiate, as well as upon the size of the mortgage. If you need $75,000 to buy a house and the existing mortgage is for $16,000, you might as well figure on getting a new mortgage for the full amount you need, unless the rate on the $16,000 is more than two percentage points lower than what you'll have to pay currently.

If you fear that you'd never qualify for a mortgage, talk to a banker before you panic (and read Chapter 4, "Borrowing with Skill and Savvy"). Don't give up without investigating certain possibilities, including that of purchasing the home with someone else—a parent, for example, who might see this as a tax advantage in his or her own right, or as a way of making a gift to you to minimize a tax burden.

A single working woman of thirty, who was tired of living in rented houses and apartments, worked out a novel arrangement for acquiring a house of her own. Her widowed father, himself weary of maintenance responsibilities and eager not to live in a house that reminded him so much of his late, beloved wife, moved into a rented apartment and gave the deed to the family homestead to his daughter. She was delighted, gutted the house and made it feel like her own, took over the tiny and very affordable mortgage payments still remaining on the twenty-five-year-old house and everybody was happy. Her father explained to his two other children that he had organized his will and bequests to take into account the fact that one of his children had already received a substantial "legacy" from him while he was still alive (see "Wills"), so that in this case even potential sibling rivalry was circumvented, and all the parties were very pleased.

A less happy and more common tale is told by a woman of forty- two, who says, "Sixteen years ago I had the opportunity to buy the one-bedroom apartment I still live in for fifteen thousand dollars. I decided that it was silly to burden myself with ownership and the whole route of getting a mortgage, and later trying to sell the apartment if my life changed, just seemed like a hassle I didn't need. My whole life then was predicated on the certainty that I would be married within a few years.

"Well, here I am, many interesting relationships later, still single—only now without the equity in a co-op apartment. And now, to buy this apartment would cost me a hundred and fifty thousand dollars! What would have been the harm in buying even if I had gotten married? None! But my thinking was so deformed—as if my brain had been bound up by false notions of what a woman's life decisions should be, in the same way Chinese women had their feet bound!" Take this cautionary tale to heart and think seriously of the advantages of owning something if it's at all feasible financially.

Buying For Fun and Profit

"Whoever said money can't buy happiness doesn't know where to shop."

*—Needlepoint pillow in a
Madison Avenue store window*

Many single women may see the act of making purchases in short- range terms only. Women as a rule have been conditioned to view their "discretionary" spending simply as ornamental; that is, they will spend on clothing, costume jewelry, personal care items and vacations, but not necessarily on such invest-ment-wise items as art, antiques, "collectibles," hobby items or negotiable instruments (stocks, bonds, stuff like that).

Why? Again, because marriage was for so long considered to be the normative state for women that all major purchases were to be deferred until they could be made jointly with the person who was to carry them (and her) off into the sunset. Life wasn't supposed to get serious until then.

No more. One enlightened mother has told her twenty-five-year- old single daughter, "Buy what you really love right now, dear. You'll never be able to do it again. If you marry you'll always have to consider someone elses's taste, and if you have children there will never be the money to spare. You work hard for your money. Enjoy spending some of it." The lucky daughter who received this advice didn't take it to mean "permission" to buy $1500 worth of silk culottes, but rather made a policy of rewarding herself with a piece of art—sculpture or a print or a wall hanging—on birthdays, or whenever she needed a lift, or as a personal bonus for some achievement at work. After a couple of years she had a significant collection of objects she really enjoyed, found that she had an interesting "purpose" when she browsed in shops or galleries in her travels, and — the added bonus — owned something that was guaranteed to go up in value. The same cannot be said for designer shoes or fur coats.

Other kinds of purchases less delightful to look at than art include investments of a more traditional nature—stocks and bonds. Again, this is an area where women and men have had very different conditioning. A father might routinely invest money for his son, talking to him about the investments frequently, so that before the boy is even in his teens he understands the rudiments of the stock market. Not so for many women. One otherwise well-informed woman in her thirties tells that when her father died she discovered she'd been left some stock in a mining firm. She opened the stock market pages of the newspaper for the first time in her life, scanned the lists until she found the name of the company, calculated from the printed price that she was about $15,000 richer than she'd thought! Ecstatic, she called the bank that held the stock certificates, and, after announcing the great news to the bank manager, was told that what she'd read as fifteen dollars per share was, in reality, fifteen cents a share! She swore that she'd not repeat her mistake, but was mortified that though she knew how to choose an appropriate vintage Bordeaux from a complicated wine list, and read poetry in three languages, she had absolutely no idea how to read a stock market quotation.

The situation is more pressing for single women because, without dependents, they are likely to have more discretionary income to invest—no matter what they earn—than women who are married and/or parents. Also, having fewer dependents, they suffer a bigger bite at tax time and therefore could conceivably benefit more than others from tax-free investments or investments linked to tax-planning strategies. Plus, married women sometimes learn about financial matters by osmosis because their husbands talk about them, because their signatures might be necessary on some relevant documents, or because they are actually part of the investment strategy.

Wills and Insurance

While most financial planning for single women suggests that life insurance is unnecessary, this is certainly not sound advice for a woman with elderly dependents—parents or other relatives who are dependent on her gifts, cash, rent payments, etc., in order to make their lives bearable. For a single woman who may not be the sole support of an aging relative, but whose assistance is crucial (or whose time and energy is contributed in large amounts that would have to be substituted for by paid help should the younger person die), a relatively small life insurance policy should be part of the planning portfolio—or perhaps an annuity payable to the elderly person for a stipulated number of years.

Similarly with wills. Even if you have no spouse or children to leave your assets to, why shouldn't *you* be the one— rather than the government—to decide how your property should be disposed of? Of course the aging relatives could be mentioned, as might any of your siblings or their children. Your Alma Mater or favorite charity might be appropriate beneficiaries, and while you're alive you might like to know that your generosity will outlive you.

Special collections count, too. (Remember the art?) A single musician decided to leave her magnificent collection of musical scores to a university library and mentioned this in her will. She also informed the university in question of her bequest, and was subsequently treated very well indeed by the Chancellor and the Board of Trustees—including receiving invitations to gala events not open to the public. We're not suggesting using your will in any Machiavellian fashion to get kudos and perks while you're still around, but such things have been known to happen. For specifics on these topics, see Chapter 12, "Life Insurance," and Chapter 13, "Wills."

Charitable Giving

Not all gifts take the form of bequests payable only after you die. Working women are finding out what men have known all along: giving time and money to charities while you're alive has many advantages. You get tax deductions, you often meet interesting and/or useful people, and you have the satisfaction of helping a cause you are genuinely interested in (often a novel change from the kinds of activities you perform in your paid work.)

For single women, the special benefits here are enormous for all three reasons—but the tax advantage may be particularly appealing for a woman in a relatively high income bracket with no dependents. Just remember that to qualify for a tax deduction you must save your cancelled checks or receipts for any monetary contribution you make.

If you find yourself making a significant outlay of money (to travel out of town for meetings of the charity, for example, or to host a large coffee party for its members), keep receipts for all your expenses, which you may be able to deduct from your income tax.

Something else women are learning about charitable giving: when you make a contribution to any cause, you are essentially buying a vote and a voice in the way that cause represents itself. Volunteer organizations are not the government, and one person does not equal one vote. Some people are more equal than others. Contributions of time and money can gain you votes (or clout) to influence the course of a cause you believe in—for example, supporting women running for political office, or contributing to political and other activities that advance women's rights as independent beings. You may also gain access to local, state or federal politicians who may be able to effect legislation that affects you and other women directly.

Do remember, by the way, that the non-profit sector is one of the worst offenders in that ultimate put-down of single women: the announcement or invitation which quotes a price "per couple"—as if we all have to march in *a la* Noah's Ark, two by two. Protest this whenever you can—it delegitimizes you as an independent entity. And while you're at it, remember to inquire about ways of beating the "family discount" prices at community centers, etc. Ask if you can join with a friend and have announcements sent to one address; anything in order to qualify as a somewhat non- traditional "family" group or "couple."

Single Women/Single Men

"It is a truth universally acknowledged, that a single man in possession of a good fortune, must be in want of a wife."

—*thus opens Jane Austen's* Pride and Prejudice

Well, things have changed a great deal since 1813. And single women and men no longer relate to each other as if the object of every encounter were matrimony (or even sex). With the change in expectations and relationships comes a whole new set of routines for dealing with money matters. Etiquette guides are now rife with advice on how to manage a business lunch when the woman has invited the man, but handling these circumstances in our personal lives is still a bit uncertain.

Men, accustomed to seeing males in the driver's seat, literally and figuratively, sometimes feel that their male prerogatives are challenged if a date offers to split the tab or pay for the meal or the movie. And well he should feel thus. There's no such thing as a free lunch (except perhaps on certain well-padded expense accounts), and men have traditionally expected a woman to reciprocate in some fashion for the attentions (read money) they were lavishing on her. Being financially dependent on a man, even if only for an evening, a woman puts herself, to some extent, in his power. Sharing the expenses in a dating relationship can be a way of signaling that the days of male-as-earner/predator and female-as-helpless-young-homemaker-in-waiting are drawing to a close.

One doesn't want to see a date as a battle between the sexes. Quite the contrary. So the question arises as to how you can maintain your self-esteem without making the evening an awkward experience for both of you. We're in a transition period. Being "taken out" makes some women feel more desirable, while others go to the extreme of our friend who always goes "Dutch" and refuses to double-date with other couples if the other woman permits her date to pay!

Some women have found it comfortable to fix in their minds the rule that the person doing the asking is the person who pays for the activity. This works at the beginning of a dating relationship, when there is formal asking going on. Farther along, it's useful to simply reach for the bill or, if the man you're with is likely to taken aback, reach and ask, "May I?" (though this does strike the ear as a bit prissy). When on a dinner date, for example, you can always use this ploy: excuse yourself from the table, allegedly to go to the bathroom, and pay the tab before a dinner bill is even produced.

It seems reasonable that with big ticket items—a vacation or a ski weekend or a party jointly thrown for mutual friends—you talk things over openly first. There's no shame in saying that some plan is beyond your financial capability. Just say, "I can't afford it," and perhaps there's a solution without your necessarily being strictly on the receiving end. Women have a lot of conditioning to overcome before all of this is second nature. Now in her forties, a sophisticated single woman says that through years of fairly equal sharing of expenses with her dates she could hear her mother's words to her as teenager, "Of course men pay for things, dear, because what they get in return is the pleasure of your company." It sounded reasonable at the time, she says, but only in recent years has "pleasure of your company" conjured up visions of courtesans.

Personal relationships can be, in fact, intensely political. One independent single woman put it succinctly when she confessed, "Frankly, I'm afraid to get married because I see marriage as a loss of power. He'd probably expect me to quit work and give up everything for him." Obviously marriage need not be thus. It's worth repeating here: the best marriages are the most egalitarian—which means equality if not of actual income then of financial decision-making. So if marriage is one of your goals as a single woman, it can be argued that sound financial planning makes you psychologically better prepared for marriage, since you have some control over your own future. (See also Chapter 6, "Living Together," and Chapter 7, "Women, Men and Marriage.")

Between single women and men, as in every other area of human relations, money has a meaning far beyond the goods and services you actually buy with it. Seeing and understanding these sometimes subtle associations may affect not only the bottom line of your financial statement but the bottom line in some social arrangements as well.

Single Women/Married Men

Aside from the potential for grief here, there are also financial costs to the single woman involved in an ongoing relationship with a man who is married to someone else. The financial costs of an affair with a married man may be chronic: you pay for entertainment because he can't afford to; you pay because he can't have your dinners on his credit card bills; you pay because you're cooking for him because you don't want to be seen in public together. There are other, hidden costs as well—not just "outlay" expenses where you directly foot the bill, but "opportunity" costs, too. What does it cost you to not attend a career-advancing course in the evenings, or not to stay late at work because you want to be available for your lover when his wife's not home?

In a relationship with a married man that feels to you like a lifelong commitment, you have to face the painful realization that when he dies (and regardless of his age the statistics suggest that you'll outlive him) you will not only have none of the emotional support a widow receives, you will also likely not have the financial cushion of receiving a bequest in his will, unless he is able to mask his bequest to you as a remembrance to a colleague or some such arrangement. To protect herself, one woman who, in a classic scenario, had been her boss's lover for more than twenty years, asked him to purchase a life insurance policy with her as the sole beneficiary. A life insurance policy doesn't "pass through the estate," as the lawyers say, and so no one would ever know that she had received anything after her lover's death except the insurance company. If you make an arrangement like this, it's obviously to your advantage for the policy to be purchased in one lump-sum payment rather than in small monthly doses, both for discretion's sake and to ensure that you really will have a paid-up policy in your hands that's yours outright.

While all this may sound crass as we spell it out here, crass is the last thing you want to sound when you raise this issue with your lover. You could say, with full justification, that you feel the man's wife will benefit in many ways from his will, and that your feelings are deeply hurt that he hasn't found some way to make provision for you as well, since your relationship has been a significant one.

In Conclusion

The main strategic focus of financial activity for a single woman must be toward greater independence both from her family and from outdated prejudices about singlehood. Your goal should be a maturity of vision that will allow you to see yourself as a responsible adult even if you don't see yourself on a nonstop road to marriage.

Your financial needs are a little different from those of women at other points in the life cycle. For example, you are freer to take certain risks financially than women who are married or who have children to support—you must just develop the independent attitude and pluck to take them. To be single and solvent you have to look at your own life closely and analytically and determine just what your own desires are. The information here should help you choose your strategies.

2

Women in the Workplace

Paradoxically, two trends emerge simultaneously when we look at working women today. The first: women are now able to advance into fields—and into positions—that would have been all but closed to them a generation ago. In other words, women are moving up. The second: another population of women is moving down the economic scale—women who never expected to be poor. Women, especially women who are the sole support of young children, are the new poor, and often because of the urgency of their situation they must enter the lowest-paying occupations, with little chance of advancement. One out of every three female-headed families live below the poverty line.

The women moving up got where they are in part because of women's rising levels of education and a new climate, including the presence of antidiscriminatory legislation that helps to support women's progress in the workplace. The women in the latter group are usually poor because of divorce and the early conditioning women get that tells them (incorrectly, it turns out) that there will always be a man around to support them and their children. Saying that women are inadequately prepared to assume responsibility for their own financial well-being sounds like blaming the victim for her own fate. But along with an insufficient system of welfare supports for families in need, a woman's own lack of perceived options early in life is certainly an important factor in her financial struggles later on.

Women from both groups share an unfair rate of pay relative to men with similar education or training. Equal pay for women and men doing the same jobs has been mandated by law since the 1960's, but since women are, to start with, often in jobs which pay less than do "men's" jobs, there is still a "gender gap" in earnings. Despite the movement in the 1980's toward an equitable pay scale known as "comparable worth" (the attempt to raise the wages of jobs traditionally occupied by women), women on the average earn not quite two-thirds of what men do for similar work.

Regardless of whether you group yourself with those on the way up or those who feel themselves moving down (or where you are on the spectrum in between) the advice in this chapter will help you make more informed choices as you shape your earning trajectory—the path you'll take through your life as a working woman.

Ironically, while many more women are now working for pay than at any other time in history (more than half of women over the age of 16 hold jobs outside their homes), the circumstances of their working lives have not changed as radically as their numbers. More women than men have their work lives interrupted by having and raising children (no surprise), and even now, after newspaper stories about women firefighters and professional weight lifters and bank executives, ninety percent of dentists are men, while 98 percent of dental assistants are women; nearly 90 percent of telephone operators are women, while nearly 90 percent of telephone repairers are men, and so it goes. More than three-quarters of all female employees work in just five areas: clerical, service, sales, health professions and teaching, the typical pink-and white-collar ghettos for women.

Through the Looking Glass: Entering the World of Work

"Some of us are becoming the men we wanted to marry."

—*Gloria Steinem*

Since having an income is usually the first step toward self-sufficiency, we begin here. Assuming that you have some clues as to how find work, here are a few guidelines to keep in mind when you are interviewing for jobs or are facing such employment considerations as to whether or not to accept the first salary offer an employer makes to you, how to evaluate competing job offers (lucky you!), and whether or not to strike out on your own.

Remember to view every job as part of your personal employment history. Many women who came of age in the 1970's and 1980's saw from the start their training and job experience as part of a lifetime of work, rather than as a string of unrelated flotation devices. For others, this enlightenment was not so easy.

A just-graduated single lawyer was furious with herself, for example, after taking a relatively low-paying government job which, despite its financial drawbacks, gave her terrific contacts and a boost over the competition for her second job. The young men she worked with, also in their first professional jobs, saw the same liability in their small salaries as she did, yet were happy with the decision they'd made because they saw their work lives as part of a continuing path toward certain goals. Our friend, despite her parallel professional training, somehow didn't see herself as having a career *per se*, and for a long time couldn't get past seeing only *this* job and nothing beyond it.

We are not blaming women for lacking foresight or, sometimes, the economic confidence to focus on long-range goals. For many, especially women with dependent children, the dollar amount on the paycheck is justifiably the most important consideration in any job. But the woman who is now single, with no dependents, can afford to take a longer view, one that will benefit the shape of her career as a whole. With your work future in mind, understand there may be a difference between earning money and gaining experience. Remember that the average twenty-year-old woman can expect to spend thirty years in the paid labor force—so it makes sense to see your current piece of work as part of the larger puzzle, as part of a career (even if you're not yet sure how it will turn out) and not just as a job.

Despite the example of our friend the lawyer, many women report being more willing to make these trade-offs than men are, perhaps because women have had less ego invested in the size of their paychecks. Women start out with the grotesquely unfair handicap of earning, on average, only sixty-five cents for every dollar a man earns (though nobody charges women 35 percent less at the supermarket to compensate). What this means—the bad news—is that women have not been raised with the same salary expectations as men to begin with.

We are certainly not suggesting that it makes sense to take a job where you are being underpaid because you are female; just try to ascertain whether the "bottom line"—in this case your take-home pay—should be the sole basis for your taking a certain job. A woman in her twenties, not recognizing this fact, tells of changing jobs for a pay difference of five thousand dollars a year. "I used to work for a small academic publishing house where I had total autonomy and really enjoyed the intellectual stimulation of my job. But publishing in general pays very poorly, and non-profit publishing especially so. I began to feel sorry for myself, earning so little, and snapped up a chance to go to work for a large commercial magazine.

"The new workplace environment felt very oppressive—for instance, a lobby receptionist who sat behind a large bouquet of flowers and smiled at me each morning was paid to keep track, surreptitiously, of what time each employee entered the building. I recognized that this might be a perfect job, but for someone else. And I've now had my first taste of what 'selling out'" means. Not that it was bad to make more money—the money isn't bad in and of itself. But what I hate is to think that I am doing work I enjoy so little for a pay raise that seems insignificant in retrospect, since my expenses aren't that great at this stage anyway. I'd be better off doing work that's more challenging and getting paid a bit less for it or, better, figuring out how I could have convinced my first employer to raise my salary to meet the new offer—which never occurred to me at the time." You may have the luxury of considering at this point in your career what experience or contacts or other benefits a job will provide. But also keep in mind these points:

• *Starting salary*   Despite what we've just said about not making employment decisions based on salary alone, know that in any particular job, early money decisions do have consequences. Your starting salary will affect more than just your immediate take-home pay. Raises can be based on a percentage of your base pay. And if regular cost-of-living increases or holiday bonuses are based on a percentage of salary, all these will be greater if you have managed to negotiate a starting salary even a tiny bit higher than what was initially offered you. Even if this is your first paying job, you may have a special skill (for example, the ability to translate into another language, or to build cabinets, or troubleshoot computer problems) which, if called to the prospective employer's attention, might justify your request for a slightly higher wage than was originally offered. It can't hurt to ask, and your forthrightness at this stage might identify you as a person who knows the value of her own work. Some employers still believe that women work for "pin money" and they pay accordingly. Do your homework: find out what comparable jobs pay. Then you have some basis for negotiating your entry-level salary.

• *Benefits*   Be sure to check on the benefits that come with your job. Some companies discriminate against women workers in both subtle and overt ways. Traditionally, the fringe benefits offered by employers have been geared toward the needs of the worker and *his* family. Women workers have often been assumed to have protection for themselves (and their children, if any) through a nonexistent husband.

Some small firms may offer nothing in terms of health insurance or retirement plans. However, many larger companies now offer "cafeteria benefits"—which does not refer to subsidized lunches, but rather to a company's willingness to let employees pick and choose among certain benefits offered. An example: one recent survey reports that single women most frequently chose an extra week's vacation time over a company-sponsored life insurance policy. Another possibility for young single working women: you may be eligible for health or other coverage through your parents' policies if you are under 21, or are still partially dependent upon your parents for livelihood, or have a disability. Check this out—it may be cheaper to pay an additional premium on your parents' policy than to pay for separate coverage through your own employer. Then, if cafeteria benefits are offered you, you can select an alternative that you'd prefer.

You may find that buying disability insurance is a better bet than life insurance. This coverage will pay all or part of your salary if you are disabled and cannot work, solving a very real problem for a single woman who has no other source of financial support. If you have no one beside yourself actually dependent upon you for support, life insurance may fall into the category of a a luxury, while disability insurance may, depending upon your assets, be a necessity.

• *Pensions*   Pension systems have traditionally had biases against single women, with the underlying assumption being that every woman belongs to a family with a male head-of-household. The rate of pension contributions tends to be fixed as a percentage of employment income contributed by both employer and employee. Most plans carry with them additional benefits which may include a survivor's benefit if a spouse or child survives, plus life insurance and death benefits. Check the terms of the plan when you first meet with the personnel department. If you're single and the plan doesn't allow you to pass along these additional rights to a parent, friend or relative and doesn't give you substitute benefits or a reduced contribution rate, you're overpaying.

It's worth noting that the federal government has proposed stronger legislation to eliminate pension discrimination between men and women. However, there has been very little said about the continuing pension-plan discrimination that often exists between singles (of whatever gender) and married employees.

• *Raises (and subtle negotiations)*   Do you have skills from volunteer activities you can bring to bear in this job which might help you to earn a raise more quickly? And we're not just referring to that awesome moment in the film, *Private Benjamin*, where Goldie Hawn, when she hears about her new army assignment, reacts with glee: "Purchasing Agent! I can't believe it! The job I've been training for all my life!"

Your youth group or religious group organizing experience might make you the perfect person to help coordinate conferences and meetings, even if this wasn't one of the reasons you were hired as an office administrator. One woman who had run several successful charity parties as a volunteer used this experience to assume the role of special-events coordinator for a bank which had originally hired her as a public relations receptionist. If you haven't mentioned this on a resume or in a preemployment interview, there's always an opportunity to suggest yourself for some task after you are hired. Just do not make the mistake—in any job—of becoming the all-purpose enabler, so that you find yourself doing ten jobs for the price of one. Try to focus on one or two particular skills that you can bring to your work environment that none of the other employees can, while trying to make sure that these skills are recognized and paid for.

Remember to keep a log of all this "extra" activity, both on the job and in your community, so that after you've been on the job for six months and you go to talk to your boss about a raise (yes!), you have all the documentation at your fingertips to support your claim of being worth more than they've hired you for. An office administrator successfully negotiated a raise after pointing out to her supervisor the many ways she'd actually saved the company money in her first six months on the job: she had used all the skills she'd had to develop out of necessity as a PTA officer working with an absolutely bare-bones budget, so she was able to cut corners in the business world too.

• *Retirement*   Recognize that there's more to any job than how to dress for success. You also have to learn how to plan, network and cerebrate for success. That means taking your work life very, very seriously, because the consequences—in income and benefits now, and in savings and retirement benefits later—are very grave.

The value of money invested over a long period of time grows tremendously. Look at this example. If you invest $1000 at 10 percent interest at age twenty-five, this money, with the interest compounded (added into the principle each year), will produce $45,249 by the time you're sixty-five. If you postpone saving for retirement until you are forty, the same $1000 will only be worth $10,837 when you reach sixty-five! Put another way, at age forty you will have to put in four and a half times the money to get the same pension you'd have if you'd started at age twenty-five. The best insurance against having this happen to you is to try to plan for retirement as close as possible to the start of your working career (see Chapter 5, "Funding Retirement"). But if you are now forty or over, don't be alarmed by these facts—just begin now. As the Sixties guru used to say, "Today is the first day of the rest of your life."

Financing Your Own Future

Part of taking your work life seriously is being prepared for it. Since you and every other woman may well be in the paid labor force for many, many years, you might as well be doing work you enjoy, and work that's suited to you. Understanding perfectly well what she wants to do with her life, a woman who'd always loved looking after animals told her disapproving parents and friends that she thought six years' training in veterinary school was not unnecessarily lengthy. "Look," she argued, "I'm going to be doing this for at least forty years once I'm out—I should at least be doing what I've always known I want to do." She wasn't afraid that the possible arrival of the Main Chance—marriage—would cast a spell over her and immediately cancel out the ambitious person she'd always been.

If you are already in the work force and want special training or retraining, or if you want a general liberal arts education that you might not have been able to afford right out of high school but that would certainly give your career and your self-esteem a boost now, remember that there are many ways to do what you want to do educationally. And unlike high school, perhaps even college, the courses you take need please no one but yourself.

Some companies offer education loans for employees after they've been with the firm for a minimum time; others actually cover the costs themselves as a company benefit. Check these possibilities first, but if they don't exist for you, don't give up. Especially if you have regular income, you should be a good prospect for an education loan from a bank. Interest on this loan may be tax-deductible if you're taking courses related to your work; so may the tuition payments themselves.

Many colleges, universities and technical schools offer courses for adult students in the evenings and on weekends. Don't think it will be difficult to be accepted to these programs. Universities need the cash from such extension students, and may need high numbers of students enrolled in these courses to continue their per-capita government funding. You may be able to get credit from previous courses toward a degree, or, as a mature or "re-entry" student you may be able to use "life-experience credits" to reduce the number of courses you need in a degree program. This new twist—allowing older students to apply work or volunteer or travel experience toward a degree—will not only shorten the time you'll need to spend in school (if getting a degree is your goal), but will also cut your costs substantially.

As a woman you may qualify for special educational assistance programs. Check with your local YWCA, or women's centers. This is as good a time as any to connect with the feminist networks and resource centers that exist throughout the country.

Aside from full-time study in work-related programs, there are free (or reasonably priced) courses offered by municipalities, religious and academic institutions, and professional associations for which your employer might be willing to give you time off or cover the costs. The training you get will make you more valuable to your current employer and more marketable when you look for your next job. If you do pay any of the costs, remember that they may be tax-deductible as a business-related expense.

So even if your current perch in the workplace isn't where you'd like to stay, try to think of ways you can parlay it into something more, with self-development as your goal.

Special Situations:
Love and Money in the Workplace

Going into a Family Business

Consider the joys and the pitfalls of entering a family business when you are planning your career moves. The advantages are obvious: you know the cast of characters already and see their strengths and weaknesses better than most. This is also, of course, the chief disadvantage. The tyrannical father may behave the same way in the boardroom as at the dinner table. Male relatives may malign your competence because they remember your feeble tennis game. But the biggest hurdle, if you think you want to have a try at this, is usually to convince them to let you in in the first place!

While sons are often trained from lowly office boys or porters all the way up, the very idea of having a daughter managing things may make the boss feel as if he's failed to attract sufficient male talent. Here, more than in any other workplace milieu, situations vary from extreme to extreme. Some fathers are very supportive, while others are like the dad who took her younger brother to business meetings from the time he was ten years old, but refused to discuss a word about his transactions with his twenty-year-old daughter.

The most important first step is to make an agreement (in writing, perhaps) that you will start on a trial basis, with a reevaluation at some fixed point in the future—six months seems too short, but a year, eighteen months or two years are quite realistic. This way, you can exit gracefully if the situation is unworkable, and any initial objections from family members are defused—it's only a limited-time offer.

Be aware that however noncompetitive the relationship of the father and daughter (a relationship generally considered to be psychologically less stressful than that of father and son), daughters in family business are almost never considered to be in line for the throne. If you "wanna be a contender" as Rocky puts it, make your goals and desires clear from the outset.

One consultant who has studied family-owned businesses gives the gloomy news that "the big issue is the father's acceptance and not the market acceptance" of women in management roles. (Since mother/daughter businesses are still so rare, we don't yet have data on what those conflicts might be.) A recent study corroborated the experience of many women who have been disappointed in family enterprises—most fathers prefer to pass on a business to a nonrelative than to a daughter. And for single women trying to make it in a family business, being denied the ultimate goal—taking over from Dad—can be devastating, because there is no new nuclear family waiting in the wings to cushion the blow of being rejected or passed over by a powerful parent.

Interestingly enough, many fathers give active support to daughters who produce outstanding achievements in other areas, though they appear not to want to have them involved in the family business. When you look at the list of women who have made it into leadership positions in family-controlled businesses, you're likely to see more wives and widows than daughters. This phenomenon may change as more women (including, presumably, the daughters of business tycoons) graduate from law and business schools, those traditional sources of entrepreneurial talent.

Spouses Working Together

From the days of the classic mom-and-pop grocery store to the husband-and-wife team of stockbrokers or lawyers, being married to one's business partner has a long and dappled history. For some women, the situation "just evolved"—as in the case of a woman who helped her husband out in his convenience store and soon realized that she was working nearly full time; her consciousness raised, she wanted to be paid a regular salary as a valued employee rather than simply seeing her work as "helping out" her husband, the "real" worker. Another woman, a schoolteacher by training, gave her stockbroker husband so much good advice on how to deal with his clients that she decided to take some investment courses and join him in business; her earnings soon outstripped his, causing them to have to do a little balancing act in the kitchen, so to speak. After she became more successful than he was at work she found

herself deferring to him more and more in non-business decisions so as not to bruise his ego.

A third woman's story reversed this pattern. A jewelry
designer, she asked her husband, a lawyer, to help her out with
legal matters when she decided to go into business for herself
at home after the birth of their first child. From handling the
basics of setting her up in business (incorporating, paying taxes
and so forth), he became so interested in her work that he gave
up his practice to become her marketing director, traveling all
over the country, negotiating with everyone from suppliers of
raw materials to the stores who carry her finished pieces.

In each of these success stories of wife-and-husband part-
nerships, certain patterns emerge, both from empirical evidence and from the testimony of psychologists and others who
counsel working couples: complementary skills help keep
peace—for example, the jewelry designer loved to work the
materials with her own hands. Her husband loved to deal with
people and manage the "outside" aspects of the business. All
this is similar to the situation for any business partnership, but
with a relationship that doesn't end when you walk out the
office door, compatibility at work is ultra important.

It's also important to get down in writing what each of you
will be paid, and who owns what. (As we point out in "Women,
Men and Marriage," this is useful both in the event of divorce
and under the more happy circumstance of ensuring that there
are no buried resentments smoldering between the two of you
in an otherwise happy and stable marriage.) The most successful wife-and-husband business duos seem to be those where the
marriage has lasted long enough for the spouses to have gotten
the kinks out and to have developed a basic sense of trust and
of sensitivity to each others' strengths and weaknesses.

The frailest arrangement would appear to be those where
newlyweds try to start everything fresh at once—the marriage
and the business relationship.

There are other pitfalls as well for the husband/wife duo.
Some employers are still reluctant to hire a wife and husband
to work in the same organization. The flip side of this situation
is reported by women who say that their own achievements

were disparaged; co-workers thought wives were aided by the fact that their husbands worked for the same employer. Especially at executive-level positions, some women have actually quit their jobs, claiming that they were never given due credit for work they did themselves.

The Wave of the Present: Going into Business for Yourself

Rather than entering a workplace situation and having to conform to it, more and more women are creating their own work environment, going into business for themselves. In fact, one of the most striking trends on the business scene today is the growing presence of women-owned firms.

You may be the psychotherapist working out of a rented room in a shared office, or a cake decorator working in your own kitchen, or a woman who has just decided to buy an automobile repair franchise. Whether you want to go into business for yourself because you want to be near your kids or because in the corporate world you've bumped up against the "glass ceiling" on women's advancement, you likely share certain characteristics with other women entrepreneurs, who are emerging as a group quite distinct from their male counterparts.

First of all, they are usually relatively young—30 to 39, in contrast to men who start small businesses, who tend to be at least ten years older. Two attitudinal factors flow from this age difference. Perhaps the women are *de facto* a little less set in their ways, being younger. More likely it means that they aren't out to prove to somebody else—the world or their competitors— that they can succeed on their own. A younger man changing jobs or going out on his own is considered daring, an older one desperate. As entrepreneurs, women have a wider range of work options available.

A woman who is a successful investment banker, putting together financing deals for small businesses, comments that "women entrepreneurs want to do more with less. They're not like men, who think that first they need a big, fancy office or an expensive car as proof of how well they're doing. Women are not showy." As a result, they tend to manage their financial resources very well and very conservatively. With less ego invested in proving their instant success to the outside world, women probably pace themselves better when starting a business than men do.

And as a woman auto repair shop owner observed about her female customers (a point equally applicable to women entrepreneurs), women are more likely to ask questions; "men are more intimidated because they're 'supposed' to know all the answers already," she says. While only 2% of women entrepreneurs have had any formal business education, they're not afraid to admit this, and take management courses and business seminars whenever they can.

Some women in their middle years who are entering the work force for the first time may not even be considered by an "ordinary" employer. ("I had a terrific liberal arts education and was a 42 year old mother. Who would have hired me?" is the rhetorical question from a woman who today is a successful manufacturer of children's toys.) Yet these same women, by dint of having had very diverse experiences in their homes, as volunteers in their communities, and perhaps through a range of part-time jobs as well, are just the breed to be able to handle the diverse tasks that the CEO (Chief Executive Officer) of any company must have. These are skills more wide-ranging perhaps than those gained by a man of the same age who has been narrowly focused on one aspect of the same job for 20 years.

Anyone who goes into business for herself is not merely fitting into a job slot. Usually she's inventing a whole new role, especially if the business she's starting involves creating a new product, or a new kind of service. According to Rosabeth Moss Kanter, who has written extensively on men's and women's changing roles in the workplace (*Men and Women of the Corporation*, among other titles), women are better than men are at the "kaleidoscope" skills—taking many bits of information and creating a new picture out of them—and it's these skills, rather than just factual knowledge, that will characterize successful business people in the future.

Women are becoming the largest single group of new business owners. An estimated 35 percent of small business are now being started by women, and women's businesses have a higher success rate than those started by men. A recent study found that only 25 percent of men survived their first year in business, while 47 percent of women hung in there to financial success!

There are a number of reasons for women's success as entrepreneurs:

• Some married women business owners have the support of families—husbands, usually—who can provide a financial cushion during the initial hard times any business faces. This was the case for a woman who recently opened up a fancy chocolate store in an affluent suburb. She knew that word of mouth would help boost her quality product, but she also knew that until business began to boom (around Valentine's Day) she'd need cash just to meet her payroll and high rent payments; her husband had agreed to help her out through this period by providing an interest-free loan.

• For single women there are other pluses in entrepreneurship. For one thing, the very long hours demanded by any new enterprise (sixteen hours every day for two years, one woman claims) may be easier for a woman without a competing set of demands at home. And single women with no dependents are in a better financial position to take the risk than are people whose losses would be shared by others. The downside for singles is that unless your new business is intensely people-oriented you might miss the social interactions of a more traditional job. (Of course for a single woman with young children to support, the risks of business ownership may be too stressful; if this is your situation you might want to consider developing contacts from a secure job, and going into business for yourself when the children are older.)

• Women with extensive volunteer experience may have a distinct advantage in the workplace. While most men who go into business for themselves do so after a period of working for somebody else, gaining knowledge and business contacts, women entrepreneurs have often gone from volunteer work into the paid labor force in one step, turning their volunteer organization management skills into business management acumen seemingly overnight. "She could run a small country," said the friend of a respected volunteer who very smoothly made the transition from charity work into running her own speakers' bureau, "so why shouldn't she be able to run a business?" (The skills that made this woman successful in running her own business might have gone completely unrecognized had she been applying for a job to work for someone else.)

• Many women turn adversity into an asset. For example, banks in the past (and some, scandalously, even to this day) have been reluctant to lend money to a woman without demanding that a man guarantee the loan. (See Chapter 4, "Borrowing with Skill and Savvy.") The women who do get money from the banks have therefore had to be extremely well prepared to document their needs and their strengths, which in turn means that they have a clear financial plan for their business, a crucial prerequisite for success.

• Other women have elected to simply not open their businesses until they can do so without bank financing. A successful women's bookstore was originally a partnership of two women who chose not to borrow from a bank at all; instead they raised money from various other sources in the community sympathetic to the idea of such an enterprise. Similarly, the publishers of a women's newspaper decided to sell stock in the operation at $100 a share to its supporters rather than going to a bank for start-up funds. Obviously these tactics work best for "movement" enterprises, and aren't the sort of thing you'd be likely to try if you wanted to start an antique business or a consulting firm.

In the private sector, bartering may be the answer to the question of nontraditional financing. Before she had any income, an artist starting her own graphic design firm traded her collages for the services of both the lawyer and the accountant she needed to organize the business. These professionals were delighted with her proposal for the exchange, both because they admired her work and thought this was a chance to acquire it while she was still an "unknown" and because each of them figured on getting her paying business once the firm was on it feet—which is exactly what happened. Don't be afraid to try bartering; it never hurts to ask, and many women have been pleasantly surprised that other business people are just as eager for the trade-offs.

• Women do tend to be fiscally conservative, if not downright risk-averse. (See "Investing" for more on this characteristic.) Never having had much money to manage, women usually tend not to gamble with what they do have. Perhaps because women, who have traditionally been the ones to meet the demands of daily life for those around them, are indeed more careful about precious resources than men are, they therefore may make better managers for small businesses.

• Aside from the economic independence it promises, owning one's own business offers a very important advantage for mothers, who make up the majority of women entrepreneurs: flexibility to manage one's own time, combining both roles with fewer pressures and guilt than if one were in a traditional job. This flexibility is so alluring that it may provide a strong incentive for women to make the business work. Women tend to be more tenacious as entrepreneurs than men, and this may be simply because the thought of going back into (or going into for the first time) the traditional work world is too awful to contemplate.

Public Policy/Women's Wages

"If women are considered economic and social dependents in the home, they will continue to be treated as subservient in the workplace. If, on the other hand, they are perceived as social and economic equals in a partnership in the home, this will be translated into the practices of the workplace. Two issues must therefore be addressed simultaneously: the way women are perceived generally in society and the employment practices that affect women in any given occupation."

—*Judge Rosalie Silberman Abella*
Equality in Employment:
A Royal Commission Report, Canada, 1984

Women who work for pay often take service jobs that repli-
cate their role in the home; in fact men have even described their
their secretaries as "office wives," referring not to sexual favors
but rather the "enabler" function of the women they hire—
which says a lot about their opinion of their wives, too. Think
about it; even the professions which were once deemed the only
suitable employment for women who "had" to work (nursing,
teaching, social work) place women as helpers, performing
what was seen, usually by men, as a glorified version of
women's "natural" role. As a consequence, women were "ghet-
toized" in certain jobs, which made it easier for employers to
devalue and pay less for that work across the board.

Another result of the transfer of attitudes about women
from the home into the workplace was the idea of the so-called
family wage, an important concept in employment practices
since the early 1900's. The "family" referred to here was, of
course, always headed by a male. What this meant was that a
man was obviously the sole support of a dependent wife and
children and was entitled to be paid more than a woman, who
either was a spinster with only herself to support or working
for a few little extras for her family and therefore not really in
need of a decent salary. (The clear message here is that if men
do it, society values the work more and pays more for it.)

While these policies would not be articulated so blatantly
today, the atmosphere of inequality in the workplace that they
have created must still be addressed. The pay gap between men
and women may be created in part by the fact that more women
than men work part time (not always by choice), by their shorter
average experience in the work force or their underrepresenta-
tion in unions which might negotiate higher pay for them. But
clearly, negative attitudes toward women by employers has
been an important factor in keeping them segregated in lower-
paying jobs, discriminating against them in hiring and promotions, and just plain underpaying them at every opportunity.

Pay equity legislation, passed and put into place in the State
of Washington in the late 1980's and currently under consideration elsewhere also, is an attempt to right this situation. These
laws mandate that principles for determining "comparable

worth" be used to evaluate government jobs in an effort to adjust upward the wages of women in typically underpaid "women's" jobs such as secretarial work and nursing. How pay equity legislation and implementation fares in the next few years will likely affect, directly or indirectly, the earning power of every woman, so pay attention!

It is against the law to pay women less than men for doing the same job for the same employer. These "equal pay" laws are not currently in dispute (although some employers clearly violate them and female employees clearly have suffered from weak enforcement standards). The current debate revolves around the concept of equal pay for work of comparable value, obviously a much more difficult concept to objectify.

What's needed here, of course, is a somewhat complex series of evaluations, based on the training required, the effort the job takes, the responsibility involved and the working conditions. Since many public and private sector corporations already apply systems of evaluation in determining salaries and benefits, adding a somewhat altered point system for evaluating gender equality in the workplace should not be too difficult or alien a process. Nevertheless, as you might imagine, employers are very creative in their reasons for opposing legislation that would make sure, for example, that in a nursing home a woman caring for patients would be paid at the same rate as a man who cleans the building. Comparing the two, one advocate for pay equity notes that at present, "Both do heavy work, but the one responsible for caring for people is vastly underpaid. It's because the job is done by women and the jobs of caring tend to be done by women."

Whole sectors of the economy—child care being the perfect example—are undervalued and underpaid because they are women's fields; any kind of reasonably just pay equity legislation must not look only to adjusting women's wages against those of men they work with, but must find ways of penetrating those job areas that have been almost exclusively women's turf. Because of this traditional occupational segregation, equal pay must be seen from the perspective of "equal value."

Legislation to bring about workplace equality must include not only pay equity, but also an entire "affirmative action" agenda including recruitment and hiring practices designed to bring women into jobs heretofore seen as primarily "male." Union membership must be extended to include more women, and pension and other benefits need to include parttime workers (on a prorated basis). This last goal will affect women particularly since women constitute almost three-quarters of all part-time workers, and as such are not now adequately covered by workplace benefits.

Ironically, while union leaders have traditionally been progressive in their thinking on economic issues generally, and have in many cases gone on record to support pay equity, the whole package of directives to equalize women's roles in the workplace is often unpopular with union members. For one thing, the idea of affirmative action, which may be viewed as preferential hiring and promotions for women, goes against the idea of a strict seniority system, which has been the keystone for unions. For another, the union rank and file is unlikely to be willing to put their jobs on the line for the other important items on the "equality in employment" agenda, such as parental leave or on-premises day care.

These are just some of the complex intertwining of policy items that affect the working lives of women today. And all of these must be in place, together with adequate and readily-available child care if we can hope to have a truly equitable and just work environment. Keep in mind that these issues affect not only younger women entering the work force, but also older women whose retirement benefits will be changed substantially if their salaries are brought up to par with men's in the last years of their employment.

To make these necessities a reality—that is, for adequate legislation to be developed and passed—women have to make their voices heard on these crucial areas of labor policy. And for women to feel comfortable with their own strength as earners (and spenders) in the economy means that they will have to learn to value themselves, and convince men of their value.

Nowhere more clearly than in the workplace are personal attitudes more closely enmeshed with political expression. It behooves all women to prepare themselves not only for financial strategizing on the micro level (how to balance a checkbook, negotiate a raise, buy a savings bond or start a retirement account) but on the macro level as well, by becoming informed about and involved in the legislation that will affect where women work and how much they earn. Especially since business leaders (inevitably male) oppose equal employment law vociferously (those in power being reluctant, always, to give any of it up without a struggle), it's up to women to be part of the countervailing force that will push through such legislation and to see that it is enforced.

Women Employing Women

This seems the appropriate place to mention the area where women most frequently act as employers themselves, and where the labor pool is usually one hundred percent female: the hiring of childcare workers, care givers for the elderly or household cleaning help. Not every woman will find herself hiring and firing on the corporate level, but the majority of working women hire some kind of domestic help.

Remember when you are hiring help that you have a moral obligation and a legal one to pay reasonable benefits for the woman you're employing. Social Security tax is due for any worker whose earnings exceed $50 in a calendar quarter; you and your employee are required to pay equal amounts of this sum, which is likely to total about 15% of her salary. You are also responsible for Federal unemployment tax on a worker who earns more than $1,000 in a calendar quarter. In some states you will be liable for state unemployment insurance payments also, the amount deductible from what you owe the Federal government, plus workers' compensation of approximately $250 a year.

You should also make explicit provisions for sick days and vacations, spelled out in advance, rather than on an *ad hoc* basis. Make sure that you yourself do not fall into the pattern of undervaluing women's work that we decry in others. It's easy enough to see the need for pay equity legislation, for example, when it will favorably affect your own life, and sometimes harder to see inequities when they affect those we hire. Workplace justice, in this case, might well begin at home.

Social Relations in the Workplace

As women begin to move out of women's employment ghettoes and into work environments where there is more mixing of men and women, a whole new range of work place conflicts emerges. Aside from outright hostility and/or sexual manipulation that we know as sexual harassment, other more normal connections between men and women may prove difficult. Women may be moving up in the work force, but there are still hidden or even overt liabilities in their relationships at work.

Office romances seem to be hazardous to the economic health of women since the woman is likely to be the one fired if management decides to put an end to the coupling at work. Also, since power is appealing, a woman may find herself romantically or sexually attracted to her boss; again the woman is more vulnerable, since if the boss responds but the relationship ends the boss may fire the employee rather than continue to see her at work every day. In relationships between equally ranked employees, it's the woman, still, who is blamed most often for succumbing to the relationship when she "should have known better."

Women, in general, are thought to be more concerned about interpersonal relations, and therefore less single-mindedly task oriented than men are. What this translates into in the workplace is that women engage their co-workers in conversation, decision-making and consensus thinking. All well and good. But the same casual networking and friendly inclusiveness that characterizes many women's natural way of doing business is sometimes misinterpreted in a coed working situation, with men either imagining the situation to be more sexual than it is or with co-workers of either sex imagining a friendly working relationship to be an intimate or romantic one. One business writer has said, "Everybody loves a lover, but not in the office."

The reason we mention this in a book dealing with women and money is that women have suffered financially from being unaware of how their ostensibly (or actually) innocent office friendships may work to their detriment. First, if the other members of the "team" imagine a romantic attachment they feel excluded, and the team may cease to function as smoothly. Second, because if a supervisor feels that there is a sexual liaison happening or about to happen, he or she may feel it necessary to transfer or even fire one or both parties. So while a woman's intuitive sense of how to relate to people may make her, in reality, a much better worker, more sensitive to nuance and need in the workplace than her male cohorts, those same assets may be read as liabilities by her boss if they are unlike the work style of her cohorts.

Sexual harassment, of course, is something quite different from the kind of subtle misinterpretations of women's behavior we've just mentioned. At its most blatant, it is represented by the male fire fighters who tried to force out a newly-hired female fire fighter by scrawling sexual graffiti on her locker. They didn't like the idea of women on the force; "It devalues *our* work," one said. Or sexual harassment can take the form of overt sexual advances which carry the implicit or explicit threat that if the advances are rebuffed the employee will lose her job. Or they may be sexual approaches which border on assault by a co-worker who may have no status advantages over the woman employee, but whose advances are just plain unwelcome.

Many states have human rights legislation which specifically outlines the procedures to follow in reporting sexual harassment. Some jurisdictions will hold an employer responsible for the actions of his employees even if he did not know of the attempted sexual harassment. Others do not hold the employer liable. If you complain to an employer about sexual harassment at work, do so in writing, so that if it happens again you may be able to sue the employer or supervisor for having known about the situation but failing to prevent it from recurring.

Family Conflicts for the Working Woman

On the one hand there is the law firm where the children of the partners and employees come to the office if their nanny is sick, and the partners spell each other when they go off on maternity leave. On the other hand we see the woman executive who says she has a dental appointment when she's really going to see her child perform in a school play. She is afraid to tell even her colleagues, never mind her boss, the real reason for her absence, because she fears being perceived as less "professional" or less serious about her work than she should be. The specter of being relegated to the "mommy track"—the career path offering lower salary and fewer benefits for women who want to handle their parenting responsibilities personally— now haunts many career women. For a country that claims to consider childbearing and child rearing as a national value, ours has not produced what could be called a family-centered workplace environment. Notice, please, that nobody has proposed a "daddy track" so that professional men can spend more time with their children while taking a commensurate cut in pay.

Canada's Commission on Equality in Employment has made a pungently eloquent statement of the ambivalent attitude toward women, work and children. Its relevance to the United States is undeniable:

> *Many women find that their current or prospective status as a mother is a powerful factor on a hidden agenda affecting hiring and promotion practices. Some companies fear hiring young women who, though otherwise qualified, are potential childbearers. The prospect of maternity leave appears to inspire alarm in a way that training leaves, extended vacations, or even lengthy illnesses do not. This alarm is communicated throughout the female candidate pool and results in a form of psychological contraceptive blackmail. Women are often made to feel either that they should not have children or that, having had them and not wishing to offend the perception of career primacy, they should act as if they did not have them.*

For women coming back to work after an absence of years or decades, or for a woman with children who didn't always assume she'd be working during her child rearing years, the double burden of role-suppression inflicted from both sides is unbearable. At work she's supposed to keep her family life utterly hidden. (Studies show that women at work lead lives much more compartmentalized than their male counterparts—they rarely even put pictures of their families on their desks.) At home she's expected (or expects herself) to become Mrs. Wonderful as soon as she crosses the threshold. While the working Dad is entitled to decompression time as soon as he comes home (the dog or wife brings pipe and slippers, goes the cartoon version). Our heroic working Mom gets no such perks. In fact, she's bombarded with requests —nay, demands—the moment she arrives home.

This kind of role diffusion is for women only. Remember that nobody ever asks a little boy, "Do you want to be a father or a doctor when you grow up?" And the little girl with the temerity to want both doesn't know until she's grown up that there are no communal kitchens where the family can all go for dinner each night, no teams of women and men who go from house to house to help one another clean each week. We have the cruel duty of telling that little girl that the practical ideas for freeing women from the burdensome duties at home, put forth by early feminists from the nineteenth century onward (see *The Grand Domestic Revolution*, by Dolores Hayden, MIT Press, 1983, among other books) still haven't become a reality. Yes, folks, there's now a cure for baldness, but no progress on kitchen or bathroom design.

For "re-entry" women the issues revolve around changing the rules at home (and, if possible, on the job) to alleviate some of the stress. For two-career couples who married with the assumption that both would work, the stresses have more to do with negotiations over whose job will take precedence. (For more about the strains on the couple, and some suggestions for how to resolve them, see Chapter 7, "Women, Men and Marriage.") Trend-spotters are now commenting on the increasing numbers of professional and business women who, having worked like demons until their mid-to-late thirties, are asking themselves, "What have I bought into?" and are taking time out to raise families. Clearly, only a very small percentage of women can afford to put their careers on hold and to take the financial losses that such a hiatus brings. But think also, from the perspective of the nation's economy, how much went into training these women, and of how much more productive it would be all around to create a workplace environment that didn't cause these well-trained women to burn out. Wouldn't it have been better all around if they'd been able to combine fast-track careers and their family lives?

Women over 30 are four times as likely as men to experience breaks in their careers. When a man has a major career interruption it's usually because he has been laid off, whereas a woman is likeliest to leave the work force because of childcare responsibilities. As of 1988, according to the U.S. Bureau of Labor Statistics, 62.7 percent of women who were not in the labor force gave "keeping house" as the reason (compared to 2.3 percent of men).

The solution is not to cry out, as some dinosaur-age, right wing groups have, that women with jobs should return to more traditional roles and not work for pay outside their homes. Aside from the fact that one cannot turn back the clock and that two-paycheck families are here to stay, reducing women's options is hardly a creative solution to the problem. Women should not have to deny to their employers or co-workers that their families sometimes need them. If we are to be the flourishing and progressive society that we can indeed afford to be, we need to find the creative solutions to help women merge their roles with minimal role strain and maximum efficiency.

At the workplace we can create more on-premises childcare, including sick bays for children whose colds would otherwise have kept a parent home from work. And on the home front, not less important, we must showcase and give public praise to those egalitarian families in which the father takes on fully half of the child rearing and other domestic responsibilities so that working women do not have to face the chronic stress of working two jobs—one at work and the other at home. Perhaps if employers realized that they could get even more work from their already high-performing women employees if their husbands did more housework than the 4 percent on average that they do now, these employers (usually male) might go out of their way to sponsor courses for men on how to clean the bathroom, how to bathe a baby and so on. (In the interests of business efficiency we might even start a revolution in the home, a nice switch).

In Conclusion

Until very recently, most women have not had the luxury of planning their lives very far into the future. Women are coming to realize in many aspects of their lives, but especially in relation to their work and earnings, that developing a future-orientation is crucial. This planning encompasses:

- setting goals for yourself and not merely settling for meeting the expectations of others;
- being able to read your own desires in order to plan for appropriate work;
- projecting present earnings and benefits in order to make an honest assessment of what your needs will be at retirement; and
- being committed enough to the doctrine of enlightened self-interest to become politically active (as much as your overburdened schedule permits) on behalf off those issues which will affect women's bread and butter, croissants and caviar.

Freud once defined the two parameters of a person's life as love and work. The 1980's saw women beginning to invest as much of themselves in the latter as they traditionally have in the former. The 1990's are likely to be a decade where the issues affecting women's work lives shift from external considerations ("making it") to those patterns that merge self-fulfillment and appropriate social policy.

3

Investing: Sending Your Money Out to Work for You

Many women have a mental block when it comes to investing. A prominent feminist we spoke with told us she left such matters to her long-time cohabitant. "He likes it, he knows about it and I trust him." This from a woman who has spent a good part of her adult life working to ensure that women achieve equal status with men.

But her attitude is not surprising. For reasons which we can only speculate about, even well-educated, liberated women tend to avoid the subject when questioned about the idea of investing their money. In many cases, it is not that they are afraid to do so, but rather they feel that their ignorance about the subject is so all-encompassing that they don't know where to start. And no wonder, since until very recently women have had little money of their own to manage. It takes "excess dollars" to be in a position to invest, and most women who might be in a position to put their money to work for them may be either too new to having money (and too surprised by their own earning potential or good fortune) or so unfamiliar with investment options that they freeze.

One who froze, widowed in her forties, had to calm her hysterical accountant when he discovered that she had left $50,000 received from her late husband's insurance policy in a non-interest-bearing checking account for six months. She figured she might need the money, and didn't know that even if it were earning interest at just 6 percent, $1,500 over the six months, she could still keep the lump sum available.

Or take the case of Paula, a single, thirty-five-year-old physician making almost $100,000 a year. "I had the same education as my male colleagues—undergraduate work in sciences and premed followed by medical school, interning and so forth. Professionally I am doing every bit as well as they are in terms of earnings. But when we sit around in the doctors' lounge of the hospital, they spend all their time talking about investments. The truth of the matter is that most of my money is tied up in bank accounts and term deposits. I suspect I'm handling my money unimaginatively, but I don't know what else to do. And I ask myself, where did they learn all about money?"

While there may be no definitive answer to that question, it is likely that in many cases they learned about it from their fathers. Traditionally, fathers have talked to their sons but not to their daughters (nor to their wives) about investing, most notably investments in the stock market. In school, the chances are that the boys were more likely to take courses in economics and business than were the girls. And the fact of the matter is that in years gone by, the making and preservation of money has been primarily a male role. Boys grow up *expecting* to earn money; some girls are still raised with the outdated notion that there will always be a man around to provide.

Things have changed and continue to change. More and more young women expect to earn salaries commensurate with men's; many are taking business-related courses both in high school and college. And women are beginning to play a very significant role in all aspects of business, including investment firms.

But while the future may be brighter for those women who are now in school and are just entering the work force, the fact of the matter is that a lot of otherwise savvy and successful women have been handling their money poorly, sometimes from a lack of time but most often from a perceived inability to do better. Yet, at least a basic understanding of the investment process is essential to a woman who wants to be in control of her destiny. The vast majority of women will spend a significant part of their lives without a man, either through choice, divorce or death. But this doesn't necessarily mean they will be without money. (Indeed, on divorce or the death of a husband, many women suddenly find themselves for the first time with substantial sums of money to manage.) When she is alone, a woman will be faced with handling her own money wisely, which means investing it to achieve her financial needs and objectives.

This chapter will not make you an investment wizard, but it will set out the factors which you should be considering when you invest and will help you find sources of outside help and information.

What is an Investment?

One dictionary defines investing as the setting aside of money with a view to profit. While this definition may be technically accurate, we should point out that many extremely good investments are not made primarily with a profit motive. For example, over the years, home ownership has proven to be perhaps the best single investment which a woman could make. Yet very few people buy a home for themselves with the idea of turning a profit. Normally, they are anticipating the pleasure of living in their own home, even though they also know that in the long run, they are unlikely to lose money buying a house. (See Chapter 1, "Single and Solvent.")

Too many people view investing only in terms of stocks, bonds, real estate and the like. Anything you buy which is likely to grow in value can be fairly viewed as an investment. In many cases, money poured into a hobby is really an investment. Serious stamp or doll collectors often find that their collections have grown to be very valuable over the years. These collections can be turned into cash if needed, and the money put into them is every bit as much an investment as is a dollar put into the stock market.

A couple we know bought paintings by Hudson River artists over the years, often at very low prices. They bought only for their own enjoyment and rarely sold anything. When they decided in their seventies to move into an apartment, they felt that they had to get rid of some of the paintings. To their utter astonishment, they were offered ten, twenty and in one case fifty times what they had paid for works which they had lived with for years. The money put into the art turned out to be a spectacularly profitable investment, though they had not purchased any piece with an eye to its resale value.

A common statement we have heard from women is that they "have no investments." With the exception of those who are entirely dependent financially upon somebody else or who are literally living from hand to mouth, this is seldom the case.

For example, a bank account is an investment. Technically, you have loaned money to the bank, which pays you interest. It just may not be a particularly good investment for you because it pays lower interest rates than you might earn elsewhere. If you've bought United States Savings Bonds, you have an investment. If you are covered by an employer's pension plan or have an Individual Retirement Account (see Chapter 5), these are also investments. The difference between these types of investments and others is that they are investments which are geared to funding your retirement.

But the mere fact that you "have an investment" isn't enough. There are good and bad investments. Where things become a little more tricky is that what may be a good investment for one person may be a bad investment for another. In the next part of this chapter we'll look at the major characteristics of investments with an eye to what type of investment is appropriate to particular situations.

Income versus Growth

One of the first things to remember is that the profit from an investment can come in one of two ways. The investment may generate cash income or it may grow in value. For example, when you lend money to someone, you get interest back on the money you loaned. Eventually you should get back the amount you loaned as well. If you put money in a bank savings account, you might get 5 percent interest a year and you have the right to get back your deposit (the amount you loaned) whenever you want it. If you buy a one-year certificate of deposit (C.D.), you have a right to interest (which will likely be higher than you would get on a bank deposit) but you only get the money you loaned a year later. If you buy a United States Savings Bond, you get better interest than on a bank deposit but less than on a certificate of deposit, because you can get your money back anytime you want it. In each of these cases, there is basically no chance that your investment will grow. You'll get back exactly what you invested, plus any interest earned.

In most cases, the longer you are prepared to tie up your money, the higher the rate of return. For example, a five-year certificate of deposit usually pays a higher rate of interest than will a one-year certificate. Recently, with interest rates being so unreliable, the longer term rates have been almost identical to the shorter term ones. You will get more interest on a savings account that you will on a checking account since the checking account is a loan to the bank which is reduced every time you write a check. Some savings accounts will pay more if you retain a minimum balance (that is, promise the bank that you'll leave a certain amount in the account at all times).

At the other end of the scale, there are investments which do not and cannot produce any income. If your money is invested in gold bars, your coin collection, or a painting, no income will be paid on your investment. If the asset increases in value and you sell it, only then will you recognize your profit. (An increase of this type if called a capital gain.)

In between, there are assets which offer both income and growth potential. As a general rule of thumb, the greater the income generated annually, the less likely it is that there will be growth in value. For example, if you buy shares on the stock market (shares being a fractional interest in the company you choose to invest in), you'll have a choice between common stock and preferred stock. Preferred stock usually offers a guaranteed dividend paid regularly (quarterly, semi-annually or annually, depending upon the company whose shares you bought). Common stock does not guarantee a dividend, though there are companies which have regularly paid dividends on common stock for decades. As a general rule, if the value of the company you invest in rises, the common shares are more likely to increase in value than will the preferred shares.

Real estate which is rented out may offer both income in the form of rents along with the possibility of substantial growth.

We'll look at real estate a little more closely later on in this chapter.

One of the first things you'll have to consider when making an investment is whether you want or need income from the investment. For example, if we return to Paula, the physician we spoke about earlier, there is a strong case to be made that she does not need any income from her investments at this time. She is single and generating substantial amounts of money from her practice. Any income she gets will just be subject to tax when she receives it, which suggests that she might be a candidate for investments which have a substantial growth potential even if they produce little or no current income.

On the other hand, if you are a divorced mother of two and received a $100,000 lump-sum settlement from your ex-husband, you may very well want to invest that money in such a way as to ensure that you get a regular flow of income to live on. Again, the desirability of this will depend very much on whether you have other sources of income (such as a job) or whether that $100,000 is going to have to support your family for a number of years.

Let's say that you are earning $15,000 a year but you need $25,000 a year for the next ten years, when your children will presumably be on their own. If you can find a safe investment which returns 10 percent a year, you can invest the $100,000 and generate $10,000 a year which, when added to your salary, gives you the $25,000 you need. Or you might want a very safe investment which earns 8 percent, or $8,000. You might then plan to draw down the difference between what you are earning and what you need from the $100,000. At the end of ten years, instead of $100,000, you might find that you have just $60,000. But with the children gone, that, along with your salary will provide more than enough to keep you comfortably.

A widow in her seventies probably will not be much interested in an investment which is going to grow over a long period of time. She'll be much more interested in getting money to supplement her pension, and in ensuring that what she has invested is safe, so that if she ever needs to go into a nursing home, or wants to take a special vacation trip or leave money to family or a favorite charity, the money is available.

A married woman who has some money of her own may want either income or capital growth depending on her circumstances. If she does not need extra income for her own or her family's needs, she may opt for long-term growth, anticipating for example, college costs five or ten years hence. If the family needs money, or if her own income or her husband's does not provide her with sufficient money for her own needs, she may want to generate as much current income as possible.

A useful measure is known as "the rule of 72." By dividing the interest you receive into 72, you can determine how long it will take to double your money. For example, if your investment earns 8 percent a year, it will take nine years for it to double in value if all the interest is reinvested at the same rate. Knowing this rule may be handy in putting away money now for longer-term goals.

Safety versus Risk

Investments can be ranked fairly easily according to risk. At one end are investments which are virtually without risk. This category would include Treasury bills and notes, savings accounts which are guaranteed by the United States and short-term lending such as certificates of deposit. There are a range of mutual funds offering investments in government securities or money market accounts which are also geared to low risk and generate interest income. The hallmark of a riskless investment is that it tends to yield relatively low income and has almost no growth potential.

On the other hand, many investments carry substantial risks. For example, common stock may drop in value. Gold has a recent record of rising and dropping in value very quickly. Real estate values in the city where you invested in property may drop if the major employer in the area closes its doors.

Generally speaking, if an investment is risky, you are usually offered a much higher rate of return on your investment (a company in poor financial shape will pay you more interest or promise you higher dividends than one which is solid) or the potential for growth in the value of the investment may be higher.

You might ask (since studies show that women as a group take many fewer risks with investments than men do) why anybody would risk losing all or part of their investment? The answer is that the greater the risk you take, the greater the chances are that you will make a big profit. The Chinese had it right; the ideogram for the word "risk" can be interpreted as either opportunity or danger.

For example, suppose you hold down a job which pays a substantial salary and you feel you are in good financial shape. You have taken maximum advantage of retirement savings plans, your house is paid for, and you have a fair nest egg tucked away in bonds and term deposits. (A fair nest egg in this context might be the amount of money you feel could tide you over the time between which you might lose your job and get another—about six months' salary.) You suddenly inherit $25,000 from a distant aunt. The safe way to deal with this money is to put it in a certificate of deposit and perhaps get 9 percent a year interest at best. So you'll have an extra $2,250 a year, and perhaps two thirds of that after taxes have been paid. Will $1,507.50 a year change your lifestyle? But you could invest in an equity mutual fund into which you can make regular contributions. If you adopt a regular investment strategy of investing on a consistent basis, even $100 a month, you achieve dollar cost averaging, namely you are not always buying at the peak of the market or at the very bottom but can achieve an average purchase price without fear of having to watch every twist of the market, and start to watch your investments really grow. Don't expect to hit the lottery in the stock market or invest all your hopes in one stock. The stock market can be a real roller coaster ride. By investing regularly and consistently, you may find yourself with a little nest egg and a new hobby of investing.

Conversely, if the loss of all or even a small part of your investment would result in your having to scale down your lifestyle, beware. The single mother or the widow of modest means probably should not be taking any risks at all, given the impact of what a loss of even a part of their investments would mean. (It is no wonder that the classic movie script maximizes the pathos factor by having the slimy villain lure the widow into a fly-by-night investment scheme.) A single woman without obligations, however, might be prepared to take substantial risks in investing, knowing that even a step down in lifestyle wouldn't greatly bother her, and anticipating that her place in the work force generates enough income to live on.

The decision to take investment risks should be based on two quite different factors. First, what would the impact be in terms of lifestyle and obligations if the investment were lost? Second, how comfortable would you be taking the risk? These are two different questions, please note. A lot of people simply do not have the psychological makeup to take risks, even if they can afford to lose money. If you'll end up with insomnia or ulcers from worrying about an investment, forget it, no matter how much money you have. The worry over investments may be another reason why women have been less likely to make high-risk investments. One study shows that men equate risk with excitement while women equate it with danger.

Alas, it is the risk-takers who make money. If you want to get rich, you may have to take chances.

Liquidity

While the term "liquidity" sounds like something sloshing around in your waterbed or wine glass, in investment parlance it means the ability to sell an investment quickly and get the money. Treasury bills and bank accounts are "liquid" in that you can get your cash back almost at once. A certificate of deposit is less liquid since you have to wait until it comes due to get your money or forfeit some interest as a penalty for early withdrawal. Investments in the stock market tend to be quite liquid, since normally you can phone a stockbroker, sell your stock, and get your money within a week.

On the other hand, real estate is illiquid. It may take months for you to find a buyer. The same may be true of paintings, your stamp collection or the interest you bought in your friend's catering business when she was short of capital to start it. When an asset is illiquid, it may mean that you will have to sell it for much less than it is really worth if you want money in a hurry.

When you are investing, you should keep in mind any particular goal you have. If you're saving to take a trip around the world in three years, don't invest in something which cannot be sold easily when you're ready to take off. The same is true if you view your investment money as an emergency fund. What good is an emergency fund if it is going to take you six months to find a buyer who will give you the cash you need?

When making an investment in something like a certificate of deposit, ask what happens if you have to get rid of it before the regular maturity date. If the potential penalty is too high, look to another form of investment.

The question of how liquid you should be is a matter of personal lifestyle. If you are generating enough cash with your paycheck to meet all your normal needs, you can afford to tie up your investments that are less liquid. But if you plan to use your money for a big trip or to buy a car within the year, make sure you can easily get the cash when you need it. It also makes sense to have an emergency fund equal to two-to six-months salary that you can tap quickly in an emergency.

Diversification

If you are among the fortunate group of women who have a substantial amount to invest, you should be thinking in terms of diversification. That is to say, you should have a number of different investments, some safe, some with more risk, some paying interest, some paying dividends, some very liquid and perhaps some which are more illiquid. If you invest in the stock market, you may want to buy shares in companies which carry on different types of businesses. (If gold or oil plunges in value, you don't want to find that all your money is in these types of stock.) If you invest in mutual funds, invest in at least three to achieve diversification of investing goals. Each fund has a different strategy which should be considered before investing. *Money* magazine regularly publishes reviews of the various mutual funds, their investment goals and their performance.

Tax Shelters

Many investments used to be sold as tax shelters; that is, they provided some extra tax benefit. Many people who invested in these shelters found themselves with more expense than benefit in the long run and have rued the day that they ever invested in them. Many of these shelters have been disallowed and instead of having a tax benefit these investors are facing taxes plus interest, penalties and more. The tax laws have changed substantially so that any investment should be looked at as a business deal rather than as a tax shelter. A good example of a safe tax shelter would be your pension plans, contributory retirement accounts through your employment (for example, a 401K plan) or an IRA.

In analyzing whether to seek tax-advantaged investments and tax-free investments, you must consider your marginal tax rate. If you are not paying tax at the top marginal tax rate, don't buy. If you want to buy part of an apartment house, for example, it may be cheaper to buy one that is not a tax shelter than one which is; most tax shelters are overpriced compared to similar non-tax-sheltered investments. In any event, get your lawyer and accountant to look at the documentation carefully before you sign on the dotted line. They should know whether this investment is wise for somebody in your position.

Saving taxes makes sense, but not if the price you pay means losing a significant part of your investment.

Rental Real Estate

One of the most common first investments for women is in rental real estate. (Interestingly, this is also true of immigrant males from Western Europe. North American-born males are most likely to make their first investment through the stock market.) The attractions are obvious. A good house can produce decent income much of which can be used to cover the mortgage and taxes of the house itself and the costs of maintaining it. And the long-term trend has been such that real estate has increased in value. Perhaps the proclivity of "innocents" for buying real estate is explained by its concrete nature. Women may prefer making investments that they can actually see (rather than just a piece of paper), and many may correctly feel that they understand the economics of home ownership better than the running of a multi-national business.

But there are pitfalls.

One woman we spoke to is a senior editor with a national financial publication, knowledgeable and very successful. She reminisced about her first investment, a duplex. "I went into the deal with four colleagues from work, all men. It looked like a super deal. The rental income more than covered the costs and the house was in a neighborhood which was 'coming up.' We figured we'd make a big profit within a couple of years. The problem was that the people living in the two halves of the duplex hated each other. They fought constantly over noise, heat, the yard and always were looking to the landlords (us) to solve the problems. The fights always took place at night and I was the only unmarried landlord, so the tenants felt less uncomfortable about phoning me. You can guess who had to traipse down three times a month to sort out matters before the police came.

"I'd drag myself into the office with three hours sleep and barely manage to function.

"Then there was a major storm and the sewer backed up, doing a lot of damage not covered by insurance. There went our profit for the year. And there always seemed to be repairs, little things. With rent controls and limitations on turning the property into a condominium, the resale value was further reduced.

"We eventually sold for a modest profit, but I swore I'd never again get into an investment where I had to do things. My time is too valuable for that!"

Obviously, everybody doesn't have these kinds of experiences when they become landlords. But this type of real estate investment is recommended only for somebody who has the time and ability to deal with the problems that always arise with any buildings.

There are other ways to invest in real estate. Some people buy shares in real estate companies which are listed on the stock exchange. To the extent that real estate values rise, the price of such shares often rises. Others who want a more direct involvement will invest in real estate which is managed by somebody else. Such an investment may be in an apartment house or office building or even a shopping mall. Often, your lawyer or accountant will know of such investment opportunities and you can let it be known through them that you are in the market as an investor.

Even if you've got comparatively modest amounts of money to invest in real estate (and you should have cash for about 20 percent of the purchase price), it is easy to find out what's available. One woman we spoke with spent some considerable time looking at rental units in her own neighborhood and talking with local real estate agents, most of whom were women and some whom she knew socially. After six months of this, she had a good "feel" for which properties in the neighborhood were good buys and which were not. She bought a house just a few blocks away from her own home, and, because she did not hold down a job outside the home, was able to give the place the attention it needed. this was the start of a career for her, and within five years, she owned five separate properties, all in her neighborhood and all of them generating a profit.

Setting Your Objectives

The secret of successful investing lies in setting your particular goals and reaching them. Almost by definition, different people will have different goals. A lot will depend upon whether you are investing to generate more money to spend or investing as part of savings. Your age will have a major bearing on your decision as will your overall financial situation. We've already touched on some of the factors in our earlier discussion. Now you have to sit down and ask yourself these questions.

1. *Do I need current income from my investments to support myself and my family?*

If the answer to this question is yes, you'll obviously want to look for investments which produce a regular flow of cash. You are probably in the market for something like guaranteed investment certificates or preferred shares in established companies which have a good record of meeting dividend payments. If the answer to this question is no, then you might want to look at common shares of companies which pay relatively low dividends but which perhaps have growth potential.

2. *Do I want to make certain that my investment is safe or am I prepared to assume some level of risk to increase the value of the investment?*

If safety is a prime concern, you may want to stay with investments which pay interest and which guarantee the return of your money, such as certificates of deposit or money market accounts, or loans to other very secure borrowers. You might also like to investigate Treasury bills, which can be very short-term (90 to 180 days) or long-term (10 to 30 years) borrowings by government. If you buy government bonds, remember that while your money is safe if you hold them to maturity, the value of the bonds may fluctuate before they mature, and they can produce either capital gains or losses if you sell them before they mature. Or you may wish to invest in the stock market but only in so-called blue chip (usually the biggest and most solid companies) shares will produce some annual dividends and some growth in capital, though there is no guarantee that any shares will not drop in value.

If safety is not a prime consideration you can start to range further afield. You may take a flyer on issues, normally shares in younger companies which are just getting established, or in mutual funds which invest in a diversity of such higher-risk companies. Or you might ask your various "sources" (which we'll talk about a little later) about investment possibilities with large growth opportunities.

We have up until now dealt only with what we might call "public" investments, those in which you lend to or buy shares of large companies. Occasionally you may be invited to invest in a private venture such as a friend's business. This form of investment tends to be both high risk and illiquid. But there is also an emotional factor which may make you want to give such an investment serious consideration. Where such an opportunity arises, the best bet is to take whatever financial and business data you are given and consult with your lawyer and/or accountant. Professionals such as these can tell you about the potential risks and problems and can, if you decide you want to make such an investment, advise you on how you can best protect yourself.

At the risk of sounding cynical, investing significant funds in a venture started by somebody with whom you are emotionally involved has been an almost traditional way for women to lose money, often in amounts far beyond what they could afford. If your lover wants money to start a business, make certain that your lawyer has drawn up documents which give you a measure of protection. This procedure is also important if your spouse wants to put your money into a risky venture his friends are starting.

You may also be invited to make "public" investments which have some sort of emotional meaning to you. For example, you might be invited to help start off a feminist magazine, a woman's co-op or a new, exclusive woman's club. There is nothing wrong with using risk money for a venture which is close to your heart, but you should recognize that all brand new ventures are financially dangerous and that part of your return, if any, will have to be emotional satisfaction. The women who bought the first shares in New York's First Women's Bank in 1974 felt like pioneers; for many, the thrill of the cause itself motivated the stock purchase.

3. *How long am I prepared to tie up my money?*

This is an important question. If you need income from your investment, you may find that the best return comes if you're prepared to buy, say, a five-year certificate of deposit. But the disadvantage of this is that your money will not be available for five years. You have to assess whether locking in at the higher rate of interest is an acceptable trade-off for not being able to get your money back soon.

Normally, if you invest in the stock market, you can sell your assets and get money in a very short period of time. But remember, stocks and bonds may decline in value. If you need the money, you may be faced with selling out and losing some money if you need to get cash at a time when the value of your particular stock has dropped.

Some good investments may take a considerable time to produce a profit. We spoke with a woman who invested $10,000 in a piece of raw land on the outskirts of a growing urban area. But, as she told us, she knew when she made the investment that it would take a considerable time and she also knew that she probably couldn't get her money out until the land was sold. Since she was just one of a dozen investors in the land, she really didn't have any control over when this might happen. She got back $50,000 but had to wait six years.

Again, remember, set your objectives before you start investing. If nothing else, having clear objectives simplifies the process. There are literally tens of thousands of investment opportunities available at any give time. If you know what your objectives are, you can probably eliminate at least 90 percent from any consideration at all. Once you have cleared the underbrush, the process of comparing those which meet your criteria becomes much, much easier, and what appeared to be an impossible task becomes much more manageable.

How Do I Proceed Now?

At this stage of the game, you'll likely fall into one of two broad categories. You may have money available for investment and putting that money to use as quickly as possible is a high priority. Or you may feel much less pressured and may want to undertake a longer learning process before embarking on an investment program beyond what you're doing now.

There is a broad range of choices available to those who want to learn about investments, though most people will want to use a combination of them.

Read Current Material

There are several basic business publications with which you should become familiar. There is *The Wall Street Journal*, which is published daily and has a regular column, "Your Money Matters," which is geared to the individual investor. Financial magazines proliferate and range in style from the readily available *Money* magazine, which may be sold in your supermarket and is geared to the individual, to magazines such as *Business Week* and *Forbes* which are more business oriented. And of course, there is the business section of your newspaper. Some of the women's magazines are including regular columns on investing—*Lear's* and *Working Woman* among them. Combined, these will give you an incredible range of material to study on an ongoing basis. While some of the articles are for very sophisticated investors, a lot are for those of modest means.

Bookstores are loaded with books on investing, again ranging from those appealing to the novice to those for very sophisticated investors. One of the very best is *The Money Labyrinth*, by Shirley E. Woods, (Doubleday, 1984), dealing almost exclusively with stock market investments. It is not an easy book to read, but the effort is worthwhile.

Stockbrokers (often listed in the telephone book as "investment dealers") have an astonishing range of free material available. This will range from detailed reports on specific companies to more generalized discussion documents. (A teenager who approached a couple of firms in New York in connection with her economics course dealing with the stock market pronounced the brokers "awesome" in their willingness to help out somebody who wasn't ready to invest at the moment.)

Attend Lectures and Take Courses

In almost every issue of your local newspaper's business section, especially on Saturday, you'll find announcements of free lectures or seminars on investments. These courses are sponsored by companies who want your business (mutual fund salespeople, stockbrokers, insurance agents and so forth) and they usually have a specific product to sell. As long as you understand why the courses are sponsored, by all means attend. They will show their particular investment in the best possible light, of course. But if you go to a number of them, you'll begin to understand the pluses and minuses of different offerings. Most of these lectures also have question and answer periods which will allow you to clarify your own uncertainties about the subject. Don't be shy about asking questions. We can assure you from first-hand knowledge that at least half the people in the audience know as little as or less than you do. Nobody expects you to buy anything then and there.

These lectures also give you a chance to meet people in the investment industry in a reasonably informal setting. Indeed, since one of the main reasons they sponsor such lectures is to get "prospects," they'll be as anxious to talk to you as you may be to speak with them. Meeting people in this milieu may help you decide on an investment adviser when the time comes to get one.

In addition to the free lectures, just about every community college and other institution of higher learning offers courses on investing, many of which are geared to those who have no knowledge of the subject whatsoever. Courses are also given by organizations. Clearly, in deciding to attend such a course, the key issues for you will be time demands and cost.

If you have the chance, try to take a course offered specifically for women. There have been a number of studies which indicate that when women and men are both attending investment courses (or other lectures), the men tend to dominate discussions and question periods (even though they may be no more knowledgeable) and the women often end up getting less from the course than might otherwise be the case. There are valid reasons for considering a segregated course.

Get Your Feet Wet

In the end, there is no better way to learn than by doing. Depending upon your situation, here are some options.

For example, let's suppose that you are looking for the best interest rate you can get from a few thousand dollars you have sitting in your bank account. The first step is to go to your bank and find out what types of accounts and certificates of deposit they have and what the interest rate is on each. (This is a particularly useful—and potentially painful—exercise when you've kept all your money in a checking account since you first got a job.) What you will find is that your bank alone probably offers a dozen different options. The rate of interest paid will vary considerably based on how long you are prepared to tie your money up and how much money you have to put away. Don't forget that if you write relatively few checks a month, you may be better off paying for each check and getting higher interest than getting "free" checks and no interest.

Having done this at your bank, look around at what other banks and trust companies are offering. Most people are creatures of habit when dealing with financial institutions, and they often are unaware that other places may offer better interest or better services at lower cost.

If you are prepared to tie up your money for a year or more, or have a significant amount of money (say $5,000 or more) which you want to invest for a month or more, start shopping around to see what institution will pay the most. This can be done by phoning around or, if you follow the financial papers or read the business section of your own paper, you'll find advertisements galore telling what rates are being paid. In addition, most papers regularly publish lists comparing the rates of interest paid by different institutions. Usually such lists will also show the differences between what you'd get on, say $5,000 put out for thirty to sixty days as opposed to what you'd get if the money were invested for anywhere from one to five years. Remember, if you get a windfall such as a bonus, tax refund, inheritance or the like, put it to work for you at once. Even if you plan to spend the money in the next month or two, you'll be able to get better interest in a short term investment like a money market account than you'll get in your bank account. *Don't let laziness cheat you of the extra interest income you might earn.*

So, intelligent investing isn't really that hard if all you want is the best rate of interest possible on your money. All you have to know is what your needs are (that is, how quickly might you need your money back?) and the time to comparison shop. On the other hand, if you want to get involved with the stock market, you might justifiably feel a little more trepidation.

Let's say that you've read a few books and articles and you want to try out your new-found skills, but you don't want to take the risk. Why not do what hundreds of high school courses require their students to do? Pretend you're going to invest $20,000 in the stock market. (If you want a very realistic model, you might take into account that on each purchase and sale you have to pay a commission to your broker—let's say one percent, though this might be high. And try to keep track of any dividends which might be received during the period in question.) At the end of a fixed period, say six months, see how you stand. If your imaginary $20,000 has jumped to $50,000 you have the makings of a financial genius. Realistically, if you have increased your money by even 5 percent to $21,000 over six months, you're doing well. If you lose (and most people who play this game do), don't despair. You'll have learned a lot. And remember that you've been operating without advice. If you really had decided to invest that $20,000, you'd have consulted with a professional such as a stockbroker.

A lot of people ease into investing as part of a group. There are thousands of investment clubs. Typically, each member contributes an agreed-upon amount (which may range from $10 to $100 depending on the group) each month and the funds are invested after discussions among the group. This approach also allows the members to have much more diverse investments than if they invested individually. Often, one or two people are selected each month to research a particular stock and to report on it with an eye to buying (or not buying) it for the club. Profits are divided pro rata on the basis of how much each member has invested and distributed according to the rules of the particular club.

Ask around. You may find that some of your friends or colleagues at work belong to such a club. If not, you might decide to form one. The beauty of the club is that the meetings have a social element, are definitely educational, and the exercise may be profitable. Most important, especially for a woman with no investment experience, is the emotional support given by club members; it cushions the initial shock of knowing that you're risking your money in the stock market.

A third option is to do it yourself, but with money you are prepared to risk. This is a variation of the imaginary investment, but for real. One solidly middle class woman we know started earning modest amounts of money from a part-time job when she was in her forties. The family had no need for her earnings. Initially, she put all her savings into term deposits and the like. But she kept hearing about the stock market and became interested.

Her first investment was based on a "hot tip" she got from a friend at work. She decided to buy 100 shares of the company at $3.50 and was delighted when she was able to sell out at $6.00 a share three weeks later. During that period of time she learned to read the stock market quotations in the newspaper and found herself starting to read business articles, something she'd never done in her life. Shortly after selling her first stock, she decided to take some of the money she had in term deposits as they matured and buy more shares. But this time she put the money into more solid companies which she thought carried little risk. (She liked staying at the Sheraton hotels, so she bought 100 shares of the company; she enjoyed going to movies and bought 100 shares in Cineplex. The idea of buying shares in companies which you think are doing things "right" is as good a way to determine quality as most others.)

Later on, the same friend who had given her the initial tip gave her another one. Again, she assessed the investment as risky and bought 500 shares of the company at $1.30, saying that if worst came to worst, she could afford to lose $650. Her approach was the proper one for a risky investment, as she found when the stock promptly dropped to $0.25.

We might make two unrelated points. First, for a lot of people the best way to learn is to do it yourself. As one woman told us, "I learned more from losing $1,000 on the stock market than I could ever learn from books. And I don't mean that the lesson was not to invest. I just learned how to invest more wisely."

The second point refers to tips. As the woman in our story found, some tips can be great and others can be terrible. Use your common sense. Did the tip come from a person who is really in a position to know something about the company? Did that person buy shares herself? And most importantly, if the tip is wrong, is the stock likely to go down (in which case will I lose money I can't afford) or is it likely just not to rise (in which case the cost of the investment may turn out to be minimal)? Be aware of the source of the information. As has been dramatically demonstrated by recent trials of Wall Street figures, insiders cannot tell you to buy their stock.

If you are now ready to get involved in serious investing, the most important single aspect is to find sources of information you can trust. In most cases, if you are investing solely to be paid a steady rate of interest, you can do the job yourself, as we noted earlier by taking the time to compare interest rates and finding terms which are compatible with your own objectives. But even if you want only to earn interest, you may want professional advice if the amounts you have to invest are substantial, say in excess of $25,000.

In the case of most investments, you need somebody to act as your agent to make the purchase. This person will normally be a stockbroker whose fees are a small percentage of the amounts you pay or receive on the purchase or sale of stocks or bonds. Generally speaking, almost all stock and bonds will be purchased through a broker, though in certain cases where the issues are new, there will be no fees charged. Your stockbroker is also likely to be your best source of information.

There are a few initial points to bear in mind. First, it is absolutely crucial that you inform your broker of your overall objectives. Without having a clear notion of what you are trying to achieve, he or she can be like an unguided missile. Second, if your broker wants you to buy or sell something, make certain that he or she explains why to your satisfaction. The explanation should fit in with your objectives. Don't forget brokers make money only when you buy or sell, so there is an incentive to keep trading on your behalf. On the other hand, many brokers, both female and male, told us that women often develop an "emotional attachment" to certain stocks, particularly if they have been received either as a gift or inheritance from a parent or husband, or when the stocks were their first purchase. As a consequence, they are unwilling to sell that stock when the time is right. Keep this tendency in mind when your broker suggests a sale. Third, find a broker with whom you feel comfortable and who deals with you as an equal, even if your investments are not huge. If you feel more comfortable with a woman, remember that there are many more women brokers around now than in the past.

Another form of investment is through mutual funds. With this type of investment, you buy fractional interests in a large pool of invested money. Mutual fund salespeople may be paid by a fee out of the money you contribute (called a "front-end load") or they may be paid by the fund out of profits. Remember, the mutual fund salesperson is just that, a person who sells. The management of the funds is in the hands of professionals you are unlikely to ever meet. Mutual funds are among the biggest sponsors of free lectures and seminars, and the good salesperson is glad to meet with prospects and to explain the funds in great detail. Do not get caught in the personal relationship. Look into "no-load" funds where there is no fee charged for investing or for selling your shares.

The best way to choose one mutual fund over another is to assess on past performance. Financial publications often run charts comparing mutual fund performance. In looking at such charts, remember that good performance over the long term, say five to ten years, means more than how the funds compare over a short period of time.

How Do You Find a Stockbroker?

The process of finding a good stockbroker is akin to the process of finding any other professional adviser. The first step is to talk with people you know and find out who they use and whether they are satisfied. Lawyers and accountants often come into contact with brokers in professional dealings and you can start by turning to them for suggestions. In the book we recommended earlier, *The Money Labyrinth*, the author, herself a very successful stockbroker, deals with the subject of choosing somebody to handle your financial affairs. She stresses the importance of face-to-face meetings as an absolute prerequisite in making your choice.

The important thing is that there must be a substantial level of trust between you and your broker, and the time you spend in finding one you are comfortable with is as important as the time you spend in considering other aspects of your investments.

We haven't yet discussed tax issues as they relate to investment. But when you're investing, remember that the correct way to measure your success is by determining what you keep after taxes are paid.

The tax rules change every year. Check with your accountant, stockbroker or other investment adviser about the tax consequences of any investment and how much you'll pay each year. The rules are complex. Most accounting firms and stockbrokers have up-to-date brochures which will give much more detail about current tax rules as they apply to possible investments.

Record Keeping

Anybody who has had substantial dealings with banks, credit cards or the telephone company knows that it's in her best interest to check the monthly statements. Everybody we know has horror stories about extra charges they've caught and the problems of getting them reversed. The same is true with your investments.

Whether you are handling matters yourself by investing money through your bank or have retained the use of a brokerage house to handle your investments, the onus is on you to keep track of your investments. You should keep a record of what you bought, when you bought it, how much you paid and what commission, if any, you paid. You should also record when interest or dividends are due and should check to make certain you are paid.

We heard of one case where a grandfather, in 1974, bought a twelve-year certificate of deposit through a brokerage company for his granddaughter. He sent the receipt for the purchase and the certificate he received to his son, her father, for safe-keeping. In 1979, the brokerage company merged with another company. In 1986, the granddaughter was in college and the father wanted to cash in the deposit when it came due but had lost the certificate. He went to the brokerage company which took over the original one to request payment. But he was told it had no record of the original purchase and refused to pay almost $2,000. However, the father had the original receipt from the purchase. It took six months of arguing, but faced with the piece of paper which showed the grandfather had turned over the money in 1974, the trust company paid up, with extra interest for the delay! The moral: keep every piece of paper until you have been paid off all you are owed.

You can get a sophisticated journal to keep track of your investments or keep the list in a $1.00 notebook, whichever is more aesthetically pleasing to you. (Some insurance companies offer fancy record keeping systems as free gifts for clients. You might ask your agent if he has one for you.) The pieces of paper you get when you buy or sell can be kept in a file folder, just so they're available. (Stock and investment certificates, bonds and the like should, however, be kept in a safety deposit box.)

You also have an obligation to retain your tax returns for past years. Usually, six years will be a sufficient period of time, but if you have space, you may find that some day it will be useful to be able to put your hands on your ten-year-old tax return.

Whatever system you use, the important thing is that the primary responsibility for ensuring that you get interest and dividends as they come due is yours. And you want to have evidence, whether for tax or other purposes, of what you bought, what you own, what you paid for things and what you sold them for.

Even if you're never asked for your records by the tax department and even if you never have a hassle with your bank or broker, this kind of record keeping is a satisfying way of measuring your financial growth.

A Final Word on Investing

The woman who would be in full control of her life must come to grips with the fact that a key part of that life is the care and preservation of whatever money and assets she has, whether they are minimal or substantial. For that reason, learning to invest wisely by setting goals and attempting to meet them is extremely important.

We know that for many, perhaps a majority, of women, the notion of investing (beyond putting money in the bank or term deposits) produces a high level of anxiety. We also know that it is easier to live with poor investing habits than to learn new ones. But the fact of the matter is that there is no reason why women can't achieve the same level of investment sophistication as men; indeed, the evidence is that many have done so. All that is needed is the will to do it.

Having said all that, a word of caution. This chapter may be viewed as an introduction to the psychological aspects of investment. An experienced investor reading this chapter might point out that we have not dealt with a whole host of investments ranging from commodities (like pork bellies) to convertible bonds or stripped bonds, with warrants or rights or options. The experienced investor would be correct. The purpose of this chapter is to explain the mental preparation which must be a prelude to any investment decisions, namely the importance of establishing objectives. Once you've made these decisions, we have suggested additional sources where you can learn the mechanics.

Learning to invest is no harder than learning a lot of other things a smart person should know: how to handle herself at work, how to deal successfully with her various relationships, how to protect herself from being taken advantage of, both emotionally and financially, or how to drive a car.

If you make some bad decisions, don't despair. Man have been making bad investment decisions for decades, and most reminisce more about the great chances they were offered and turned down than about whatever their successes may have been. If you lose some money as you learn, remember that it's part of the process. (Just think of how many car fenders have been dented along the way as people learn to drive.) Or remember this advice, overheard at a skating rink: "If you don't fall down a few times, you're just not trying."

4

Borrowing with Skill and Savvy

It is no surprise, given their economic power, that men borrow more often than women. The paradox of borrowing is that a person of substantial means is more likely to borrow large amounts than a person who has just enough income to get by. This stems from two facts: lenders are more likely to advance funds to somebody who they are certain will be able to repay, and most people of wealth understand that more money can be made using somebody else's funds than using their own. (We'll look at why this is the case a little later.)

Curiously, though, even women who appear to have substantial incomes and assets are less likely to borrow money than are men. This may be because even apparently successful women are less confident about retaining their economic status (and thus their ability to repay a loan) than are men. Or it may be that given the traditional economic subjugation of women in our society, they are less confident than men in dealing with the major commercial lenders—banks and trust companies. (It is also arguable that even with women becoming financially successful, these lending institutions remain essentially inhospitable to women. The stories of financially independent women being told that they could have a loan only if their husbands guaranteed the debt are legion.)

Whatever the reasons, it seems apparent that women are not availing themselves of their ability to borrow, which in turn means that to a significant extent women are curtailing their ability to earn more. In addition, because women are not borrowing and creating a "track record" as a group, it makes it harder for those who do wish to borrow money to do so. A woman clearly moving up in the ranks of one of the major banks substantiates these observations.

She was, at the time we spoke with her, in charge of a special banking program for high income individuals. For a fixed annual fee they would receive a range of benefits which included no charges for any banking services, a "free" safety deposit box, "free" traveler's checks and so forth. But the biggest plus of the program was that every participant was given an automatic personal line of credit at very favorable interest rates. This meant that even if a participant did not have cash available, he or she could write checks up to the amount of the line of credit, which could range from $10,000 to $50,000. The beauty of the system, our friend felt, was that when an opportunity came along to buy something at a bargain or to make an investment, the member need not consult with the bank in order to get money. The funds were there, available simply by writing a check.

But to her amazement, this woman found that more than 95 percent of the members of the plan were men. An active networker, she approached many women who were eligible to join and almost every time she did the idea was rejected. The concept of a line of credit, so attractive to men, had considerably less appeal to women. The most common comment she heard was "I don't like to buy anything I can't pay for" and "I don't like to go into debt."

Why Borrow Money?

Essentially, there are two types of indebtedness. The most common and most unattractive is the indebtedness you get into simply because you don't have enough money to buy what are perceived to be the necessities of life. There are many thousands of people, for example, who are permanently indebted to Visa, Master Card, department stores and the like, making the minimum monthly payment, incurring interest charges and always being at the limit of their credit line. This form of debt is a type of financial death with the debtor forever juggling payments, unable to get ahead of the game. But there is another type of debt—debt incurred to acquire assets which increase in value.

Almost any person who has ever owned a home can appreciate the benefits of debt, since a mortgage represents a debt incurred to buy an asset (the home) which usually increases in value. Suppose, for example, you bought a house in 1976 for $100,000 and had a $75,000 mortgage. In 1987, you sold the house for $200,000. You might think that you doubled your money, but you really did better than that. In fact, (putting aside the small amounts which you paid monthly towards the principal of the loan) you invested $25,000 and got back (after the $75,000 was repaid), $125,000. Your profit was four times the money you invested.

By the same token, suppose you had access to a line of credit of $20,000 under the bank's plan. You buy shares in the stock market for $20,000 and six months later, the shares are worth $30,000. You sell the shares and pay back the loan. The net result is that you have made a $10,000 profit with no direct outlay of your own funds. You will have paid interest on the loan, of course, but that will be deducted up to the amount of net investment income when you file your income tax return for the year.

The using of borrowed money to supplement the funds you have to invest is known as "leveraging" your investment. The greater the "leverage," the larger your potential profit and the greater your risk in the event of a loss. If the investment goes down, then you may lose not only your investment but must also repay what you borrowed. The point is to invest wisely and leverage prudently.

While both these examples are simplistic, they do demonstrate the importance of borrowing money for the purpose of building your own capital base. Remember, most male investors become rich by using borrowed money and most rich men are in debt.

On the other hand, if at all possible, *you should only go into debt to acquire assets which have growth potential.*

Dealing with Banks or Trust Companies

Television commercials besiege us with promises of friendly, helpful banks waiting to offer service to one and all. We see images of women and men of every walk of life being approved for loans. Believe it or not, those were attempts by the banks to attract new business from women. So right from the start we note that the banks might have the right idea, namely that women count, but still haven't the foggiest idea about how to appeal to them. But if the banks labor under misconceptions about women, the fact of the matter is that most people similarly misunderstand banks.

Do you remember the old potboiler movies where the villainous banker is prepared to foreclose on the ranch? Or where the hardhearted manager won't give a loan even to save the life of the heroine's child? Do you think of a bank as a place where you have to get down on bended knee to borrow money?

Forget it!

Banks make their money by lending money, and they face fierce competition to lend, not only from other banks but from an astonishing array of other institutions, including trust companies, insurance companies, finance companies, stockbrokers, and private investors. Banks are so anxious to lend that they extend money to virtually bankrupt countries and companies alike, hoping against hope that they will get their interest—if not their principal—back. These lending strategies created problems for the savings and loan institutions which we have not yet finished paying for. However, banks continue to solicit the traditional business and lend money for the kinds of investments that have always made banks profitable.

The most important thing in trying to arrange a bank loan is to understand what banks perceive they need. In a nutshell, they want to know how the loan will be repaid and when. They also want to know if you have assets which they might seize if the loan is not repaid (they call this collateral), or whether there is somebody else who would repay it for you if you fail. (Don't worry; they don't really expect to get all of this, although they would if they could.) If you go in with a clear explanation of what you want to do with the money you borrow, how you intend to repay it, and (preferably but not absolutely necessarily) some collateral for the loan, you are more likely to get what you want. Indeed, bankers today are much more sophisticated than they were in the past, and in many cases they will be able to provide some expertise to help you in your endeavor, especially if you're using the money to start a business. Businesses started by women are less apt to fail than those run by men. Bankers notice things like that.

Which is not to say that you might not be turned down. This may happen because your proposal truly does not meet the bank's criteria. (If this is the case, the loan officer should be in a position to spell out exactly where your proposal falls short.) But there remain a fair number of antediluvians in the banking system who don't think a woman should be in business or investing, those activities clearly being "men's jobs." Very often, they will make a loan if a man guarantees it; but no woman with a practical business or investment proposal should be forced to accept those kinds of terms. Be careful about having your husband guarantee a business loan, particularly when he has been opposing your business activities. If you subsequently get divorced and your business is valuable, he may use evidence such as having guaranteed a loan to counter your arguments that he never contributed to your business.

Discrimination against women customers should diminish, as more and more women are rising through the banks' chains of command to senior positions, just as discrimination against minorities tended to disappear as they began to flex their economic muscles.

Whether you have been dealing with a bank for a long time or are just starting to deal with a new bank, take the time to meet the key people. One woman we know said she always made a point of meeting her bank manager and talking to him a couple of times a year (although she never thought about herself as a candidate for a loan). She did this by asking to see him, rather than a clerk behind the counter, whenever she had questions, most notably about the pros and cons of the myriad types of accounts and investments offered by the bank. She just liked the idea of consistent personal contact—something she remembered her mother had always had at her neighborhood bank. When she decided to open a store, she went directly to "her friend" the manager about a loan. The entire process, culminating with the approval of the loan, was markedly expedited by the fact that over the years she had spoken with the manager about her financial situation and he had a "feel" for her prospects of success in her new business.

Types of Borrowing

The cost of borrowing money is, of course, the interest you pay. Generally speaking, the easier it is to borrow money, the higher the rate of interest. For example, it is easier to get a Visa card than to arrange a personal loan at a bank, so the interest on the card is higher than the interest charged by a bank on a personal loan. Similarly, it will likely cost you more if the interest rate is fixed at the time you borrow than if the interest rate fluctuates. Finally, as a general rule, the longer the period of time for which you borrow, the higher the rate of interest you will pay.

Let's look at these principles more closely. Probably the easiest borrowing you can manage is through using your credit cards. When you use a credit card to buy goods from a merchant, you are borrowing money from the issuer of the credit card. The beauty of the credit card is that you can "borrow" simply by using it, up to the limit assigned by the issuer. This is why we say it is the easiest form of borrowing. The real advantage of a credit card is that, if you pay your bill within the time allowed, there is no charge for the borrowing, meaning you get an interest-free loan.

The issuers, of course, would prefer that you did not pay on time. One bank president actually referred to people who paid up on their credit cards within the time limits as "freeloaders," probably the only time in history fiscally responsible people have been so categorized. But his frustrations were understandable. The interest rates charged on credit cards are often six or eight percentage points higher than the rate at which the same person could borrow from the bank in a more conventional way.

Check the rates charged on your credit card statement. You'll likely find that the rate (usually printed in very small type) is over 18 percent. You may also find that you could negotiate a loan from a bank or trust company large enough to clear your credit card indebtedness for, say, 14 percent. Logic dictates that you take a bank loan, pay off the credit cards and substitute regular payments to the bank. But even when people recognize this simple financial fact of life, they don't do it. And the reason they don't do it is because negotiating a loan at the bank is undoubtedly more difficult than using the "loan" through the credit card. For this ease they may be paying over 4 percent more a year in interest charges. (A little tip if you plan to borrow to pay off your credit card balances; go to a bank other than the one which issued your card. The bank won't be keen on lending you money at 14 percent to pay off a loan on which it is earning, say, 19 percent. Another bank may well give you a loan, and suggest that you start using its bank card.)

Sometimes you can get "easy money" cheap if you can present quid pro quo. If you are investing with a stockbroker, you may be able to open a "margin account." In effect, the broker lends you money against the assets you purchase from him, holding the assets as security. The interest rate is usually attractive compared to what you might have to pay the bank. But the amount you can "margin" is limited by law; and if the stock you have left with the broker decreases in value, you may have to ante up some money right away, or the broker has the right to sell off your stock to make good the debt.

If you have whole life or paid up insurance you may have the right to borrow money against the cash surrender value of the policy. (see Chapter 14, "Insurance.") Usually the rate at which such funds can be borrowed will be quite attractive, especially if the policy is an older one. Remember, the reason you are able to borrow this money at a low rate is that it belongs to you! If you chose, you could cash in the policy and get the money outright. But you may choose to borrow so that you can keep the insurance coverage.

Let's look now at the issue of fixed versus floating rates. The Federal Reserve regularly sets the rate at which it will lend money to the banks. This rate is usually set in response to the strength or weakness of the dollar or other national fiscal issues. But the rate is also a signal to the lending institutions. If the Federal Reserve rate is on the rise, it is a signal to raise interest rates. If the rate drops substantially, it is a signal to lenders to drop rates.

The key rate set by the banks (as opposed to the Federal Reserve) is know as the "prime rate." This is the interest rate which the most credit-worthy (read rich) borrowers will have to pay for their loans. Other borrowers often have their interest rates set in relation to the prime rate. For example, a businessperson might be able to borrow from the bank at "prime plus one" which means one percentage point over prime. Thus, if the bank's prime rate is 9.5 percent, a person borrowing at prime plus one will pay 10.5 percent interest on a loan.

If you are offered a loan on which the interest rate is linked to the prime rate, the interest you pay will vary with the prime rate. If the prime rate rises, you'll pay more interest; if it drops, you'll pay less. Obviously, given the chance to get a loan which is linked to the prime rate, you'll have to make a guess as to whether interest rates are going to rise, fall, or stay steady. With the experts having trouble predicting the direction of interest rates, the shorter the term of the loan, the less risk you will bear of being locked into a pattern of increasing rates.

You can usually get a comparatively better initial interest rate if you agree to a floating rate tied to the prime, since the lender knows that it will be protected if interest rates rise substantially.

Conversely, you can get a fixed rate of interest on a loan. You might negotiate a loan at, say, 12 percent, and that rate is fixed for the length of the loan. If other interest rates rise, you are protected by your fixed rate. But of course, if other rates fall, you are stuck paying 12 percent. Most mortgage loans (loans secured by real estate, such as your home) are fixed rate loans. The real benefit of such a loan is that you know exactly what you have to pay each month in interest for the term of the loan and thus will not be surprised in the future, either happily or unhappily. The home mortgage market has changed substantially with adjustable rate mortgages and it is important to evaluate the financial benefits of both types of mortgages in light of your particular financial circumstances.

The third element in a loan is its term. There are two basic types of loans. One is a demand loan. With such a loan, the lending institution can demand that you repay it whenever it wants. Generally speaking, this type of loan is used by people financing a business or using the funds for investment. While the lender has the right to "call" the loan at any time, it is unlikely that it will do so unless it believes that circumstances have changed in such a way that its money is at risk. Demand loans tend to have floating rates linked to the prime rate and, generally, the combination of the floating rate and the ability of the bank to "call" the loan when it wishes will result in a lower initial interest rate. Very often, the lender will not even require you to make regular payments reducing the loan but will be satisfied so long as interest is paid monthly or quarterly. This can be extremely useful if you have used the money for an investment and plan to repay the full loan when you sell the asset at a profit.

But the lender may offer you a a term loan. This is a loan usually at a fixed—not floating—rate for a fixed number of years. For example, let's say you want to borrow $10,000 to pay off debts you ran up while you were in college. You figure you can pay the loan off in five years. The bank says it will lend you the money at 11 percent interest and you'll have to make a monthly payment. The payment you make will be a blend of interest and capital repayment. Using mathematical tables known as an amortization schedule, the loan officer would be able to tell you that if you pay $216.21 a month (and don't miss a payment), at the end of five years, the loan and the interest will be paid off. If you wanted ten years to pay, the monthly payment would be $136.38

With these two possibilities, the difference in interest you'd have paid is considerable. If you used the five year plan, you'd have paid a total of 60 months at $216.21 or $12,972.60. Since $10,000 is what you borrowed, the $2,972.6 is interest. If you used a ten year payment schedule, you pay 120 months at $136.38 or $16,365.60, with $6,365.60 as interest. This example clearly demonstrates the benefits which flow from paying off a loan as quickly as you can.

The most common term loan (though it is seldom called that) is the home mortgage. Most mortgages have an amortization period of anywhere from 20 to 35 years; that is, if the regular monthly payments are made for that length of time, the mortgage will be paid off. In addition, there are adjustable rate mortgages which provide a fluctuating interest rate based on a formula. But because lenders do not want the rate of interest fixed for a long time, the rate generally must be renegotiated every five years or less. That is why most adjustable rate mortgage loans (ARM's) you see advertised have different periods for payment. The difference between a regular term loan and an adjustable rate mortgage loan is that at the end of the fixed period, say five years, you will not have paid off the loan but only a small fraction, with a new loan having to be negotiated at the then prevailing interest rates.

As a general rule, you should reduce a home mortgage loan by as much as is feasible whenever you get extra cash. When negotiating a loan, check out your right to do this. Some lenders will allow you to make a payment on account toward the outstanding principal anytime; some on the anniversary date of the original loan; some will allow a maximum annual prepayment; and others have no rules limiting prepayment. Some will not allow any prepayment. Different states have different rules on the right to prepay. Prepayment can save tens of thousands of dollars in additional interest charges.

As you can see, there are many options available to those who want to borrow money, depending upon your own needs, the lender's assessment of your ability to pay and your own guess as to which way interest rates are likely to go in the future. But always bear in mind that banks, trust companies, and other lending institutions make their money by lending it. *They want to lend you money*. This being so, remember that when you look for a loan, *you are a customer, not a beggar*.

Shop around. Banks and trust companies may look like monolithic entities from the outside but decisions about lending money are made by the individuals inside. And there is a surprising diversity of views among loan officers as to who is a good credit risk.

A woman lawyer we interviewed told us of her experience in setting up her practice in Burlington, Vermont. She had had no previous contact with banks in the city and had spurned her father's offer to make arrangements to help her through the bank he used. She knew that she needed access to about $20,000 to set up her office and support her until the clients started coming in. As she told the story, she walked down Church Street, where there were branches of four different banks. One bank turned her down flat. A second offered the money she needed if she could "find someone" (read husband or father) to guarantee the loan. The third offered her a $10,000 line of credit (that is, she could take up to $10,000 from the bank, which would credit her account as she needed it) at a rate of prime plus five, an extraordinarily high rate of interest! The fourth bank offered her $20,000 at prime plus one. And, she marvelled years later, "all these banks were within two blocks of each other, each heard the same story, and each reacted differently." Ten years later, she is still using the same bank.

One more tip about choosing banks. Don't pick a bank simply because you like the loan officer you are dealing with. Look for the best deal. Loan officers are moved with such rapidity these days that you may find that within a year you have to deal with two new people. Because they may want to "review" your loan, ask the loan officer you deal with to make certain that your file contains all the documents pertaining to your original loan application as well as his or her comments as to why the loan was approved on the terms offered. More than once we have heard of situations where new loan officers attempted to renege on deals which were in place, arguing that they didn't have the data available to them to "justify" the loan on the terms which were given.

A Word About Taxes

Earlier in this chapter we touched on the deductibility of interest paid on a loan in computing your income. The basic rule is that if you borrow money for the purpose of using it in a business or for investment, the interest expense is deductible to the extent of your net investment income. You cannot deduct more in investment interest expenses than you have earned from the investment.

Except for home mortgages, if you borrow money for personal purposes, based upon the current phase-out of interest deductions after 1990, the interest on your loan will not be ordinarily deductible. Interest paid on a car loan or for your credit cards is no longer deductible. However, the interest you pay on a mortgage for a building which you rent out can offset your rental earnings.

You should always keep this rule in mind when borrowing. Suppose, for example, you plan to buy a car costing $10,000 for personal driving and you also want to invest $10,000 in the bank. Car loans are quite easy to get, and your initial reaction might be to invest your cash in the stock market and borrow to buy the car. This is a mistake. You should use the money to buy the car (since the interest on the car is not deductible) while borrowing the $10,000 for the stock market investment, since that interest can offset your earnings.

As a general rule, if you have money in hand and debt outstanding, always use your money to first pay off the personal debts where the interest is not deductible, and only thereafter reduce or pay off your business or investment-related debts.

Getting back to the issue of the house mortgage, remember that the key to deductibility is the purpose to which the money is put. Suppose you are fortunate enough to have your house, which is worth $150,000 fully paid up. If you want to start an investment program, you can mortgage or "refinance" the house (bearing in mind that mortgage interest rates tend to be lower than just about any other loan rates) and use that money for investing. If the amount of the mortgage does not exceed $100,000 ($50,000 if you are married and filing separately), usually the interest you pay on the mortgage will be fully deductible. Mortgaging a house for investment purposes—even by taking out a second mortgage—is sometimes advertised by lenders as "unlocking the equity in your home." This is a useful technique to allow you to invest money in a substantial way providing, of course, you are satisfied with the safety of the investment you make with the borrowed money.

We strongly advise that if this technique is to be used, you check with a lawyer or accountant to make certain that you follow the correct steps. A mistake can result in the interest not being deductible, which would seriously undermine the attractiveness of the scheme.

Some Final Observations

Among canny investors, the use of borrowed money to leverage an investment and thus increase the potential profits is standard practice. Thousands of investors have used the technique to increase their wealth substantially in a way that plain hard work couldn't do.

Women have been slow to use borrowed money. As we suggested, this may be a combination of fiscal conservatism conditioned by women's general economic uncertainties, a lack of knowledge and a hostility to (and by) major lending institutions. Each of these barriers can be overcome by a woman who really wants to build her capital. The opportunities for borrowing and investing are readily available and the financial institutions are now anxious not just for new business, but specifically for womens' business.

All that is needed are the will to do it and an understanding of what factors go into successfully applying for a loan and what types of loans are available. Clearly there are poor ways of borrowing and smart ways. The difference may only be a few percentage points or the ability to deduct interest for tax purposes because of how the loan was taken out. The system works for those who use it well, and you owe it to yourself to learn how to use it to your financial benefit.

5

Funding Retirement

The Feminization of Poverty

One of the realities of life for women today is that they absolutely must not (to the extent they ever could) rely on a man to take care of them throughout their lives. For this reason, every woman should take whatever steps possible not only to ensure that she can support herself, but also be sure that she will be able to retire on an adequate income when she gets older. Please note that the concept of "retirement" is very male-oriented. Women either continue to do the things around their home which they have always done or, having left the work force, substitute unpaid work in the home for paid labor. Few women simply cease, say at age sixty-five, to do what they have always done as do men, so we can fairly say that few women ever "retire."

Perhaps the saddest and most pervasive problem faced in Western industrialized countries generally is that older women make up a very large percentage of the impoverished. This is primarily true because women live, on average, seven years longer than men. And part of the problem stems from the breakdown of the extended family in which it was a familial obligation to care for older members. But part also stems from the fact that people past sixty-five are usually supported by savings and pensions. Traditionally, women who stayed at home to care for the family had no savings in their own names. To the extent a woman had worked in the home exclusively, she was unlikely to be eligible for any pension. If she was married to a man who did have a pension, she often found that upon his death the pension stopped or, more often, was significantly reduced. And since almost all pensions are linked to earnings, those women who do have pension coverage may well find it inadequate.

There are three main sources of retirement income: that which comes from tax-aided private savings (such as an individual retirement account or a 401K plan where you make contributions through your employment); a pension plan contributed to by both employers and employees; and from Social Security. It is worth pointing out that generally you can do little planning in connection with Social Security. Either you are eligible to get it or you are not. But maximizing your Social Security eligibility should be a goal. Keep retirement in mind even early in your working life. If you are ever faced with a situation where you can earn money which carries with it Social Security eligibility, as compared to one which does not, remember that the chance to get Social Security in later years is a very real plus and should not be disregarded, even if you're living for the moment and retirement appears to be decades away. To be fully insured and entitled to Social Security, you must have been employed forty quarters, with a "quarter" of coverage being a three-month period beginning January 1, April 1, July 1 or October 1.

How To Get What You're Entitled to From the Government

The Social Security System

One of the first things a woman will notice when she takes her first job is that her paycheck is significantly lower than her stated salary. This is because the employer must deduct money for the estimated amount of tax she'll owe, unemployment insurance and for F.I.C.A. (Social Security) payments, along with any other deductions which might be authorized such as union dues, private pension plan contributions or charitable donations. While everybody learns to live on the basis of "take-home" pay rather than "gross" salary, each of these deductions does represent a real monetary asset which, although it is invisible, you do own. The most valuable of these is the accumulation of pension plan contributions.

The Social Security system is a "real" plan in the sense that individuals and employers contribute to it and employees ultimately receive payments based on their contributions. Both the employer and the employee make contributions on an annual basis. If you are self-employed, you will make a double contribution, in effect paying both parts. In 1989 deductions were made from your pay towards Social Security at the rate of 7.51 percent (with a wage base of $48,000; wages above that amount were not subject to Social Security), and in 1990 the rate was 7.65 percent (the rate has gradually been rising).

The contributions are not deductible for the purposes of computing your taxes. Usually, if you are employed, your employer simply deducts the appropriate amount from each paycheck. If you are self-employed, you must make the payments directly.

While on the face of it the government plan has no sexist bias, as with the Internal Revenue Code, a distortion occurs simply because women tend to earn significantly less than men. We can see this distortion in several areas. Because women generally earn less than men, even those women who are covered as a group end up with lower Social Security benefits, since the benefits are based on the amount earned. Because many women drop out of the work force for years while they rear a family, they tend to lose contributory years, which in turn means that their final payments will be lower than those received by men. A woman depending upon her spouse or former spouse for coverage, may not realize that her benefits will only be one-half of the employee's while he is alive and, if there are payments being made to a second wife and to dependent children, there are limits on the amount a family can get in total benefits on the basis of the earnings record of the employee.

Women tend to get very low Social Security payments. Most of the men receive at least one-half of the maximum retirement pension while far fewer of the women reached even that level. And, of course, women working in the home receive no Social

Security benefits except by virtue of their husband's employment.

Since the value of a Social Security benefit is a function of the contributions and the number of years contributions have been made, these benefits are comparatively modest. However, they will grow in value over time both because contributors will have extra years of coverage, because the rate of contributions will rise and because the basic benefits are increased by inflation.

Here are examples of specialized Social Security coverage:

- If you are disabled and unable to work, you can get disability benefits, and benefits are also payable to your dependents.
- If your spouse dies, (or your former spouse if you were married at least ten years at the time of divorce) you will be entitled to what is known as survivor's benefit. This is equal to your spouses's benefit if you are of full retirement age, or at least 75 percent of your spouse's benefit if you are under age 65 and caring for a young child. A person who is receiving a survivor's Social Security benefit and who remarries after age 60 will continue to receive the payments.

(Note that a single woman who has no children is paying for benefits she or her heirs will never receive. No reduction in premiums is offered for singles, however.)

- If you are disabled and have children aged 18 or under, or up to 22 if they attend full-time school or university, your children will receive a monthly payment. The same applies if you die.
- On your death, a lump sum of $255 is payable to your spouse or your eligible surviving child, presumably to help cover burial and other costs.

You should also remember that Social Security benefits you receive may be subject to income tax if your benefits and other income, including tax-exempt income, exceed $25,000 for a single woman, or $32,000 for a married couple filing jointly. If your income is less than these amounts, then the benefits are tax free.

Some points to remember about your Social Security benefits

Perhaps the most important, is that if you and your spouse are getting a divorce, the Social Security benefits are determined by the Social Security system. It is unnecessary for any further action to be taken by you at the time of divorce.

All Social Security benefits must be applied for. They do not come automatically. Therefore, if as a result of a death, disability, divorce or retirement, you think you or your spouse have the right to a payment or benefits, contact the Social Security office nearest you. In addition, you can contact the Social Security system prior to retirement to ascertain what benefits you have accrued. You will not get that information without asking, and the time of retirement is too late for planning. You must fill out form SSA-7004-PC-OP2. To get this form, just call 1-(800) 937-2000 and a copy will be sent to you.

If you are employed, it is your employer's obligation to make payments and deduct your payments from your paycheck. If you make an arrangement to work casually (say as a babysitter or as a plumber) and are paid in cash, when you file your tax return you should declare the money and pay into the Social Security system. The contributions you make will come back many times over in the future. If you are self-employed, you also pay for Social Security coverage. But remember that self-employed people make double contributions, paying both the employer and the employee portion themselves. (A very high-powered lawyer we know reached age 65 and started getting a Social Security check monthly. She claimed she had never made a contribution. Later on, she found out from her long-time secretary that the contributions were made through her law firm, and the secretary, in his usual efficient manner, had applied for Social Security benefits in her name six months before she reached 65.)

There is a range of easy-to-understand publications about Social Security benefits (and other plans we will discuss below) which are available on request at no cost. Even if you are not contemplating retirement from the paid work force now, the pamphlets will be extremely useful to you as an aid to understanding the range of benefits offered by the plan. Contact the

U.S. Department of Health, Education and Welfare, Social Security Administration for further information. They will be listed in your local telephone book under United States Government Offices.

Social Security has other benefits besides the basic ones discussed. There is a special minimum benefit if you have worked many years and would otherwise get a small benefit. There is a delayed retirement credit if you postpone retirement past full retirement age. In addition, if you are over the age of 65, and eligible for monthly Social Security benefits, you are entitled to medicare hospital insurance benefits, and if you are over the age of 65 and not eligible for monthly Social Security benefits, you are entitled to medical insurance benefits. Enrollment in the medical insurance benefits is on an automatic basis for the elderly and the disabled as they become eligible for hospital insurance coverage, but they can decline coverage. Others can enroll in the medical insurance plan during the seven month period beginning three months before and ending three months after the month when you turn 65. If you enroll later, the premiums will be higher.

The plan may have significant weaknesses, especially insofar as women are concerned, but it offers the income-earning woman a very good basic level of income security for her old age. The key is to maximize contributions whenever possible and to contribute for as many years as possible. We anticipate that as more women enter and remain in the work force and as pressure builds for homemakers' coverage, the number of women getting substantial Social Security benefits will rise significantly, making the current statistics about the elderly seem obsolete, we hope.

One of the objects of this book, of course, is to help women arrange their financial affairs so that they will not be faced with the need to use welfare when they get older. But for those who need the funds, it makes absolutely no sense not to make application.

If you don't need the money, it is almost certain that you know people who do. Many older people have their income supplemented by children or other relatives. One woman we spoke with told us that for years she had been giving her elderly mother upwards of $5,000 a year to help make ends meet. This was particularly draining on the daughter's finances because she was not entitled to deduct any of the money she gave except to claim her as a dependent.

Government programs are available to help ensure at least a basic level of security for those who have reached 62 or who otherwise qualify because of need. But in the end, the various programs only provide a minimal base, not a level of income which would mean a financially comfortable old age. That means that any financially savvy woman must consider other means to ensure that there is enough money available for her future needs.

Private Funding for Retirement

What we have been discussing up to now are government programs, a key element in what is known as the "Social Security net," but they can only deliver enough money to allow an older woman to live just above the poverty line. Retirement plans are failing to meet the reasonable needs of most of the elderly. Statistics indicate that only 7 percent depend upon pension checks for half of their income and many people report that company pensions have shrunk to less than one-fifth of their retirement income. There has been a substantial decline in the number of employees covered by the defined benefit plans and lower benefits available through defined contribution plans. The critical fact is that individuals must increasingly rely upon Social Security payments and their own savings to provide for their retirement. Planning for retirement is important at any age and cannot be put off to the future. Remember that before you reach retirement age, you have an obligation to yourself to enhance the income available to you in your old age.

Unfortunately, the ability to provide for one's own retirement using tax-assisted programs is primarily limited to those who earn money for their work, whether they are self-employed or are employees. And the amounts which can be saved for retirement are linked to your earnings, which means once again that, given the fact that they tend to earn less than men, women are likely to end up with significantly lower pensions than men do.

The brighter side of the picture, however, is that the percentage of women in the paid work force is at its highest level in history, which means that more women than ever before are in a position to save for their old age. While everybody has competing demands for every dollar he or she earns, saving for retirement should be a very high priority, even for a young woman. If you are a member of an employer's pension plan, you will have no choice about this type of savings; it is forced upon you by the rules of employment. But in many cases, it is possible to put aside more because of discretionary retirement plans, (known technically as 401K plans), than what is provided by the employer. If you are self-employed, a Keogh plan (another private retirement savings scheme), allows you to save money and tax dollars at the same time.

Before getting into details, let's take an overview of the types of plans. A qualified employee benefit plan is a retirement plan which meets the standards set forth in the Internal Revenue Code. Most large companies have such plans, though they are much less common among smaller employers. The plan will set annual contribution limits (usually a percentage of salary), and your contribution will be deducted from each paycheck. Your employer will normally also make a contribution, most commonly equal to what you contribute. Both contributions are deductible in computing income for tax purposes in the year they are made. The money held in the plan will be invested by those administering the scheme (usually known as the "trustees") and will be accumulated tax free.

The plan will set out the terms upon which a benefit will be paid. Different plans have different rules but all will have to meet minimum standards set by the government. Eventually, presumably, you will qualify for a retirement benefit—an amount paid out to you on a regular basis after your retire— which will be taxable when it is paid to you.

An individual retirement plan is primarily a way to allow people who are not covered by an employer's pension plan to save for their old age. You can set up such a plan by going to any trust company, insurance company, bank or stockbroker. You can join a plan and pool your money with hundreds if not thousands of other people, or can set up a "self-administrated plan" which allows you to direct how the money will be invested. But no matter how your money is invested, each plan is individual and, within the rules set out in the Internal Revenue Code, is controlled by you. Thus, you can decide when you want to receive the funds invested or even if you want to cancel the plan and take your money out.

If you are not covered by an employer's plan (and, if you're married, your husband is also not covered) contributions to the plan of up to $2,000 ($2,250 if there is a non-working spouse) are deductible from income for tax purposes within limits set by the Internal Revenue Code. The income earned on an individual retirement account is not taxable until withdrawn. Any withdrawals from an individual retirement account become taxable in the year the money is received.

Many options are available as to how you take your retirement income. Nevertheless, benefits must start to be distributed no later than April 1 of the year following the calendar year in which you attain the age of 70 ½

Before looking at both types of savings plans in more detail, remember the most important bit of advice in this chapter: *put away for retirement as much as you can possibly afford and the law allows.* This tactic provides tax benefits now and offers the best chance for financial security in your old age. It is important to start saving for retirement as soon as you start earning, since the longer your contribution to a plan stays in and earns tax-free income, the more money will be available for retirement. Most younger people put off starting to save for a goal which may be 40 years away, but the most savvy of them start early. Remember $1,000 put into an IRA earning 10 percent a year for 40 years will grow to $45,249. The same $1,000 put away for 20 years will only grow to $6,727. And that, in a nutshell, is why it is better to start saving at 25 for an age 65 retirement than at age 45! But if you're 45 now, remember that $6,727 is far better than $2,593, which is what you'd have if you start putting your money away at age 55. You're never too young (or too old) to start saving for retirement.

Qualified Retirement Plans: Moves Against Gender Bias

While retirement plans have been an increasingly important aspect of employment in the past thirty years or so, there are aspects which clearly have worked against women. The most important single negative factor for women has been that most such plans end up paying a lower pension to women than to men. This is principally because women have tended to earn substantially less than men, they enter the market later, or they are dependent upon their spouse's benefit which is reduced upon his death.

Certain pension plans provide life annuities when you retire. In many cases, the plans take the amount of money standing to your credit when you retire, and the money is used to buy an annuity which normally provides a fixed monthly payment for the rest of your life. Because women live longer than men, an equal amount standing to the credit of a man will provide a higher monthly annuity (since presumably he will die sooner) than it will for a woman. Statistically, they would get the same total amount of payments over time if they lived to precisely their life expectancies after retirement; but that is little comfort to a woman who gets a couple of hundred dollars a month less than a man who had the identical lifetime earnings record she did.

There are other biases as well. For example, most pension plans will not cover part-time employees working less than 1,000 hours. And since women are more likely to work on a part time basis than are men, there are cases of women who have worked thirty or more years for the same employer without receiving any pension at the end of that time.

Because women are much more likely to survive their husbands, if their husbands were the principal wage earner, they will be relying on their husband's pension benefits after he retires. When a woman was widowed, the pension that she and her husband were living on would stop or be substantially reduced depending upon what type of plan was making payments.

Most pension plans still discriminate against unmarried people, be they women or men, since most do not provide for payments to anybody other than a surviving spouse, if indeed there are any survivor benefits at all. An unmarried woman who was a partner in a large law firm recalled a partners' meeting called to discuss how "wives" would be compensated when a partner died. She dryly pointed out that not all surviving spouses were women, and then drew to their attention the fact that she (like a couple of other of their colleagues) was not married. Interestingly, she tells the anecdote as a joke, noting that the final form of the agreement took into account all possible situations. But she was clearly startled that men with whom she had worked for more than two decades could have been so insensitive to her situation.

Understanding Pension Plans

The rules relating to pension plans fall into two distinct categories, qualified and unqualified. If a pension is qualified, then it falls under the Internal Revenue Code rules and must meet its stringent requirements. If the plan does not qualify under the Internal Revenue Code, then the pension plan may have rules controlled by the employer and are unlikely to have the benefits which the Code provides.

Every employee should have an idea how his or her pension plan works and what benefits are available. Like computers, pension plans can come with a complete assortment of bells and whistles and can be top-of-the-line or cheap. But they all fall into a couple of very basic categories, based primarily upon how the pension is computed and who pays for it.

There are two main categories of plan—the "defined benefit plan" and the "money purchase plan." The defined benefit plan pays a pension on the basis of a predetermined formula. While the formulas used may differ from plan to plan, a typical one might be 2 percent for each year of work times the highest earned salary in your last five years.

For example, if you worked for the company for 26 years and your final year's salary was $42,000, your pension would be 52 percent (26 years times 2 percent) of $42,000, or $21,840. This type of plan is attractive for a number of reasons. First and foremost, the plan itself is not sex-biased in terms of the payout, because the pension would be paid according to the same formula no matter whether the employee is a man or a woman. Second, it gives a distinct bonus to people whose salaries rise. With the recent trend to promoting women in business, many women who had been in relatively low-paying jobs have seen their salaries increase rapidly, which translates into substantially higher potential pensions. Third, if the funds of the plan are poorly invested, this will have no negative effect on your pension. Rather, when you retire, the plan (or the employer) will just have to come up with additional funds to meet its obligations to you.

The other principal type of plan provides significantly less security. The defined contribution plans, which may include money purchase plans, profit sharing plans and other types of contribution plans, consist of a fund usually based on the joint contributions of both the employer and employee, as does the defined benefit plan. But the amount of the benefit you get on retirement is not guaranteed. Rather, whatever money is standing to your account at your retirement is distributed based upon the terms of the plan, which may include purchase of an annuity or lump-sum payment. The monthly value of the annuity, as we mentioned earlier, has traditionally worked out to be less for a woman than for a man; thus, this type of plan has been unattractive to women.

A second drawback of annuity plans is that the amount of money available to buy the annuity upon retirement will depend to a great degree upon the investment skills of the trustees and factors which may be beyond their control. If the plan is heavily invested in the bond or stock markets and these happen to be depressed at the time you retire, you pay the price in the form of a reduced annuity. Of course, if the markets are at an all time high, you'll reap a bonus.

A third drawback of these plans is that the money standing to your credit at any particular time will relate directly to your salary up to that time, since the contributions made by both you and your employer will be a percentage of salary. So if you worked twenty years at lower than normal salary and five years at a top salary, your pension will reflect twenty years of low earnings—exactly the opposite of the case with a defined benefit plan.

Why, you might ask, would anybody have a defined contribution plan? The answer is that under such a plan, the employer has no real obligation beyond making its contribution. The amount of the retirement benefit then becomes a function of the investment skills of the trustees. But under a defined benefit plan, the employer has to ensure adequate funds are available, which means that it may have a commitment in the future beyond its annual contributions to the plan. Many non-profit employers, such as universities, use the defined contribution plan simply because they have no source of income out of which to fund additional payments to the pension plan if the investment policy produces a shortfall under the defined benefit formula.

Generally speaking, if the plan you are under is a defined contribution plan, it is important for you to take whatever steps are available to augment your pension savings.

As we pointed out, normally both the employer and employee contribute to the retirement plan each year, usually an equal amount which is expressed as a percentage of salary. You pay for what you get. A contribution level of, say, 3 percent of income (which is deductible for tax purposes) probably suggests a very basic type of plan.

But there are variations. There are a few plans which are referred to as noncontributory. These are plans in which only the employer makes a contribution. Very often special noncontributory plans are set up for the executives of major companies, and are considered to be a very desirable perquisite in the employment package. But other employees may also be covered by noncontributory plans. If you're ever offered a membership in a noncontributory plan, grab it!

You should bear in mind a few other features of pension plans. If you leave a job with a pension plan to go to another job, find out whether it is possible to transfer your pension credits from the first plan to the second. This is particularly valuable under a defined benefit plan since each qualifying year of service gets you a pension based, normally, on your career-high income.

Suppose, for example, you are working for a company which offers a pension based on 2 percent a year times your highest year. After ten years you are earning $25,000. Your pension entitlement at that time would be $5,000, 20 percent of $25,000. You then move to a company with an identical plan and stay there ten years, and your top year's earnings were $40,000. Your pension from that company would be $8,000, 20 percent of $40,000. So at the end of twenty years, your combined pension income would be $13,000.

But if you could have transferred your pensionable years from company one to company two when you switched jobs, you'd have had 20 years of credit. This would translate into 40 percent of your top year's salary, $40,000 or $16,000. As this example shows, even a transfer of credits between identical plans will give you a big bonus if your salary continues to rise. The ability to transfer credits, especially between employers in the same field, is quite desirable and an important issue to raise if you're considering a job change.

If you are transferring credits from a plan with lower contribution requirements than the one you are entering, you may have to make up the differential. The personnel office can tell you how much "extra" you'd have to pay and you can then decide whether it is worth your while to make the transfer.

If you cannot transfer from one plan to another, you may be able to transfer your funds to an IRA. This may be attractive to you in that the IRA will give you more flexibility in handling the funds, and you don't have to leave them in a plan to which you no longer have a link.

Check to see what other benefits your plan has, whether mandatory or optional. If you die, will your husband and/or children get any benefits? (If you have neither, ask whether your contributions can be reduced; the answer will be "no," but it is worth doing this to make a point about the bias against single employees inherent in such plans. Remember the lawyer we referred to earlier.) Is there any insurance associated with the plan? If so, do you pay extra for it? Before you opt to take it, find out whether you can get the same coverage cheaper by buying it personally. Does the pension you get from the plan get reduced when you start receiving Social Security payments? (Many plans do reduce their payments when the government payments cut in.) This is important to know in order to assess whether your government payments represent extra income or not.

Does your company's plan have inflation protection for its pensions? If it does, you are in a Cadillac plan which offers extensive protection for your old age—though you'll probably be making a higher than average contribution.

You can get this sort of information from the company personnel office, either when you start a job or at any other time. Realistically speaking, the area of pension coverage is not negotiable unless you are taking a job as a very senior executive. But when you are moving from one job to another, especially if you've been in the first company for a number of years, pension coverage is important. Every year many people turn down otherwise good offers because of what they stand to lose with regard to potential pension coverage.

Individual Retirement Accounts

These plans—a government sanctioned method of putting away nontaxable dollars now to withdraw when you retire— are popular for a number of reasons. First, if you aren't covered by an employer's pension plan and are not self employed, this is your only method of tax-deductible saving for retirement. Second, the plans are easily accessible, with almost every financial institution offering them. Third, you have much more flexibility in being able to get your money out of an IRA than out of a pension plan. (Indeed, many people use it as a form of tax-deductible savings account with the money earmarked for nonretirement use. We do not recommend this technique since it may jeopardize future financial security.) Fourth, you have great flexibility in the investment you make. As with non-IRA investments, you have a choice between turning the funds over to managers (the most common technique) for investment in particular types of assets (mortgage funds, common stocks, bonds and so forth) or you can actually arrange to choose specific investments yourself if you set up what is known as a self-directed plan.

The Mechanics

We'll start this discussion off with a word of warning. The following material appears very complex at first reading, and it is. Yet an understanding of the ins and outs of IRA's is very important for most women who want to save wisely for retirement. Don't forget that if you have any questions about IRA's, you'll be able to get answers from people at almost any financial institution you have dealings with. But it's worth the effort to try to absorb as much as you can before turning to somebody else for advice.

An IRA is a trust under which you are the annuitant or beneficiary. You must have a trustee, which is the role played by the financial institution you select. The trust requires that the funds be converted into one of the various retirement options (discussed below) no later than the end of the year in which you turn seventy and one-half. And when you take money out of your IRA, all funds received are taxable the year you receive them.

You can set up an IRA for yourself or for a spouse. The idea was that men would have an incentive to contribute to the establishment of a pension plan for their wives since they would get a deduction in a year when their taxes are presumably high and the money would eventually be taxed in the hands of their wives.

Contribution Limits

The government has made significant changes to IRA's, which has significantly curtailed their usefulness. Since limiting contributions to IRAs to those people not covered by an employer's retirement plan, contributions to IRA's plummeted.

If you are a member of an employer's pension plan during any year, you cannot contribute to an IRA in that year unless the adjusted gross income of you and your spouse is less than $40,000 ($25,000 for single taxpayers).

If you are not covered by an employer's pension plan in the year, you may contribute an amount equal to the lesser of $2,000 ($2,250 if there is a non-working spouse) or 100 percent of compensation.

Where to Get a Plan

As we mentioned earlier, almost every financial institution offers IRA's. Banks, trust companies, stockbrokers, insurance companies and mutual funds all want you to invest with them—and don't forget, an IRA is first and foremost an investment. A quick walk around your downtown area, or a few phone calls, will yield a plethora of brochures which will describe particular plans. A visit to a number of these organizations is worthwhile since they will have people available to answer any questions you might have.

Investments

The main distinction between IRA's is in the way they invest. IRA money can be invested in almost anything you can think of, though there are some limitations. (You can't hold gold bars or paintings, for example.) You might want to review Chapter 3, "Investing," because many of the criteria you'd use in making an ordinary investment will apply equally to an investment through an IRA.

The most common type of investment is the certificate of deposit. The funds are invested in certificates paying a fixed rate of interest for anywhere from one to five years. These are very safe investments, but don't forget, if you invest in a five year certificate and need the money from the plan in three years, you won't be able to get it out.

You can select plans which pool your money with others and invest in specific types of assets, such as common stocks, bonds, preferred shares or mortgages to name just a few. You can invest in mutual funds through your IRA.

As with other investment vehicles, the "carrier," as the organization you buy from is often called, gets paid. In some cases you pay an annual fee; in other cases the carrier gets paid indirectly from the fund of money it's managing. If you want a self-directed plan, you'll pay much higher fees than you would if you just arrange to have the money put into a trust company five-year certificate.

While the choice of an investment is a personal matter, bear in mind one aspect. Because IRA's are tax free, many of the tax benefits associated with investments are not germane. This suggests that for most people, the best investment is the one which generates the highest cash income, and this usually means bonds or other forms of debt. By all means, discuss the options with the various carriers you speak to. Ask them how they would invest your IRA money. Generally speaking, each one offers a range of investment alternatives, and therefore they have no particular vested interest in pushing you towards one type of investment over another.

Retirement Options

If there is one area where the IRA is clearly superior to a pension plan, it is in the range of retirement options which is available to annuitants. On the other hand, the amount which can be contributed to an individual retirement account is so limited that you cannot rely upon an IRA to provide effectively for your retirement.

First, with an IRA you can just "collapse" the plan whenever you choose. The effect of this is that you get all the money in the plan and pay tax on it in the year received. However, you might find at some stage that you have an emergency which forces you to tap your IRA funds, and this choice is available.

Second, you can buy a life annuity, which guarantees you an income for as long as you live. As we noted earlier in this chapter, life annuities tend to discriminate against women because they end up paying a woman less than a man on a monthly basis. There is a huge range of variables with these annuities. For example, you can get an annuity with a guaranteed payment term of anywhere from five to fifteen years. The guarantee means that if you die before the term expires, your heirs will get the monthly income until expiry. Or you can get an annuity which pays a monthly income for so long as you or your spouse live. Or you can get an annuity which has inflation protection built into it. Any and all options other than the straight life annuity will cost extra—which means less monthly income.

If you're considering buying an annuity, shop around. The rates vary from week to week and different issuers of annuities (normally insurance companies) have different rates. There are annuity brokers around who will shop the market on your behalf.

The third option is to buy an annuity which will pay you a monthly income until you (or your spouse if you so desire) reach age ninety. This is somewhat cheaper (i.e., you'll get higher monthly income) than is a life annuity, but if you go to this option, you'd best be certain that you have the wherewithal to meet your requirements if you live beyond age ninety.

While you may not have any need of professional advice in setting up a plan and using it to maximum advantage, it is advisable to consult an accountant or tax lawyer before you make any decision as to which retirement option you choose.

IRA's and Women

While IRA's are not particularly designed to benefit women, there are a number of factors which make them particularly important in a woman's financial planning.

1. Because women tend to work on a part-time basis more than men and many of them are not covered by an employer's pension plan, the IRA is the appropriate vehicle for retirement savings.

2. Because women tend to earn less than men, even when they are covered by an employer's plan, the amount of their ultimate pension is likely to be on the low side. The IRA may

be a vehicle which they can use personally to enhance what might otherwise be a paltry retirement income.

3. In the event of a marital breakdown, the tax rules allow for the tax-free transfer of IRA funds between spouses. If you're getting a divorce, look into the question of splitting his IRA into two parts, one of which is in your name.

4. While we feel that IRA's should be used primarily for the purpose they were created, namely retirement savings, there are situations where they can be used advantageously for other purposes.

Jennifer had worked for several years after getting her B.A. and put the maximum amounts possible into her IRA. Five years later, she quit her job to go to law school. She then withdrew her IRA, paid a 10 percent penalty and taxes (in a tax year when she had little other income) and used that money to finance her education.

This sort of planning is particularly useful to younger women who are more likely than men to withdraw from the work force for extended periods f time. It may be useful in a situation where a woman works to put her husband through professional school prior to her returning to school herself.

And the IRA offers flexibility in that if she decides not to return to school or if her husband finances her education after he graduates, the funds in the plan simply continue to accumulate on a tax-free basis whether or not she continues to contribute. IRA funds might also be used at some time in the future to help finance a new business venture or to provide living expenses during the start-up period when the business is not generating enough money.

But remember that withdrawing funds from an IRA is an irreversible step. If you've contributed for ten years and then withdraw the funds to use the money, you've lost ten years of tax-sheltered retirement savings and there is no way those years can be recouped in the future. Therefore the decision to withdraw from a plan rather than let it mature into a tidy retirement fund should be weighed very carefully. If you are going to collapse the plan, be certain that the benefits you get (a house, education, a business) at least equal the future benefit of a financially secure old age.

A Final Word on IRA's

In this chapter we have touched on the basics of the IRA. The specific rules governing them have been changed and will continue to change in the area of employee benefits.

While the concept of the plans is easy to grasp as are the basic rules, there are myriad varieties of plans, options and planning techniques, and these change on an almost annual basis. Each year several books appear which discuss employee benefits in detail. The carriers themselves also have detailed information available, not just about their own plans, but about the rules in general and possible planning techniques.

All these sources should be used to the fullest to increase your understanding of these plans, which are an indispensable part of good financial planning.

PART II

LOVE AND MONEY

6

Living Together

You don't appreciate all the older generation of women has done for you," says a mother in her forties to her 23-year-old daughter. "You don't realize how many women had to sleep around just so you and your boyfriend could live together."

Fortunately, we've come a long way from the days of the disgusting threat that "no man will want to buy the cow when he can get the milk free"—with its assumption that women's sexuality was a commodity to be withheld and then bartered for. Quite the contrary; living together, in the past twenty years, has become a matter of choice independent of the sexual involvement of the parties concerned; you don't need to move in together to have sex.

The number of women and men living together is growing; as of 1988, a U.S. Census Bureau figure puts the number of "unmarried couple" households at more than two-and-a-half million. Lovers cohabit sometimes for convenience, sometimes as a testing ground for a future marriage and sometimes as an ideological statement of freedom from the bondage some women and men consider marriage to represent. "Just" living together in our culture is one way women and men can achieve a degree of intimacy while postponing or deflecting or avoiding marriage.

Living together is different from marriage. The same rules don't apply, and the emotional weather may be different too, partially as a result of the more fluid nature of most cohabiting arrangements. After living together for a while, some couples find themselves more attached to each other than they imagine they would be with a marriage contract binding them by law.

Such couples feel that they renew their commitment afresh with each day that they decide, existentially, to live under the same roof. (They'd agree with Aphra Behn, the seventeenth- century feminist who wrote, "Marriage is as certain a bane to love as lending money is to friendship.")

We have all been exposed to a more or less full understanding of what marriage entails. Most of us were raised in homes where marriage, if not present, was at least likely to have been part of the past experience of the grown-ups around. In addition, fiction and film have given us explicit information about marriage (and divorce). We have, therefore, some inkling of what to expect, and even what to avoid, when we contemplate marriage. As many women have discovered, cohabiting is not the opposite of marriage. It has its own rules and consequences, in some ways more perilous for women then marriage itself because they are not often discussed, nor portrayed on the silver screen.

The carefree delights of a sleep-over date ultimately become the daily realities of trust, shared financial arrangements, and who does K.P. A living-together arrangement does carry with it some of the same complications as marriage if there's a break-up and creates other, lesser known complications while it's in progress.

The Legal Aspects of Cohabitation

"We love each other, trust each other, and want to live together. We don't see that a piece of paper will make any difference to that relationship" goes the common rationale for living together rather than getting married.

While the idea of a couple "living together" has achieved considerable social acceptance, from a legal point of view marriage is the norm, and those who live together without the formalities should recognize that any rights or obligations between them may eventually have to be established by a court of law, either when one of them dies or when the relationship ends.

We should establish that except in a very few states there is no such thing as a "common-law marriage." This is a widely used phrase which connotes a long-standing cohabitation and which implies some sort of legal recognition. To the extent that any such relationships are recognized by law, they are recognized because some state has gone out of its way in statutes to define the situation. Merely passing through a state that recognizes common law marriages or even living there for a period of time will not establish the relationship. But let's first look at the "norm," married status.

If you had a license and were married by somebody empowered by law to solemnize the union, such as a clergyman or judge, that marriage would be recognized as legal. As a married person, you'd have certain rights and obligations, a few of which stem from the "common" or unwritten law, and many more flowing from the myriad of statutes which govern our everyday lives. For example, certain tax benefits (and drawbacks) derive from a couple's being "spouses." Under the Internal Revenue Code, only legal marriages are recognized; the fact that you and your cohabitant may have been living together for twenty years and have three kids is not an issue for the purpose of that legislation.

So as a starting point, you can accept that whenever the law refers to a "spouse," that term will at the very least refer to partners who are legally married to each other. You can also assume that in this context no other status offers as much overall legal protection to a woman as marriage. The nonwife will always have to prove her entitlement to rights by demonstrating that the relationship met the applicable statutory requirements, while a wife normally will only have to prove that she was legally married.

The attempt to determine what relationships should be viewed as equivalent to married has created real problems, both for legislators and for the people who are affected.

Because so many people have lived together for extended periods of time without being legally married, various pieces of legislation have attempted to recognize such relationships for various purposes. The problem is that there is no single definition which applies to all statutes, and while your relationship may be recognized as the equivalent of marriage for the purpose of one law, it may not be so recognized under another law. Indeed, even within a particular piece of legislation, there may be variations.

When we examine the local laws which deal with support obligations, we find that there is no recognized obligation for a man to support a woman to whom he is not married. Children of the relationship must be supported (provided, of course, that he has been recognized as the father).

What you have to recognize is that the legislation gives a legally married person more rights (for example, the right to split the family assets upon permanent separation) than it gives to a nonmarried person, who has rights only to child support payments if the relationship ends.

If You Are "Living With a Man"

If you are embarking on (or are in the midst of) a long-term relationship involving cohabitation, you're being less than wise if you don't take steps to find out what your rights are in your particular jurisdiction.

The issue of your legal relationship goes beyond rights and obligations with regard to "family" property and support. For example, you will have no rights as a spouse to the other person's pension benefits. One woman who had lived with a man for eight years and was being supported by him, found herself on welfare when he suddenly died from cancer and his long-lost family suddenly claimed all of his pension benefits because he had forgotten to name her a beneficiary. If she had been married to him, she would have been protected regardless of what the husband did. If your "domestic partner" has a wife from whom he is separated, she will collect his retirement benefits unless she has waived her rights in writing, a highly unlikely scenario unless they have a written separation agreement.

What rights do you, as a cohabitant, have under health and hospital insurance plans? Are you entitled to coverage under his plan (or vice versa) in the same manner as a spouse? Unlikely.

What is the legal status of the children? Are they your children, his children or both? Did he adopt your children at some stage?

One couple we spoke with told us that the prospective birth of their first child was the factor tipping the balance in favor of marriage after having lived together for several years. Getting married was the easiest and most certain way to protect his rights vis a vis his own child in such a case, and her rights also. She put it this way, "Getting married was our shorthand for a cohabitation contract." And as it happened, they felt they had no guarantee—except for marriage—that a court would honor their agreement that the father would get custody if the mother died and that she would be supported if they separated.

Where you have a relationship of some permanence, it is absolutely crucial to look into all these areas if you are going to protect yourself. If you find that the law or other governing documents (such as the company pension plan) will not give you adequate protection, consider using a contract, an agreement which legally requires him to provide some level of financial and other support for you and perhaps your children. For example, if you find that you have no rights to a pension or other death benefits, the contract might require him to take out an insurance policy and keep it in force, naming you as the beneficiary.

There is, of course, the possibility of cohabitation which falls between marriage and the type of relationship we have been looking at. Many couples live together with no intention that the relationship be permanent. Generally speaking, the law will not recognize rights or obligations in such a case. The reasoning is that if the parties view the relationship as casual or impermanent, the law should not interfere.

The key thing to bear in mind is this: if you are legally married, the relationship carries with it rights and obligations which will be protected by the state itself. If you are not legally married, any rights and obligations can only be obtained if you fit into definitional categories, either under statute or agreement. But since the rules are different from state to state, and from statute to statute, the important thing from the point of view of self-protection is to learn just where you stand legally.

Remember that there is no legal recognition of a "common-law marriage" in most states, only statutory extensions to the concept of what is recognized as a marriage. Don't let your financial security hinge on your belief in a legal myth. If you have the funds, consult a lawyer privately. If you don't, free legal aid is available in every state.

If, after investigation, you find that your position is not all that you might have hoped for, give some consideration to using a contract to ensure that you and any children who might be involved have adequate protection. If you don't have that "little piece of paper" which makes you a legal wife, think about creating with your co-vivant a piece of paper which at least marks you as a knowledgeable woman able to protect herself.

The Living Arrangements

Because living together requires no formal arrangements— a wedding license, physical examinations, meeting each other's families—there is usually little time between the decision and the act. Actually, many cohabitation arrangements "just happen." While the spontaneity may be terrific for the relationship as it's evolving, many women ask themselves, after the couple has settled into a cohabiting unit or after the relationship breaks up, why more was not made explicit at the time they moved in together—whether financial arrangements, housekeeping details, signatures on the lease, responsibilities toward one another in the future, or whatever.

One woman describes a very common situation when she tells of her first living-in relationship. "He was a guy I'd been dating very intensely and exclusively for about five months. He'd been living with another woman and had a child with her, whom he'd promised to support and never did, I later found out. As their relationship was winding down, he came over for dinner one evening with a small satchel of clothing and said that, since he'd likely spend the night—which he'd done often in the past—he might as well leave some clothes at my place. I thought the whole idea was really cozy, so I emptied a small drawer for him, and that's how it began.

"The overnight date lasted for several weeks. I continued to pay the rent, and out of sympathy for his difficult situation with the 'other woman' (who is really the one I sympathize with now!), I didn't ask him to pay for groceries or anything which I continued to buy. He began to get phone calls and mail at my place too. Mercifully, in a way, just as I was beginning to wonder how I was going to deal with this encroaching relationship without a real showdown, he got transferred to another city. After a few months of separation we just drifted apart, but the drifting itself was a little scary because it showed me how little the relationship itself meant to me in emotional terms, yet how easy it was for me to fall into a totally nurturing and supportive role with this guy."

One way to handle the beginning of a live-in relationship, particularly if it appears to be casual, with one party still maintaining another residence, is to say, "If we're going to do this for a week or so as a lark, that's fine and fun. If we're thinking now of something longer, or if after a week or two it feels as if we want to continue living together, let's agree now that we'll talk about it and try to get organized about it then."

Certainly you have to trust your own instincts about whether or not you're making too big a deal about a casual guest. But especially if the man begins to feel that he's at home, and has moved in a substantial portion of his clothing and comforts, it's time to formalize the relationship in some way. At the very least this protects the relationship itself—with the host (whether you or your lover) much less likely to feel put upon by taking on all the expenses and/or all the work.

There are pitfalls, however. At the other extreme from our friend who just drifted into cohabitation (and was just as happy to drift out again) is the story told by an executive who, after her divorce, began a years-long relationship with a colleague. All along she resisted having him move into the large house she'd retained from her marriage, claiming the presence of her teen-aged children as the deterrent. But, she admitted, she really wanted to make sure that no man was going to overwhelm her "space"—literally and figuratively—as her ex-husband had.

When her youngest child left home and she felt ready to have her friend move in, she drew up an elaborate set of premoveing conditions which she had him sign. He had permission to use her son's bedroom (which was to be the man's room; she didn't want him moving into her bedroom), but only while her son was away at school. At other times he was to move into her study. She also spelled out in detail what household tasks she expected him to perform, and made it quite clear that in no way would she schedule her life around his.

Not surprisingly, this relationship, which had endured for many years when the partners maintained separate residences, fell apart after about six months of living under this carefully articulated contract. This is not to say that all such agreements are inherently faulty or will imperil the couple's happiness. But with precohabiting contracts (as with some premarital agreements as well), the person in power is usually the one pulling the strings and calling the shots, which means that there is an inherent inequality in a situation which is supposed to foster greater equality.

In this particular case—which has about it many elements that will recur throughout this chapter, including the woman's concern for her children and her own autonomy—the woman held most of the cards. For openers, it was her house, and she was the one whose children were around and whose interests she wanted to protect. He was so glad to be able to force some commitment from a woman he'd been in love with for years that he didn't foresee some of the interpersonal difficulties that would be spawned by this particular contractual arrangement.

Danger Points for Lovers Only

A living-together agreement that's in writing may give your partner some unexpected legal or financial claims on you if you separate. With the existence of a written contract, the idea of a casual relationship seems to be replaced (at least in the eyes of some legal interpreters) by the concept of an intentional coupling. Any advantage you may see in a live-in contract could become a liability under the law at some future date, so you might want to put in a disclaimer of any future responsibility for each other after you split.

With so delicate an emotional connection at stake, the very act of enforcing the agreement usually means that the relationship is over. Which is why, if you do have a written contract, it should cover circumstances surrounding the termination of the relationship (by consent or by the death of one partner) rather than the conditions, per se, under which you'll live happily together. If the woman is the younger of the two partners, she is often the party whose interests are underrepresented. If she is planning to live with a man who is her peer or even a few years older than she, he is likely making more money than she. For this reason, and because single men feel more entitled than single women to "establish" themselves in apartments or houses despite their single state, she is more likely to move in with him than vice versa. (She is also, for reasons of safety and economy, more likely to have a roommate at her own place, which would make his moving in with her a little awkward.)

If she lives with him and does not insist that they spell out in the beginning who will pay for what, and explicitly what her contribution will be, she falls into the awkward and politically unacceptable situation of singing for her supper, so to speak. She feels dependent on this man for the very roof over her head if she is not contributing to its upkeep, so she is likely to fall into the traditional female nurturing role, doing more than her share of shopping, cooking and cleaning, without the roles ever being made explicit as they are in the traditional marriage situation wherein Pa goes out and earns the bread and Ma stays home and sweeps up the breadcrumbs.

So, as close to the beginning of the cohabiting relationship as possible, while trying to keep your compulsiveness at bay, spell out mutual expectations and obligations. This means that at least there will be no hidden agenda, where he pretends he has a kept woman at home, or she pretends that they're playing at being married (or vice versa).

Cohabitation as a lifestyle offers the alluring possibility of reduced spending (the old two-can-live-as-cheaply-as-one routine), and the wonderful opportunity of being more intimate with someone you care for. The downside risk is that it's a style of living which can make women economically much more vulnerable than men. Here are some of the reasons why, and some pitfalls to avoid.

First, except for the situation of younger singles described above, the man more frequently moves in with the woman, especially if it's a casual (unplanned) cohabitation. Sometimes social sanctions play a role here, with the woman feeling more comfortable in a nonmarital relationship if she retains control over the domicile. More usually, the stereotype of women as nesting little homebodies is at work: her place may appear more comfy or homey. And if one or both are divorced with children, typically his ex-wife and kids have retained his former home, while if she's divorced, she has custody of her original family dwelling, so it makes more sense for him to move in with her. Yet there are certain trade-offs or disadvantages for the woman if the action takes place on her turf.

If you are planning such an arrangement, check first with a lawyer to make sure that your partner will have no vested interest in your home just from having lived in it with you for a certain length of time. (Women need to be protected from implications of "palimony" decisions as much as men do!) Second, make sure that if you receive alimony or child support payments, or have a custody arrangement with an ex-husband, that none of these will be jeopardized by your having a man living in your home with you. If you are in reduced circumstances and receive government assistance of any kind, make sure that neither the live-in relationship nor the income of your partner will be counted against you in determining payments.

If she cares about the relationship a lot (and evidence reveals that a majority of single women say they would like to get married or be in a long-term relationship) a woman may foot the bills for food and rent without proposing a split of expenses, lest she appear to her partner too eager to put the relationship on more formal or permanent footing than he feels comfortable with. This differential approach of women and men, with men wanting to avoid or escape the very intimacy women seek, is captured well in the title of Barbara Ehrenreich's book, *The Hearts of Men: American Dreams and the Flight from Commitment*. This is the hateful dilemma of the jokes and sitcoms—a man ostensibly trapped into unwanted domesticity by some scheming woman.

In the face of these fears, the cohabiting woman is understandably reluctant to scare the man away, since popular imagery has so convinced people of women's unstoppable desire for an inhibiting and claustrophobic domesticity. But it is certainly possible to create a script which acknowledges the freedoms of the partners while at the same time not trapping the woman financially. (She'd be the one to suffer right from the start here, since she is at first supporting both of them while, as typically the lower earner of the two, she is less able to withstand the additional expense.)

The best way to talk about the financial aspects of living together is simply to recognize and state the fact that "we are both adults and we don't have any expectations at this point that his relationship is anything more than the casual and pleasurable connection that it appears to be. But since we are adults, I want to make sure we handle the money side of our living together as equitably as possible without making a big deal out of it. How shall we organize things to split our expenses?" Clearly the earlier in the living-together arrangement this is said, the less awkward it will be to put things on a "businesslike" footing. If you are a woman living with a man, and are so happy to have him with you that you are uneasy at the very thought of suggesting "Dutch treat," examine your motives. Not every solution will work for every woman, and you know what stresses you yourself can tolerate. But you owe it to yourself to be aware of how your emotions or anxieties may be in conflict with your financial self-interest. You need at least to know what emotional factors (fear that he'll reject you—that you'll be seen as too assertive or too preoccupied with money?) are getting in the way of making reasoned judgments about your future.

If you are uneasy about raising issues so basic to equality as resolving who will pay for what and how the simplest household finances will be managed, you are, by your very silence, condemning yourself to an inferior position for the duration of the relationship. What you are saying—to yourself as well as to your partner—is "I care more about this relationship than about my own well-being or self-esteem." You are, in effect, condemning yourself to being a doormat. And although one ancient piece of religious verse has a woman praying to be her man's "footstool in heaven," we are convinced most modern women set higher sights for themselves both in this world and beyond. Know the consequences of your own timidity and temerity.

Practical Steps for the Smart Cohabiting Woman (Or, Learn from the Mistakes of Your Sisters)

Aside from the financial considerations of having him move in with you, be aware also of any clauses in your lease, if you rent your dwelling, which restrict the number of people who can live there. If he's there for anything less than a month, you can probably legitimately claim he's only a guest, but anything over that time and your landlord (or lady)—especially if living gin the same building—may have cause for suspicion. We're not talking bourgeois propriety here, but about such genuine landlord concerns as extra water or electricity usage, insurance liability, etc. And if you live in a city where apartments or rented houses are hard to find, be sure you don't jeopardize your tenancy.

For example, a woman who has just ended a live-in relationship of three years' duration tells this chilling tale. Eleanor and her boyfriend of many years finally found themselves in the same city at the same time—both had been roving photographers. Her best friend found them a terrific apartment. The couple moved in, with the man's signature on the lease; his job was permanent and her work was free-lance, and they thought this looked better to the landlord. Besides, he agreed to be responsible for the rent and she for the other household expenses, since he was earning far more than she.

When they perceived, three years later, that their relationship was coming to an end, Eleanor realized that she was in a grim situation regarding housing. Rents had escalated sharply in those three years, and she soon discovered that while "his" rent (on "their" apartment) had been going up in only small increments each year, if she were to rent an apartment as a new lessee, she'd be getting into the market at its current inflated level. She also saw that if she were to fight him on keeping the apartment, she'd be no better off because she couldn't even afford the rent he'd been paying; she had not felt financially pressed enough to look for a higher-paying permanent job in the time they'd been together, because he'd essentially been subsidizing her career, and she hadn't foreseen the economic consequences of a breakup, the suddenly "overheated" urban housing market and so on.

What were the solutions to her problems? Relatively few. In fact she was forced to move in with a friend for a year until she stabilized her finances, while her ex-boyfriend continued to live in the comfortable apartment she had located and decorated for them. Had she known in advance what she found out through bitter experience, Eleanor could have taken certain self-protective steps. With the benefit of hindsight, we present some of them here:

• Put both names on the lease even if he's going to pay the rent, so that at least you have some rights to the apartment if you split. You might not be able to afford the rent, but at least you could then consider taking in a roommate, taking on more work, or asking your family for funds to tide you over. With keeping the apartment option, you have more choices available to you. You may still decide not to fight him and to let him hang on to it (after all, he'd have an equal right to keep it), but at least you would have some bargaining chips.

• Write a contract when you move in that specifies how he'd compensate you for your loss of a share of the apartment in the event of a split. He could pay for the first three months of your rent elsewhere, or split it with you, or give you a lump sum to help you relocate, or whatever. Of course, bringing up the possible dissolution of a relationship just at the very point when you are ecstatic about being together may dim the roman-

tic glow a bit, but considering the events that befell Eleanor, a
little cold fluorescent light on the situation might be wise.

Even partners with nearly equal earning power need to
consider similar buy-out arrangements in the event of a break-
up, agreeing (while still feeling tender toward one another) how
they'll handle the rights to the common dwelling if they part
company. If it is his apartment she moves into, she needs to be
especially concerned about negotiating some compensatory
arrangement, preferably before she leaves her own cozy little
hearth for his. Some women have even decided to keep their
own apartments or homes for years after moving in with a man,
subletting or renting them out all the while, just to ensure that
they'll have a roof over their heads if the relationship sours.

• Even better would be to sign an agreement at the beginning that you automatically get the apartment if there's a
breakup. He is probably the higher earner, stands to continue
to make more throughout his work life, does not necessarily
have the same safety factors to consider in choosing a dwelling
as a single woman does, and therefore could relocate or resettle
more easily.

However, if you've been through a scene like Eleanor has,
unless you face grave financial dangers, don't excoriate yourself
over the financial cost of a live-in relationship that has ended.
Some people have been badly burned, it's true, but the scars
seldom last forever. With anything less than third degree burns,
it's probably better to tell yourself (and to believe) that you have
bought an experience. You likely didn't enter the relationship
imagining that you'd gain financially, and it makes no sense to
poison your present and future by trying to extract some monetary gain now that the relationship is ending. The recommendations above are intended to guide you in the financial aspects
of the relationship, but finances alone obviously aren't the
relationship's reason for being.

Gender Role Rules

Subtler aspects to consider at the beginning of a cohabitation relationship: if in her own digs the woman already does all
the chores, it may be hard for her to ask any guest to share

them—least of all a potential Serious Relationship (although these are the very people it's most important to get it straight with, since the garden-variety overnight guest is leaving soon anyway).

We don't mean here the superficial "sharing," where you are permitted to call him at four to ask, "Please pick up a nice chilled white Burgundy for dinner tonight on your way home from work." We are talking here about serious sharing of the maintenance chores that are the underpinnings of every household. We mean such hard-to-utter statements as, "We have to scrub out the bathroom before you go to your racquetball match." And if you can't spare yourself the odious tasks of physically maintaining this man, you are likely to be equally disabled when it comes to confronting him on money matters as well.

It is very hard for a woman living with a man in her own home not to act out the nurturing roles she was raised to perform, even if this means acting against her self-interest. And it's equally hard for a woman living rent-free with a man not to feel that she must render services in exchange for room and board.

Even the most perfect relationships may end, and despite recent suits for "palimony" awards, the settlements for live-ins who break up are considerably less equitable than even the limp attempts at equality in divorce settlements. So don't let your nurturing instincts go too far. The above examples about cleaning and cooking are intended to be read as analogies to your general financial well-being in cohabitation.

Single Woman/Divorcing Man

Not every cohabitation situation can be neatly organized in advance, and almost all are constantly evolving until they reach a state of equilibrium with some kind of "understanding" between the parties, or until they dissolve. But one of the most common cohabitation situations arises in the wake of a divorce when, for example, a single woman's long-time lover finally separates from his wife and moves in "for a few weeks." The situation is of necessity uncertain, since he isn't sure when his divorce will become final, whether he'll have the use of the former family home, and just what his discretionary income will be after alimony and child support, if any, are agreed upon.

In a case like this, very little is negotiated beforehand because of what appears to be the *ad hoc* nature of the living-in situation. But especially in situations like this the woman who is playing hostess to her lover should beware of the ways in which her emotions will affect her financial arrangements. She is likely to see the man as vulnerable and needy, and may be very glad that he's finally free of his marriage and is turning to her. She feels that to seek some financially equitable agreement between them at this point would endanger their fragile new status as a couple, since he is so uncertain of his own financial future, and feels so much at the mercy of his wife's financial demands. A situation of this sort also plays into the competitive roles women are forced to enact with each other—in this case the "new" woman may feel that she must be especially conciliatory to the man in light of his recent experiences, and she may go out of her way to disabuse him of the notion that "all" women are as demanding as his soon-to-be-ex-wife. Competitive strivings might lead her toward this indulgence of her lover, but self-interest does not. Inertia is hard to overcome; patterns set down early in the relationship can and do persist for its entire duration.

We are not preaching that all newly separated men are to be avoided like the plague, but remember that if you and he do get married and he has financial obligations from a previous marriage, there will never be a time when he's going to be really delighted to sit down and work out financial arrangements with you without being a little defensive. Since there will never be a perfect time, do it now!

Long-Term Live-Ins

The terms of a live-in relationship vary with the length of time it exists. What changes first is the security the partners feel with each other, buttressed by time and shared experience. If the relationship has endured for more than two years, this is usually testimony to the fact that it's a good one—"good" in that

it has been meeting the partners' various needs as it has pro-
gressed. The secure feelings that this induces means that one's
guard can be down a little more. One woman sums it up very
well in her answer to the question, "why," as a very knowledgeable feminist lawyer writing frequently about women's financial hardships at the hands of men, she lets her live-in lover of
fifteen years manage all her finances, she says, "I trust Harry."

Even with this growing and quite natural trust, there are
certain guidelines for a woman to keep in mind as the relationship progresses:

• Keep separate bank accounts. Even for married couples,
with built-in safeguards according to law, separate accounts are
a good idea. But they're even more important for the cohabiting
couple, because in the event of a breakup, to prevent claims on
you afterward by your ex-partner, you do not want to have
given the impression of a permanent relationship.

In addition, to make sense of each party's expenses and
deductions at tax time, separate records are a must. You may
want to keep a joint household account for food and other
shared items, into which you each deposit an agreed-upon sum.
This can be an equal percentage of income, or a fixed amount
from each of you per month. But an account like this might not
be necessary if each of you agrees to be responsible for separate
items.

Aside from their other advantages, separate accounts mean
that you have absolute and independent control over your own
money—a very important fact for every woman. Since funds
from a joint account can be removed by either of you without
the consent of the other, if you should break up acrimoniously
or even have a disagreement, you may get the unpleasant
surprise of discovering that he's drained your joint account!

• Don't pose as a married couple, or suggest that you're
married. Under some circumstances you could be held responsible for his debts—if, for example, he seeks credit from a store
where you have an account and the management had been led
to believe that he was your husband.

• Find out, if you can, whether your partner has any major
debts outstanding, and then try to assess, given your local

legislation, how you can avoid being held responsible for those debts. One way would be not to hold anything in common—because if his creditors come after what he's got they could end up taking what belongs to you too.

• Pay for major purchases by check or on a charge account if you save your charge receipts. This will furnish proof—or even just a reminder—of who bought what if you reach the point of having to divide the household.

• Keep your will up to date. With the developing nature of your relationship, you might want him to inherit from you, whereas in an earlier will he wasn't on the scene yet, or you didn't feel as strongly about wanting to make a bequest to him. But after he's seen you through tough times, or you feel that your lives are becoming enmeshed in more powerful ways, you may want to consider such revisions.

On the other hand, if you have children or other dependents and you want to leave your estate only to them, it would be wise to spell this out explicitly in your will; he might at least be able to challenge your will in court if you don't explicitly exclude him from inheriting. The flip side of this is that if either of you is married to someone else, even if you've been living with each other for years, your estranged husband or his wife would probably automatically have a claim against your estate.

• Consult a lawyer or your insurance broker or your employer's benefits office to see if your cohabitant qualifies to receive survivors' benefits when you die. You may want him to, or you may prefer that your children or other dependents receive these benefits instead. Just make sure that whatever your wishes are they can be acted upon in the event of your death.

• Speaking of insurance—while of course your dwelling should be insured (preferably by both of you jointly—see our discussion of this in Chapter 1, "Single and Solvent"), something you might not yet have considered is health insurance. It is possible—though not generally likely—that you or your partner may be able to arrange coverage under each other's policies. If, for example, you are the earner and your co-vivant is a student, you may be able to cover him under your insurance.

Just remember that if the relationship dissolves, you will need to arrange independent coverage immediately.

Joint Ownership

One of the biggest financial changes in a cohabiting relationship as it develops concerns housing. In the beginning, as we've said, the party of the first part moves into the home of the party of the second part, and negotiations proceed from there—with the person who was there first having more leverage in the power game. But the ground rules change as trust and, usually, income increase. For reasons of tax and equity, as well as for other reasons, owning the place they live in might suit the couple better than renting.

There may be several ways to buy a home that would work for you. One of you might make the purchase and rent a portion of the dwelling to the other. Then expenses for the part of the house that's rented become tax-deductible. Depending upon your own specific circumstances, there are ways to make your nonmarried status a financial plus.

The joys and complications of owning something this large together while at the same time keeping your finances separate (not "comingled," as that luscious legal term describes it), may call for some interesting maneuvers. A single woman in her middle thirties tells of her confusion when, after she and her boyfriend had been living for four years in the house they'd purchased together, her mother died and left her an inheritance of $45,000. Since she had no other major projects in mind, our friend decided she wanted to pay off the mortgage on her house, which was rising in value, and which she wanted to own outright without being locked into the high interest rates she was paying on her bank mortgage (even though the interest was tax-deductible).

But how to do it? She couldn't decide. Should she just pay off her share of the mortgage? Buy the house outright from the bank and her boyfriend and have it all in her own name? She finally decided to pay off the whole mortgage, and her boyfriend paid her each month for what his share would have been had the bank still held the mortgage, and they retain joint ownership of the house.

An arrangement like this one seems perfectly equitable while the couple is living together, but should have some built-in safeguards in case they part company before he has finished paying off his share of the mortgage. In fact, joint ownership like this—whether of a house or of a business enterprise—should always build in safeguards and stipulations anticipating what will happen if the partnership dissolves: who can buy out whom, and how this would work.

Another consideration when buying something jointly is that an arrangement which works while you're "just living together" may become awkward or feel unwieldy if and when you decide to marry (each other). Faced with the situation just mentioned, for example, some women would find it strange to be accepting a check from their husbands every month for rent or mortgage payment, whereas the slightly riskier or more distant living-together relationship can more readily absorb such a businesslike approach. (See Chapter 7, "Women, Men and Marriage," for the traditional—and perhaps misguided—distinctions between marriage arrangements and other business ventures.)

Sometimes parents who plan to leave a sum of money or a piece of property to a married daughter insist that the daughter and her husband sign an agreement that any inheritance will not be considered communal property in the event of the dissolution of the marriage. Or they give the inheritance to their daughter in such a way (through a trust, for example) that it cannot fall into her husband's hands. But while parents might (and do) say "I don't want my son-in-law to get my money," and make their feelings very clear to a married daughter, thereby alerting her to her rights, parents almost never take these precautions in the case of a daughter who is "just" living with a man. Perhaps this is because they fail to realize that the individuals comprising a cohabiting couple may have almost the same rights to each others' property as a married couple, or perhaps they don't imagine that the live-in relationship will outlive the parents themselves.

Living Together with Children

If you are living with a man and have children from previous liaisons, you'll want to protect not only your own interests but also, presumably, those of your children. We've already mentioned how important it is not to let your live-in situation jeopardize support payments (or, God forbid, custody). How you do this will depend in part on the laws in your area and in part on how vindictive the children's father is. (See also Chapter 11, "Divorce: Coaching in Battlefront Tactics and Strategies".)

You'll also want to be clear about any financial commitments your lover may make to your children. If yours is a long-term relationship, he may feel as much responsible for them as you do, but it is a good idea to get his feelings down on paper. For example, if he has said that he will help pay for their support or their tuition, perhaps you can say, "I am trying to work out a realistic budget for what our needs will be over the next few years. You've always said that you want to help pay for the kids' college education. How would you feel if I asked you to put that in writing? I am just so nervous about these upcoming huge expenses that I think I'd feel better if we had a formal understanding about this." Or you could, even if it's a few years in advance, ask him to cosign a college loan from the bank with you. Managing day-to-day expenses is much simpler if he has agreed to share the costs of child rearing; if he has had a change of heart about helping to feed and clothe your children you'll know soon enough—it's his promised help with the significant long-term expenses that may cause you some (understandable) anxiety.

One of the most difficult problems in dealing with such financial arrangements within an ostensibly loving family-like arrangement (or even, for that matter, within a more traditional family itself) is that one feels that one is moving in and out of the relationship's intimacy when one schedules a confrontation, of sorts, to deal with financial matters. In daily life you may function as a loving team, tightly bound up with one another and with the children. So it's unsettling to have to draw back a bit and say, to yourself or out loud to your partner, "We are essentially discrete units; our connection is not much greater than skin deep; I'm not sure I trust you to act in my best interest always." You know how much of this confrontation you want to enact in representing your own needs to your lover. But when it comes to your children, you may have to be tougher.

Make sure, as we've mentioned above, that your will and your arrangements for life insurance and the like take into account what you want, which might not be found in some standard, boilerplate policy. You don't have to favor your children over your co-vivant, nor vice-versa, but you do owe it to yourself to make sure that your own wishes are set out in your will and other estate-planning devices. (See also the section on legal guardianship in Chapter 13, "Motherhood: Financial Strategies.")

If the two of you have a child or children together, you will also want to ensure that, if you so choose, both parents are listed on the birth certificate and other records. In most jurisdictions, children born "out of wedlock" have the same rights of inheritance as all other children. Where complications are likely to arise are in those cases where either one of the parents is still married to someone else. If this is the case, be sure that your child's birth records make clear who the father is—for many reasons, obviously—but among them to ensure appropriate inheritance from the father's estate.

While for some couples an unplanned pregnancy is the trigger to a long-contemplated marriage, for others it can be a terrible cause of dissent. It's never easy to predict how anyone will respond in the existential situation of actually being pregnant and facing the decision of whether or not to continue the pregnancy. But you should ask yourselves certain questions in advance: who will pay the costs of an abortion, if necessary? Will he accept responsibility for the legal paternity of the child? Will he enter into an agreement regarding child support?

One callous man tells his own story (without remorse, one might add) about what happened when the woman he was living with got pregnant unexpectedly: "I told her not to worry when she realized she was pregnant. She could have the kid, and I'd always take care of her. Well, of course after the kid was about five months old we could see that we weren't getting along. Times were hard for me financially, and when I moved out of town to take another job I really couldn't afford to send her anything or I'd be living too close to the bone myself."

Do not let this happen to you!

One way around such a situation is to insist, when you agree to proceed with the pregnancy, that he make a lump-sum payment into an account to which only you have access. Ideally, the amount should be at least equal to what you'd need to live on for six months if you had no other means of support. If he doesn't have the money, suggest that he get a loan or take a cash advance on a line of credit at the bank. If he balks at all of this, you have some notion of how much financial responsibility he'll feel toward you after the baby arrives; if he says he simply cannot understand your anxieties about possibly facing parenthood alone and without money, reconsider whether this is the time for the two of you to have a child together. (See Chapter 17, "Modern Problems" for information about motherhood without marriage.)

When it comes to negotiations between consenting adults about their own interests and needs, there's some leeway—you may not want to push your partner to a point where the relationship loses its savor. But when children are concerned, especially a child he has fathered and for whom you will be the custodial parent if the relationship crumbles, you must get a statement of paternity and of intent to provide support even before the baby is born. (Not that enforcement of child support agreements is ever as sufficient as it needs to be, but recent legislation in Canada allowing men's salaries or tax refunds or savings bond interest to be withheld until child support is paid is a step in the right direction.) As an unmarried mother, you would find it easier to exert some clout in getting the father to support you if you could produce such an agreement.

As you can see from what you've just read, the financial and legal complications of living together vary enormously for each couple, depending upon where they live, how long they've been together, whether there are children involved (hers, his or theirs) and whether or not either of them is married to someone else. The factor common throughout is the woman's need to retain a sense of herself as an independent being—a "singloid," so to speak—even in the closest moments of the relationship. For most relationships defined by desire and not by law, the tension of committing to the relationship anew each day adds to its allure. But living together provides a woman with even less financial security than marriage, so it requires vigilant self-interest in order that she may feel secure enough to enjoy it.

7

Women, Men and Marriage

Before there was romance, before there was a tradition of courtly love, even before there were caterers and banquet halls and soap operas, there was marriage. What was marriage without the trappings of love? It was an economic agreement, usually between the families or tribes of the principals involved, but sometimes just between the husband- to-be and the bride's family. The economic contract, with clauses that have changed through the centuries but which are in some form still built into our marriage laws, predates our current expectations that marriage is a pact based on tender feelings.

Even though many couples view the contractual aspects of marriage as antithetical to its "higher" purpose—the union of two people who care enough about each other to want to build a life together in a formal, legally sanctioned fashion—there are financial responsibilities to being married, and usually financial consequences to ending a marriage. The economic basis of marriage as a contract between two parties (who may or may not have been consenting) still exists.

Marriage is not all lilies of the valley and a champagne reception. It is a legal state which may be entered into with more fanfare and festivity than most corporate deals, but which is, in its bare bones, a legal agreement between two people which can remain in force for life. Therefore, it makes sense to think about the legal (as well as the emotional) consequences of the change of status you are about to formalize when you apply for a Wassermann test. No longer are you the romantic couple trying to "psych out" each other's needs and desires. Now your relationship has formal and legal obligations, responsibilities and consequences, both as the marriage proceeds and if it ends in divorce.

Marriage is likely one of the longest-lasting legal arrangements a person enters into, yet it is the one about which the parties probably know the least. Often a woman investigates more thoroughly the warranty terms on her microwave oven or her home computer than she does the legal and financial terms of the agreement she's making with the person she marries. One specialist in marriage law, Lenore J. Weitzman, warns in a *Columbia Law Review* article that,"The marriage contract is unlike most contracts; its provisions are unwritten, its penalties are unspecified, and the terms of the contract are typically unknown to the contracting parties."

The very fact that you've gotten married creates mutual legal obligations which may not exist in any other arrangement. In most states, the marriage creates a legal obligation of each to support the other financially, creates rights which automatically come into play upon divorce or death, and offers tax concessions which do not exist for unmarried couples. While various rights may ultimately arise between unmarried partners which are similar to those of a married couple (see Chapter 6, "Living Together"), they will not be as comprehensive in scope and will not be in place instantly, as happens when the minister, rabbi, priest or judge says, "I now pronounce you husband and wife."

Nobody wants to eliminate love, passion and other tender feelings from the marriage picture and return to a time when individual preference was never taken into account. But whether or not we enter marriage swept away by feelings of passion, devotion and harmony, there are certain legal and financial aspects to being married which can (and often do) affect the emotional quality of the relationship at some point along the way. Money matters have the potential to strain a continuing marital relationship, even a happy one. Whether a first marriage or a remarriage, whether both spouses are earning or only one, we can see certain patterns emerging in the ways that wife, husband and money interact.

Who Marries?

Even now, in the closing decade of the twentieth century, women tend to marry men older than they, taller, better educated and earning more than they do. All these culturally induced "preferences" lead to a certain imbalance in the marriage partnership. While women tend to want to marry "up" in every sense, men may be drawn to those women over whom, in subtle ways, they can exert mastery.

While some of the older patterns of marriage preference may be changing slowly (six examples of older women marrying younger men may constitute a "trend" for journalistic purposes), statistics show that most marriages still follow the more conventional pattern. Until the age of 35, there are slightly more single men in the available pool than there are single women; from then on, the proportions reverse. At age 35 there are 84 single men for every 100 single women; past 65 there are only 26 single men for every 100 single women. The reasons for this are complex, and at the older end of the age spectrum one must take into account women's greater longevity. But the numbers are useful as a reminder of the power structure of marriage: husbands still tend to be older and richer than their wives. And they are likely to stay that way throughout the marriage.

What does this predict for the balance of power in the relationship? Each marriage obviously has its own issues, but certain patters emerge. Concerning power and money, most marriages fall into one of three categories, sometimes depending on the age of the partners. The classic pattern has Pa at work and Ma at home managing house and kids, a pattern shifting nationally as the cost of living rises and more families are dependent upon two paychecks to make ends meet.

The middle ground, which gives families more income but usually not much shift in roles at home, has Pa at work full time and Ma at work either part time or full time, but with the shared understanding that her work is just "helping out" and isn't what gives the whole family its self- definition or status.

The third type of economic arrangement in marriage is characterized by couples in which both partners have fairly equal earning capacity, and who choose to share both economic support of the family unit and the tasks of maintaining the family's support systems. This financial arrangement between wives and husbands is also not without its financial crises, particularly when the time comes to reassign priorities as children appear on the scene or are being planned.

The At-Home Wife in a "Traditional" or "Asymmetrical" Marriage

Let's look at some examples from the lives of couples in which the wife, even if she does earn some money, is not considered—by either spouse—to be a significant contributor to the family finances. These families represent what economist Julie Matthaei has called the "complementary" model, in which the man and woman specialize in different spheres, he the economic and she the family.

• *Case One*   They've been dear, trusting friends for most of their married lives—which have been spent together. Then he says, in annoyance, when she disagrees with his plan to make a major investment hastily, "Just keep quiet. You don't have any voice in this. I've been in business and you haven't and I know what I'm doing." She knows he's acting precipitously and stubbornly, but his words seal off all her reasonable arguments.

• *Case Two*   Another woman, whose husband feels she indulges their teen-aged children, wants to talk with her husband about saving for their education. He says, in anger, "*You* want them to go away for college, *you* make the money to finance it. As far as I'm concerned they can stay home."

In these and in many other marriages, *purse and power seem inextricably linked.* In every marriage in which the wife does not work outside the home for pay, or in which she earns substantially less than her husband, or in which there are dependent children from a previous marriage, beneath the surface always lurks the hidden threat that he will pull rank because it is "his" money that keeps the family afloat. The prevailing fear is that he will throw up to her, explicitly or indirectly, that she is a parasite who is supported by him, and therefore not his equal. A nineteenth century writer describes this in words that ring true today for the lives of many women: "Even where a woman does all the work of a family—performing all sorts of housework, her husband will talk of 'supporting' her, and never seem to think that he owes her any wages for her labor."

The woman may in fact be contributing substantially in ways other than household labor, as we'll see, but the perception she and her husband share is that he is actually the sole breadwinner; her earnings, and/or money she saves the family through good management or her own labor at home don't seem to be figured into the family's economic equation. They don't "buy" her any more power at home. The husband who challenges the opinions or desires of his nonearning or underearning wife with the finality of, "*You* want it, *you* go out and get the money for it" (whether it's orthodontia for a child, a course for her, or some small luxury for an aging parent) is not seriously suggesting that she retool and earn more money. In fact, he may even have discouraged her from full participation in the work force all along. What he really means is, "Accept the facts: we'll do it my way or not at all."

Not all marriages have the same kinds of conflicts over money, of course, and some may have none. (If you're lucky enough to have a marriage that fits the latter category, stick around anyway—this chapter has advice for avoiding financial quicksand, as well as strategies for getting out if you're in already.) Hidden or implicit or covert contracts about money in marriage exist both in marriages where the husband works for pay and the wife supports him at home, and in marriages where both agree that the husband's work is the important and chief-earning job, while the wife, who works part time or at a substantially lower rate of pay than her husband, still provides all the support services at home. The implicit contract in these situations says, "he provides, she serves."

One woman, in a recent magazine cover story on the plight of wives today, said with resignation, "I don't know anyone who has a 50-50 relationship. His attitude is, 'Well, if you go out and make as much as I do, then we'll be equal.' It seems like men just want to dominate you. I love my husband and I want to make it work...but...." Many of the women interviewed,

including this one, wanted more tenderness and companion-
ship from their husbands—no matter what the men earned—
and the response of the husbands was often some variation on,
"I work hard to earn the money to keep this operation afloat
and I need time and space for myself; don't lean on me to give
you more than I feel like giving," as if giving financial support
were all that mattered, and constituted a license to withdraw
from human contact.

Clearly, money is a metaphor for other issues between husband and wife. It's very concrete and, as Dr. Spock says about
children's bedtime, it comes around so frequently that if you
don't deal with it smoothly it can make a wreck out of you.
Many nonmaterial conflicts (such as issues of control and dom-
inance) are expressed through conflicts over money management, and there's never a scarcity of opportunity to find some
financial matter to do battle over.

Money becomes the weapon of choice in many duels between husband and wife. He may withhold money as an act of
hostility; she may spend money for the same reason; more
rarely, these roles are reversed.

We are only at the first stages of exploring the meaning of
the money battle between "traditional" wives and their husbands. In many ways it was easier to deal with sex, because even
the most conservative, retrograde men believed that the so-
called sexual revolution would ensure that their wives would
"give" them "better sex." When women strive for economic
equality, it's not nearly so clear to the man (usually in the
superior position) that he has anything at all to gain.

And yet he does. As opposed to divorce negotiations, in
which the partners become genuine adversaries and in which
they are playing a "zero-sum" game, where a gain for one of
them means a loss for the other, there are plenty of opportunities
in a relatively stable marriage for mutually beneficial financial
arrangements—in effect, a situation where both parties win.

We suggest that you read this whole chapter, regardless of
your present status. If you are married and working for pay, this
may change when you have a child, and in any case chances are
that you grew up in an environment influenced by "traditional"

views of women's and men's roles within the family and out-side it. If you are yourself an at-home wife—for whatever reasons—you may be working in the future, or you may want to manage your money in ways more closely approaching that of the two-paycheck couple.

The big question in the traditional marriage is how to help women and men overcome an essential difference in attitude. Women report feelings of being trapped, of feeling claustrophobically dependent upon husbands, some of whom hold their wives accountable for every cent spent. ("My friend, whose husband is a very rich businessman, can't even buy a pair of stockings without asking his permission," moans a woman from Indiana.) Some men say that they think their wives are perfectly happy this way—or should be. One man an-nounces, "She should be glad not to have to go to work every morning." In other couples, the running gag is, "My wife helps me a lot with money; I earn it and she saves me the trouble of having to spend it—she spends it all!" Of course, the hidden subtext in this latter situation is that the man is secretly pleased to have so much disposable income (another form of macho) that he can boast of how much his wife spends.

In the cartoons of the 1950's, the biggest crises between Blondie and Dagwood were over her spending habits (symbol-ized by the hatboxes hidden after a shopping spree with the boss's wife). Money issues in contemporary families are more likely to revolve around independence or interdependence, a sharing of responsibilities so that each partner feels valued and respected by the other, rather than being polarized into the dependent/infantalized/spendthrift wife and adoring/irri-tated/bill-paying husband of the past. *Thus, the crises in tradi-tional marriages today are more likely to be over the wife's desire to earn rather than her desire to spend.*

Women who want to get out of these traps, especially if there are no dependents needing full-time care at home, are eager to enter or reenter the work force. More than two-thirds of Amer-ican women with children between 6 and 17 have already gone out to work. The majority of women in the work force work for

the same reason men do—because they must in order to support
(or help support) themselves and their families.

Self-worth, for both sexes, is an extra benefit of working
outside the home. Yet many men still don't believe that they will
gain from having their wives in the paid labor force. Even the
lure of shifting some of the family's heavy financial burden onto
other shoulders isn't convincing enough for some (see the
Chapter 10, "Myths About Taxation: Their Impact on Women,"
for the fascinating reasons many men use for dissuading their
wives to work for pay). Such men correctly equate women's
paid work with their greater independence, which suggests
why patriarchal systems have wanted to keep women financially dependent on men. That's the barefoot part of "barefoot
and pregnant."

The balance of power in a marriage changes radically when
the partner who has heretofore been earning little if any money
begins to earn, and then wants to transfer her newly discovered
sense of her own value into family decision- making as well.
When both partners recognize the value (or necessity) of each
other's earnings, they must also recognize joint authority in the
family, and the patriarchal premise under which most "traditional" marriages have operated is thus eroded.

The immediate reason for this shift in power when a pre-
viously unemployed woman enters the workforce is not myste-
rious. A woman who has money of her own to draw on can
afford to be more honest, less conciliatory and even more con-
frontational in her relationship with her husband, because she
is not totally dependent upon him for a roof over her head and
food on her plate. This may be why many two-career couples
(about which more in a moment), in which the wife and husband are equally committed to their work and earn more or less
comparable salaries, are likelier to have made explicit agreements about sharing money and support tasks in the home. The
women in these marriages can afford to set forth their plans and
needs in a forthright way because they see themselves as their
husbands' equals. While perhaps most women would not describe their home lives in strict terms of economic give-and-

take, the underlying ideology is certainly built into every marriage.

There are countless stories of women who stay in marriages that are not only loveless but also downright abusive because they cannot see any economic alternatives, especially if they have dependent children. An example from Gail Singer's film, *Loved, Battered and Bruised* (National Film Board of Canada): a farm wife with five young daughters is trapped in rural isolation and cannot get away from her violently abusing husband. Finally escaping with her children to the city, she works gruelling hours as a waitress to support the girls. When the narrator comments that she must be glad to be out of that situation, she replies, "I'm not sure."

The marriage need not be abusive for a wife to feel that she had better stay in it. One woman, separated from her husband, realized that not only was she better off in the marriage for the sake of her own and her children's economic well-being, but also that her much-valued freedom not to work full time meant she could visit her ailing parents every day and see to their material needs. All this would be sharply curtailed if, as a divorced woman, she had to work full time to supplement any support payments she might receive. So, reluctantly, she acceded to her husband's desire to continue the marriage, for her parents' comfort as well as her own.

We can conclude from these examples of women's frustration and economic helplessness that every woman, if she can manage it at all, must have as a goal putting some money of her own aside and keeping it absolutely sacrosanct to her own desires.

Even if you aren't planning a divorce in the near future, let's face it, there are adversarial moments (and weeks and months) in most relationships. Since you've learned by now that money is a form of power, you might want to have some in your corner when you and your husband disagree. Perhaps it's knowing from personal experience how important such a nest egg can be to a woman's sense of having options that leads some mothers to earmark money especially for their married daughters, and to give it to them in such a way as to keep it out of the hands of their sons-in-law. (See Chapter 15, "Wills".)

Financial Independence in a "Traditional" Marriage

The traditional marriage begun in the 1960's and earlier featured a man focused primarily on his work and a woman focused primarily on the home; their roles were highly differentiated from one another. Note that this definition does not take into account the fact that the man's earning role gives him more importance in the family dynamic than his wife has.

In our imperfect world we should all be struggling to recast the gender definitions that declare that whatever men do is more important than what women do, and to put a halt to attributing status to high earners for their money alone. But until the world is remade, women (especially in traditional marriages) need a good defense; one such protective shield is money.

Where to get the money? The simplest but in some ways most absurd way to tackle the situation is to ask your husband for it. To support your argument that you are entitled to money of your own (from a practical point of view, aside from the ideological issues) you can quote from *What's a Wife Worth?* and tally up how much he owes you for the services rendered in a typical week.

At least one woman did actually manage to extract a regular monthly salary from her husband, but only after they negotiated it via a professional marriage mediator. Out of her salary she was to contribute to some of the household and child-rearing expenses. She felt that with her earnings came an economic vote in the management of the family's affairs, because "her" money went into the family pool, too. Odd as it sounds, they reached a good solution to their family dilemma, and built into the agreement an understanding that after their small children were grown and in school, she'd go back to school herself and take a job outside the home. (The catch here is, of course, that not every household has the positive cash flow to sustain the payment of a salary for a woman's labor.)

Another woman, who had always kept the small sums she earned in a separate account for her own use—with her husband's blessings—decided that she felt demeaned to receive cash from him at the beginning of each week for the household expenses. She felt that having the money doled out to her in relatively small sums made her feel that she was more an "errand girl" than a family manager. When she mentioned this to her husband (sending "I" messages, as the marriage counselors suggest, rather than "you" messages such as "you make me feel like a beggar" and "you make me so angry") he proposed that he deposit a lump sum directly into her bank account at the beginning of every month, or that he would try to depersonalize the "giving" even further by setting up an automatic bank-to-bank transfer of funds the same way he paid the mortgage. For some women, who are just trying to get to first base in communicating their feeling about money to their husbands, this couple's concern with such intricacies may seem baroque, but each couple's sensitive points are different.

What if you don't want to risk being labeled "abrasive" or "strident" (men's code words for women who assert themselves) by asking for wages for your housework? Or what if there is simply no extra cash in the family system even though your husband has all the goodwill in the world and would gladly make it available to you if it existed?

For many women, particularly women in their fifties and older who have never worked for pay since being married, receiving an allowance from their husbands may be the only autonomous money they've ever handled. It is not uncommon to see middle-class, middle-aged women who actually receive a weekly allowance from their husbands for their personal expenses, just as children do (note the comparison). In other families, women have simply approached their husbands saying that they feel uncomfortable having no funds of their own—even if it's money to buy family gifts—and have asked their husbands to open a bank account, with a certain sum deposited at the beginning of each month, over which the wife has sole discretion.

It's a good idea to expand this account to become the household account, to cover grocery bills, or clothing bills, or whatever, so that you will also have the experience (if you haven't before) of actually managing money. (This will be a particularly useful experience if your marriage dissolves or, as is the case for most women over 65, if you are left a widow. It's much easier for you to gain this experience under your husband's loving tutelage than after he's gone, for whatever reason.)

But watch out! If you pay the bills without having any earnings of your own and no control about household financial decision-making (no vote, for example, in whether or not there's a new car this year, or if the kids go to summer camp), then you have responsibility without any authority. You may be the one who worries every month about how to balance the family budget, and you may also be the one to be blamed if your husband puts his card into the cash machine and finds no balance left in the account. Until you can say, "Look, we don't have any money because you decided we needed a luxurious night on the town with your cousin from Chicago," and don't feel panicked or guilty, you'll have the ulcers and often the blame without ever being able to show in a clear way how the family's money is being budgeted.

There are, again, differences among couples in how the actual money is managed and who manages it. There are ethnic and cultural distinctions as well, so these differences can sometimes be explained by asking about how money was managed in their own families of origin. A Caucasian artist from the Pacific Northwest describes his Japanese wife, saying, "All those allegedly self-effacing Japanese women actually control the purse-strings." Men in other cultures sometimes say the same thing about "their" women. We don't have sufficient data to know whether this is true or merely a projection of power onto essentially powerless people, but it may be true that there are cultural and ethnic differences in the way couples relate to money. For example, former U.S. vice presidential candidate Geraldine Ferraro, when asked about her husband's financial dealings, claimed he'd never informed her of them. "Anyone married to an Italian man will know what I mean, "she said.

If your husband refuses to share financial information or actual money with you, either out of general unwillingness or because the money just isn't available, consider the following sources:

• Get a part-time job or a full-time job, and try to make sure that it provides you with some retirement benefits; at the least, make sure that Social Security payments are being made in your name.

• Save from household accounts; figure out what you normally spend on groceries, etc., each week and spend less. You know all the tricks from consumer magazines; now you have a real incentive to use them. Some married women spend more than they need to as a sometimes unconscious way of punishing their husbands or rewarding themselves. Now your reward can be more direct—pocket the savings.

• Try bartering, or exchanging something you can do for something you need to have done—household repairs, clothing alterations, etc., and pocket the money you'd have had to spend. An aspiring concert pianist we know gives piano lessons to a student who can't afford to pay cash, but who cleans the house and babysits in exchange.

• Ask for a gift of cash when your husband wants to know what you'd like for a present.

• Return gifts your husband gives you which you don't want and keep the money—you can even say why. "I'm so sorry that the jumpsuit didn't fit me properly. I've put the money away, and I promise to buy something special with it when I see it and have that be your gift to me." You can use the money for a course to upgrade your skills, so if you look for a job you'll have some new options available.

• With the money from the household's next income-tax refund, get him to set up an individual retirement account (IRA) for you. It'll give you some independent assets, and it'll provide a tax advantage to him. You're entitled to something out of that refund check. Read Chapter 8, "Myths About Taxation: Their Impact on Women" to find out why.

- Consider turning some of your assets into liquid form before you're faced with an emergency: hold a garage sale or go to a consignment or estate jewelry dealer and sell off the items you never wear and don't feel attached to. Rent out your empty garage to a commuter looking for a monthly daytime parking space, or rent out an extra bedroom to a university student desperate for accommodations. Your husband might not approve of your keeping money from these rentals for your own personal use if he's carrying the mortgage on the property you're renting out, and he'd obviously have to be consulted on such ventures. But even if you don't keep the cash yourself he's bound to begin to see you in a new light, as a financially wise and imaginative person who's a financial asset to the family and not merely a passive somebody to be "supported."

- Then think about investing your nest egg, or part of it. (See Chapter 3, "Investing.") There are two advantages here. First, your money can grow. Second, tying it up for a while keeps it out of reach not only from your own impulse to spend it, but also from your husband's or other people's rationalizations for having you deplete it. It's easier to say no, to yourself or your husband, if the money isn't easily accessible—that is, if you'll have to sell stock or cancel a bank's term deposit account to get to it.

- Ask for cash payment if you do any work to assist your husband's business—whether keeping the books, creating place cards in calligraphy for his boss's luncheon, buying his professional Christmas gifts, or whatever. Your time is valuable; see if you can get paid for it. And the business can claim your charges as a deductible business expense.

Once you have begun to put aside money of your own, try to pretend that it doesn't exist in the family's scheme of things. Try not to draw on it if, for example, the family overextends itself one month. Remember the wonderful story "Mama's Bank Account?" The children in the story feel very secure knowing Mama has a bank account which, fortunately, they never have drawn on because their large family can always make enough sacrifices to get through each crisis without touching the sacred money being put aside for "real" emergencies. At the end of the story, one of the children, now grown, learns that there never was such an account—it was an imaginary safety net Mama had created so that the children would feel more secure in their severely straitened circumstances. Your money will be real, of course, but you should be just as vigilant about finding other sources of emergency funds.

Think of the nest egg you're building as your *ideological* money—perhaps to be used only for those purposes on which you and your spouse might disagree. Or, on the positive side, to provide both of you with some luxury that he might not think he can afford; in this case you are the provider, and both of you become aware of this new role.

This savings account (or term deposit or whatever) may be the only liquid asset you'll have if he walks out suddenly (it happens—read Chapter 11, "Divorce:Coaching in Battlefront Tactics and Strategies"), or if he refuses to pay for something you *know* is essential either for you or for the children. ("I never had orthodontia—why do *they* need straight teeth?") Make sure to keep this money in your own name, not jointly with him or anyone else!

You can build up this fund openly or secretly, and there are arguments to be made each way. Openness is, in theory, "better" for the marriage. It also allows you the opportunity to wave your bank statement in the air and to renegotiate some of the points in your "covert" contract. But wanting to keep your own money as something only you know about isn't necessarily the sign of a bad or failing marriage; if you feel you have some flexibility and independence you may find yourself less furious at your husband than when you were completely at his mercy financially. (Of course if there's a real emergency and you want to use your money to alleviate the distress, be prepared to explain how you came to have this secret stash.)

An advantage to secrecy is that it protects your money from your own ability to be manipulated by your husband. Imagine a scene in which he says: "We're low this month and we really need it. You're hoarding in a very selfish way. I have nothing I keep separately in my name." Actually, in the vast majority of cases, this last statement is utterly false. If he's holding down a job, he has a credit rating and a chunk of retirement income or a vested pension which, if you divorce or are widowed, you may never see a cent of. If you have no regular source of income yourself you have no financial stake for your own future—which is a very good reason to begin pressuring your local politicians to support wages for housework, or at least to insist that your husband provide you with coverage under a retirement plan or annuity, recognizing the value of the unremunerated work you perform for him and your family.

One possibility is to put your money into household needs—new carpet, great family vacation—very concrete pleasures, so that your contribution is recognized. The advantage of doing this is obvious, in both psychological and practical terms. The disadvantage is that you have no money of your own once it's spent, and you're back at square one. Only you can evaluate what will work best, and protect your interests best in your own marriage.

One important warning if you do decide to use your money for family purchases: try *not* to use whatever money you have to help pay *directly* for the family home. This may sound absurd, since usually when a family is purchasing a home, especially a first home, every single cent they can put their hands on is desperately needed. But please hearken to this message.

Since in several states the house you live in while married is the one asset which, by law, has to be split evenly at the time of divorce (unless you've signed an agreement to the contrary), you might put up the lion's share of the down payment on your house with the only substantial sum of money you'll ever have. If you put the money itself into the house, goodbye nest egg! In the case of a divorce, your husband will get 50% of the house or its proceeds, regardless of whether or not you were the one who made its purchase possible.

The idea in this situation is to avoid putting the money directly into the house, while still making funds available for the purchase. Suppose you have $25,000 to put into a house, enough for the down payment. Instead of just making the payment directly (to the seller or the bank), you can lend the money to your husband. This can be an interest-free loan if you feel more comfortable with this, as most spouses would. He then buys the house. In the event of divorce, you are entitled to one-half interest in the house and whatever other split of assets is called for under the applicable state laws, plus the repayment of the $25,000 he owes you. If you are thinking of contributing money towards buying that dream house for the two of you and your family, check with a lawyer as to how you can best protect yourself while still contributing to what will probably be the family's largest purchase.

The irony in this whole situation is that a law which was put into place to ensure that dependent wives and children have a roof over their heads in case of divorce may in some cases create a trap for women who have put their own money into the family house. The benefit for women under the law was based on the implicit assumption that *he* paid for the whole house and she was still entitled to the use of it. If *she* paid for any of the house directly, the upshot may well be that if they divorce he gets a financial bonus.

So, you now understand the pitfalls, and you want both to contribute to buying your family's house and to protect yourself in the long run. Here's a suggestion you can make to your husband which illustrates our contention that there's often benefit to *both* parties with financial strategies that protect the woman's interests.

You tell him, as one woman did, that her nest egg was providing him with "cheaper money" than if he had to go to the bank, since she'd provide the money as an interest-free loan. The note, or statement of his debt to her, stated that the loan was "payable on demand." Obviously, if they continue to be happily married she might never call in that note.

Now, the ideologically feminist approach might be to declare that, once again, the person paying the piper calls the tune, and that by allowing him to be the purchaser of the house you're appearing to be a kept woman. Remember, again, that your services to the household (if you're not working for pay) are worth a great deal, and that if you have that note of indebtedness in your hand—or in your safe deposit box, where it ought to be—you have proof of your financial contribution as well, and neither of you can forget it.

What Do Men *Want?*

Not all disputes over financial control occur when the woman wants more power and the man is reluctant to grant it. In fact, some difficulties arise when a man doesn't want to continue to handle the finances but doesn't know how to turn over the reins. Here is an instructive story about the inability of a man to communicate (or even be in touch with) his own feelings, told spontaneously by a mild-mannered, gracious, middle-aged woman, a "career" volunteer for good causes whose husband had been a successful businessman before he retired.

"I took over our family finances a year ago. I do all the management now. Why? Terror and anger. (I'd have had to have had pretty strong motivation, wouldn't I?)

"My husband retired and sold his business for a very great sum of money. Then he made a series of huge, exciting, high-risk investments which might pay off twenty or forty years from now. I didn't know about this, but I did sense that something was wrong. All our security was in jeopardy. He hadn't told me. For two months after I found out, I couldn't even sit beside him without being *furious*. Then I took it all over. I actually think he was relieved. Now he's begun to understand his own motives: the retirement thing—proving he could still manage risky investments, all of that. But I had to start from scratch.

"I interviewed lawyers and accountants—six lawyers! I really wanted to find someone I could work with. After I found the perfect person I said, 'Here's someone I think you'll like,' and my husband and I went together to make the final decision. The lawyer I chose is a hardbitten, tough guy. The nice friendly ones made me nervous.

"I had to figure out how to approach the lawyers and accountants in the first place. As an innocent? As a little girl? Finally I realized I could say, 'Listen, I don't know anything about this, but I *am* a very intuitive person and I know this is wrong for me.' They can't argue with that—whereas if I'd tried to challenge them factually they'd have argued back.

"I've learned so much from this, and I feel so much more powerful and in control (though my husband says it's a false sense of power because I should have been more in tune to these issues all along). I remember when things were out of control. Today I was walking with a friend who said she had to stop at the bank. I looked up and shuddered—I'd had to go there with my husband to renegotiate payments and so on, and of course had to play the dumb little woman.

"I feel all this has really changed my life. Last night when I was soaking in the tub making notes for my meeting with the accountant today I felt positively jubilant!"

How To Communicate About Money (This Ain't Just Pillow Talk)

Women traditionally have been reluctant to talk about their own financial concerns with their husbands in a marriage in which the man is the family's sole or major support. Even in more egalitarian earning situations, women report their uneasiness about discussing money, reluctant to appear money-hungry, reluctant to have their husbands think they're contemplating divorce. But as one activist woman puts it, "nobody much likes to talk about contraception, either. That's also not a very romantic subject. But you do it. It's the same with talking about money."

It may help you in making up your mind to have more openness about money in your traditional marriage if you present your husband with data that shows that there is joint mutual benefit in having things understood more thoroughly between you; you want to be able to tell him that he has something to gain here too. You might want to quote to him these comments from a (male) financial adviser who believes that men have everything to gain from sharing financial information (and not just money itself) with their wives. This man, a noted money guru speaking off the record here, says: "You have to get away to talk about money regularly. It keeps you sane. My wife and I try to go out for brunch once a month or so, and since I'm the major earner I keep her up to date on our income and we talk together about any major expenses. We also go over what kinds of investments we've made for the children.

"When we know that we have a financial 'appointment' coming up, we're spared a lot of dinner table arguments over money. One or the other of us will say, when some potentially explosive subject arises, 'Well, make a note of it and we'll talk about it at brunch.' The advantages of going out are obvious—not the least being that our conversations are more focused and less distracted than they are at home. Doing this out of our usual context also gives them a vignette-like quality that helps us remember them very clearly later. And making notes in advance about what we want to discuss gives us a written record of the things we've discussed; this can be a very useful spur to the memory if one or the other of us claims that a subject was never put on the table.

"Frankly, I've found these discussions a stabilizing feature in our marriage. We fight less about money now because there's less room for blame or recriminations after the fact. I used to hate it when she'd second-guess me. 'Why did you lease the car instead of buying it? Why did you put the kids' birthday money into worthless stock?' and so forth. She can't get angry with me over financial decisions if they've been made jointly or in consultation.

"I also see that especially when money is tight my wife understands much better the family's need to cut back on expenditures. The more aware she is of these things as they're happening the more economically we can manage the household.

"There's another, more painful, aspect to these sessions, too. I always have at the back of my mind the sense that if I'm disabled or die suddenly, she'll be better prepared to take things over completely now that she's much more familiar with our family finances. It's not that in the past she knew nothing, but now she knows and understands the thinking behind some of the arrangements we've made over the years."

Two Paychecks, But Only One "Career"

More than half of all married couples qualify as two-earner families, and the number is growing.

In the case of a married couple where both parties are working for pay, the problems are a little different from those we've just discussed. The "political" issues are not as clear-cut, but they exist nonetheless. Since women still earn only 66 cents for every dollar a man does, pay inequities are a reality of every working woman's life. Combined with the caste privilege many men feel is their birthright (why, even in this day and age, do so many feel entitled to be looked after much as, perhaps, their nonworking mothers looked after them?), pay inequities contribute to the situation in which a woman with a job outside her home may feel that, as one woman tells it, "I've taken on two jobs. I still have as much to do at home as ever before, with less time to do it, and no time at all for myself. I love my job, and especially the feeling of earning money of my own, but I can't figure out how to get out from under the burden of being the Superwoman around here."

Statistics bear out this woman's complaint. A time budget survey shows that as of 1981 (and we have no reason to doubt that the numbers are less true today), even when women are employed outside the home most continue to have primary responsibility for family and home care. Women in the labor force average almost 4 hours each day on domestic and child care duties. The men surveyed spent only half that amount of time on domestic responsibilities—and in household where the men are in professional occupations where they are entitled or required to bring their work or at least their work worries home with them, we can surmise that the hours spent on domestic or child care tasks are considerably less that this. More women are working outside their homes, but reality inside hasn't yet caught up.

Many couples unconsciously accept income as a basis for assigning household duties. As Philip Blumstein and Pepper Schwartz point out in *American Couples*, the woman who earns money isn't expected to do quite as much housework as the woman who stays home full time, "a sure sign that she is elevated in her own and her husband's eyes." Note that house-work seems to have a meaning quite apart from its necessary performance as a maintenance task for the machinery of the household. It is the lowliest job in the family pecking order and performing it often reinforces a wife's suspicion that she is merely the family enabler, whose work permits the other mem-bers to live in comfort—and it's clearly women's work. The image of a man wearing an apron and wielding a dishcloth conveys to every reader of comic strips that this man is stereotypically "henpecked"—or worse, unmanned.

For many married women, especially those for whom the rules weren't carefully worked out in advance (for example, in a first marriage where she might not have had clear career goals at the outset, or was still in graduate school, or was supporting her husband with the understanding that she'd quit work and he'd support her once they had children) the old rules were clear—whatever the man does is what's considered important. Her wages are not important in defining the family because it's only the woman who's earning them. Never mind that they may be what is keeping the family afloat. When he starts to earn, however, his salary is all- important, and gives him the right to establish the rules of the manor in many cases.

One woman, a social worker, puts it quite plaintively when she describes how the money/responsibility dynamics work in her family. "Every time I ask my husband to do something for the kids—take them to a lesson or leave work early to go to a school play—his response is, 'Would you like me to quit work altogether? How can we live on your salary alone? It's OK for you to take time off from work because you aren't supporting the family. I don't have the luxury of doing that. I pay most of the bills around here; now you want me to fold the laundry, too?' He says that if I want him to spend more time at home or doing chores I'd better be prepared to face the financial conse-quences. It's as if his time, because he is getting paid more per hour than I am, is inherently more valuable *in every situation,* so that I end up doing most of the housework, almost all of the child care, and still trying to squeeze in a full schedule of my own work. And my work is important not only because it keeps me sane, but also because, although it doesn't pay as well as his, it does cover about a third of our living expenses."

The situation this woman describes may not be based simply on her husband's assumption of male privilege, or of any generalized misogyny on his part. The actual financial reality is that as long as women continue to earn less than men (because they've been tracked into lower-paying professions, because they've lost seniority in taking time off to have and raise children, because our whole economic system undervalues what women do, or for whatever reasons) there is more incentive for the whole family to view the man's work as more important. Therefore, the care and feeding of this partner is more important than any value placed on the wife's work. The implicit agreement between wife and husband in a marriage in which the wife's earnings are substantially less than those of her husband, or in which she works only part time, are not too unlike the understood gender-role distinctions in a traditional or complementary marriage, except that in many cases the working wife may have a greater awareness of the inequity of her situation as a juggler of home, work and children than her nonworking cohort does.

Are things different in those rare families where the woman earns more than her husband? Sometimes not since wives in such circumstances often claim that they fear their husbands' resentment of their higher earning power, and don't want to "unman" them further; they therefore do even more around the house than they'd be expected to given their earning power, just so as not to rock the marital boat further.

Working wives may still threaten the psychological equilibrium of their husbands. A 1986 study of some American couples found that husbands of working wives feel less adequate as family breadwinners than do husbands of housewives. The researchers discovered that a man may begin to feel that he could not support the family on his income alone and that "his sense of adequacy of himself as a man is eroding." Which should lead them (and us) to ask how we should be reworking our definitions of "man" and "woman" if a man's gender identity is so fragile that it hinges on his being the sole support of the family when there is another breadwinner able and willing to share the task.

What may also be going on is that husbands fear for the stability of their marriages because their wives work. The men know that women, if they're in the labor force, are exposed to other men, and that their lives are less circumscribed and less controllable by their husbands. They also suspect that one factor motivating a woman to work outside the home is her heightened awareness of the fact that she may at some point in the future have to support herself and/or the family on her own if the marriage ends.

The Two-Career Couple

When we examine the lives both of women in the paid labor force and of women working in their own homes, whether newly married or in long-term marriages, we realize that to speak of the "traditional" and "contemporary" styles is a distinction more appropriate to a furniture showroom than to a marriage. Even those media darlings, the yuppie couple, find when they have, or even contemplate having, children that some of the self-same difficulties arise (with different refinements) as with an older and more traditional couple.

A successful career woman in her early thirties, for example, claims that she is terrified of having a child because, as she puts it, "I've worked so hard to establish an egalitarian marriage that I'm afraid if I quit my job and stay home with a child I'll lose a certain status in my husband's eyes. Frankly, I feel I'll lose power if I'm not earning money anymore." Just as the married woman who has never worked (or who has been out of the workplace most of her adult life) needs to make financial provisions for herself (as we've seen above), so does this woman.

To diminish your realistic anxieties about an anticipated loss of income and status, what preparations can you make in advance of leaving your job (whether to raise a child—the most common reason—or because your husband's career necessitates an agreed-upon relocation, or because you are laid off or retraining)?

• First of all, air your anxieties with your husband, with the goal of coming to an understanding that you will be reimbursed in certain specific ways for the undeniable financial losses you will suffer if you are the one who will withdraw from the labor force. (If you are leaving your job to have a child, we presume this is a mutually desired child.) Minimally, he should make payments every year into *your* IRA just as you might if you were to continue in the work force, so that your private retirement fund won't suffer from this hiatus.

The same goes for memberships in your professional associations or unions—you may need the benefits these confer even if you are no longer actively working—financial as well as psychological and career benefits (for example, cheaper life insurance through your union, or special discounts or insiders' newsletters). Think about arranging with your husband that he will continue to pay these dues and membership fees while you're not bringing in a salary, especially if you have kept your earnings and expenses separate until this point. If you have had two paychecks and separate accounts for everything throughout your marriage, renegotiating such matters when you decide to become parents is almost like getting married all over again.

• Whether you plan to resume work at a specific future date or not, remember that no one can read the future accurately, and you need to make your possible reentry as smooth as possible. Find out if you can continue to participate in your pension fund, if you belong to one, and whether or not you need to make payments into such a fund even while you're not working. If you have to have worked a minimum number of years in order to have a vested interest in the pension, you might want to plan your childbearing leave accordingly (without working for so long that you jeopardize your fertility, obviously).

• Check to see what employment benefits you can continue to receive while on maternity leave. These may include low-cost life insurance, private health care coverage or the continued use of a company car. If continuing availability depends on your making payments, try to show your husband that it may be to your mutual advantage for him to pay.

- Remember to maintain credit in your own name even after you quit working.

The Hardheaded and Softhearted Task for All Married Couples

These money issues need to be addressed not the way a court of law might settle them in the case of divorce or separation, but in order to make satisfactory financial arrangements *within* what you both hope will continue to be a stable marriage—clearly a different matter entirely.

This distinction between how matters would be settled in a divorce court and how they can be negotiated in a continuing marriage raises the real question marriage partners must answer: *How to merge autonomy with intimacy?* In money matters, there must be some degree of financial autonomy for the woman, especially, not to feel like a disadvantaged dependent. Yet there must also be some degree of financial merging for the partners to function as a marital dyad.

In marriage, the rules of the game are allegedly the opposite of those for a business arrangement. Common wisdom says that people who agree to business deals on a handshake alone are fools; yet the same wisdom suggests that marriage partners who don't want to proceed on trust alone lack true passion for one another. But having money matters out in the open need not mean that romance is gone from marriage. In fact, open discussion and joint resolutions can mean that both partners are clear that it's not merely financial dependency that bonds them.

State legislation dealing with family property tends toward a more businesslike approach. More and more situations are arising where neither spouse can deal with family property (which may also include "his" business assets) without the consent of the other. These days, for example, in most states neither spouse can mortgage the family home without the consent of the other, even if the house is in the name of only one. More to the point, in order for that consent to be valid, the consenting spouse (who is almost always the wife) has to have had independent legal advice (her own lawyer, not his) and must sign a certificate to that effect before a loan will be made.

This leads to a situation where husbands have to be prepared to discuss key financial situations with their wives or risk not being able to wheel and deal the way they might have done in the past. The need for the husband to get his wife's consent to certain types of transactions gives her real leverage to get concessions she may desire in return—the basis for a contractual agreement.

Should You Use a Contract?

Sam Goldwyn, the great movie pioneer, once said, "An oral contract isn't worth the paper it's written on." The real question you have to ask yourself as you enter a relationship is whether a written contract is worth any more than an oral contract.

In recent years partners in marriage (or romance) everywhere have begun to negotiate contracts. There are three reasons for this. First, marriage contracts, or nonmarriage or prenuptial contracts, have become more visible as celebrity couples air their differences in public. Second, younger people marrying today are themselves more likely than in the past to be the offspring of divorced parents. Having seen the chaos marriage and its dissolution can entail, and remembering the financial battles their own parents waged as they pulled apart, they opt for getting it all in writing from the start. And finally, women today, marrying later, are more likely to have assets to protect than their mothers did and are more likely to see the need to protect them. Many working women have delayed marriage because of education or career advancement (also, one hopes, because of higher expectations about marriage). Women are entering their first marriages much later than they have in previous generations. In 1982, for example, the average age of a woman marrying for the first time was 23.7 years; by the time you read this, the average age will likely have crept up to almost 25. These women are also likelier to become part of a two-career couple when they do marry. This is the kind of marriage most likely to make its contractual obligations explicit rather than implicit and therefore likelier to spell them out not just in conversation but also in the form of a legally binding marriage contract.

Marriage contracts are nothing new, of course; in many societies the husband's family paid a sum of money as a bride price, or the bride brought a dowry of money or property into her husband's household upon marriage and in return received promises of support. In exchange for a dowry, one sixteenth-century Jewish scholar insisted that his son-in-law spell out in a contract that his daughter was not to be burdened with household tasks, but would remain free to pursue her own studies. In fact, the ketubah, the Jewish "wedding license" still in use today, is a marriage contract, couched in legal terms, traditionally stipulating under what circumstances the couple might dissolve the union, and how much the man owes the woman if this happens. Couples (or, earlier, the families of the bride and groom) have been inserting their own conditions into these contracts for centuries.

Contracts between spouses or spouses-to-be have not been the rule but have gained a great deal of notoriety as a result of celebrity break-ups (e.g., the Trumps). They are not unusual in a second marriage or when one party to a marriage has significantly greater assets than the other. Many couples have used them to opt out of the division of property rules which would otherwise apply in that jurisdiction, which may require an equal split of family property on the divorce of the spouses. They have also been used by older couples contemplating a second marriage to ensure that property built up during the first marriage goes to the children of that marriage and cannot be claimed by the second spouse.

What guidelines will be useful for women coming to grips with these new situations? Where should they look to find their advisers, especially since, if they are already married, their husband's advisers will not be acceptable? How will a woman negotiate, recognizing that a particular business venture may be important to the man in her life, and on the other that it may be risky to her? And is this legislation really a step forward or are there lessons to be learned from other jurisdictions which suggest that this sort of progress may, in many situations, be disastrous for women?

Despite the rising popularity of cohabitation and marital contracts, there are those who oppose them. In contract-making as in other areas, one party (usually the man) has more clout than the other, and in many cases women sign away rights which it might have been to their advantage to retain. The situation is exacerbated because a woman seldom has lawyers of her own to provide independent advice, relying on "his" adviser. This is a classic situation where emotions and ignorance rule over reason, often to the detriment of the woman's subsequent financial security. Because of her more dependent status, or her greater desire to marry, a woman may be all too willing to accept the man's terms without thoroughly investigating their consequences in her own life.

In a letter to Ann Landers, a woman writes of having received an inheritance just before she was to be married. At the urging of her parents, she and her husband-to-be signed a contract under which each gave up any rights to the other's assets. Twenty years later, he was extremely wealthy. As she wrote, her marriage was a happy one, but now wondered whether the agreement was still valid. (The answer, of course, depended upon the law of where they lived.) But this is an example of the person with more power (or more money, often the same thing) insisting on an agreement, though in this case, it seemed to have backfired on her. In seeking to address a limited issue—protecting an inheritance— the agreement drafted went much further and excluded this woman from sharing in the wealth which was created during the marriage. This story also points up another issue. It may make sense to have a clause in any agreement which allows either party to ask for a renegotiation after the passage of several years.

In considering whether you should have a contract you need to think about two very different aspects of contract making. First, the act of negotiation of an agreement is very useful even if you never expect to go to court and, indeed, even if the provisions are such that a court would not enforce them. (In the business world, if one party is in breach of a contract's terms, the other party can sue. Implicit in signing a business contract is that, if necessary, a judge can be called upon to enforce the terms of the agreement.) The negotiation process is one which opens up the areas of potential conflict as well as identifying areas of substantial agreement. At least you'll know in advance what you're getting into. And discussing the issues in the context of writing a formal contract about financial matters (which can legitimately be contracted about) forces the partners to recognize potential areas of disagreement about substance or style. One lawyer who regularly draws up marriage contracts says that even though some stipulations are useless from a legal standpoint because they're unenforceable, "They have moral force. People forget promises they make, and these things serve as reminders."

There are other issues, exclusive of strictly financial considerations, you should consider working out in contractual form also. For these, a neo-contract, or mock contract is not a bad idea. Not just who will take out the garbage when, but potentially more consequential matters such as will you have children? In what religion will they be raised? Who would you want as their legal guardians? Which parents, if any would you ask to live with you if they needed care? Would each of you be willing to help support the other's aged or infirm parents or other relatives if they needed funds? Which one of you would move to take a better job? And will such moves be rotated? Would you ever consider a commuting marriage? Where will you live? How will expenses be shared? Who will do what work around the home? Whose name will property be registered in? Do you expect total sexual fidelity? These are just a few of the scores of issues which you might want dealt with in an agreement. If you can settle these issues by negotiation before you start living together, the chances are greater that the relationship will last.

Second, when it comes to ownership of property or the right to support in the event of a break-up of the arrangement, it is much more likely that you (or he) would go to a court to enforce the agreement and that the court would agree to do so. For example, if the agreement states that all property acquired during the relationship will be held jointly and he secretly acquires assets in his own name, given a properly drafted contract, you should be able to get your one-half interest when the relationship terminates. If he promises to pay your way through graduate school after he becomes a doctor, a court would probably enforce the agreement if he tried to renege. These may be steps which a court would order even without a contract, but having the signed agreement will make it much easier for a judge to give you what you want and what you bargained for in the beginning.

In several states now, a spouse's professional license is considered to be a part of the family property and may partly belong to the other spouse in the event of divorce. This means that a percentage of, say, a lawyer's income could forever belong to his ex-wife if she contributed to his support while he was earning that degree, though that percentage would probably be paid as a lump sum, and vice versa. A marriage contract might stipulate that the partner being supported through school will repay the investment with interest shortly after graduation, and this might get around the possibility that the spouse would have a share in all future degree-related earnings after divorce.

"How can I tell the man I love that I want him to sign a contract?" There has probably never been a woman who contemplated such an agreement who didn't ask herself this, though we have never heard from a man struck by similar qualms when it came to self-protection, especially with regard to finances. *If you are afraid that talk about protecting yourself will cost you the relationship, you are dooming yourself to second-class status before you start.* Remember the analogy to birth control: You don't have any qualms about discussing and setting the ground rules relating to birth control. That's more intimate than money. If you can talk to him about that, you should certainly be able to set out your feelings about other important areas without having to worry that you'll alienate him.

Another crucial issue is to get legal advice from somebody you have hired. You want to make sure of several things. First, does the contract cover everything it should deal with? Second, does the wording of the contract reflect the arrangements you two have agreed to? Third, is the contract one which would be enforceable in your state? Four, if you sign the contract, have you given up rights which you might otherwise have? If so, have you achieved other protections which make giving up some rights worthwhile?

Remember that for a marriage contract to have any meaning economically it has to be pegged to a full disclosure of your assets and his; its validity depends upon both parties making full disclosure and each having independent legal advice. Otherwise a woman (or a man, for that matter, but let us assume here that the common condition remains: women make less money and have fewer assets than men) might unwittingly comply with a plan to limit her access to her spouse's assets.

One woman, for example, agreed to her husband's suggestions that they sign a contract stipulating that, in the event of divorce, she'd accept a lump sum payment of $15,000 in lieu of other support; she based her agreement on her understanding of her husband's assets. What she didn't know was that he was the beneficiary of a trust fund due to fall into his hands within a few years. He wanted to make sure that if their marriage didn't last she wouldn't be able to touch that, and he could well afford to offer her apparently generous settlement terms to help her start a new life.

Since he was the one proposing the marriage contract, however, she didn't feel comfortable about challenging the terms, which seemed reasonable to her given her limited knowledge of his present, apparently modest circumstances. She didn't want to appear overly interested in his money, especially at the start of a new relationship. Yet when they did divorce a few years later, she was of course heartsick that she hadn't questioned his stipulations. Whereas at the beginning she was concerned only for the happiness of the relationship, when it ended she had to think of her own best interests—a not uncommon shift for women as they pass into and out of a marriage. With the new legislation requiring full disclosure, this contract would probably not now be considered binding upon her; she'd have the option of suing him for more support.

Don't use his lawyer. You don't know where his lawyer's main loyalties lie but you can figure that the lawyer is looking out primarily for his or her regular client. If the agreement is to cover significant property, if not now but perhaps in the future, be prepared to pay somebody who is on your side alone. Lawyers love to pick out loopholes in agreements and that is what yours should be doing. The money you pay the lawyer now will be nothing compared to what you might lose if you have unwittingly bargained away your legal rights. A poor contract may very well be much worse for you than no contract at all. And finally, if he reacts with shock and horror to the idea of a contract, beware. It may be because he understands very well that without anything in writing he is in effective control of the money and property and, thus, effectively is the power in the relationship.

Remember that, with or without a formal contract, every licensed marriage is a legally binding agreement with mutual obligations. You would investigate thoroughly, seek sage advice and think very carefully before you'd sign an apartment lease, a mortgage agreement, a summer sublet or a car loan. Make sure that you examine with at least as much care the financial consequences of a relationship that will, you hope, outlast the summer, the car, the apartment lease, and maybe even the house.

But I'm Already Married

"If I were going to get married, there sure are things I'd want in a contract. But I've been married for almost fifteen years and I don't know how I'd ever be able to get my husband to agree to a contract at this stage of our relationship. I mean, he's got everything the way he wants it now—why would he agree to any changes?"

A married woman who thinks that a contract might be useful clearly has less negotiating strength than does a single woman who is in a position to dictate, at least to some degree, the terms upon which she is prepared to cohabit with or wed a man. Very often, many of the issues which might otherwise be the subject of negotiation have, in fact, been settled, though not necessarily to the complete satisfaction of either party.

It may be possible to get your husband to enter into an agreement after marriage if you can show him it might be in his best interest. If you are about to start your own business and he does not want to be liable on any of the debts of the business, suggest an agreement that, in the event of divorce, he will not claim any interest in the business and you agree that he won't be responsible for any debts of the business. If he is about to leave a job and has the option of taking his retirement benefits out, he may require your signature; this may be a time to discuss provisions for *your* retirement and to set these out in a written contract.

It is now very much in the interest of many businessmen to get their wives to agree, for example, to allow an interest in a business to be sold to a partner if he dies. (This is a standard clause in most shareholder agreements.) But now, in order to do this, the spouses have to agree to waive their rights, since the business assets which are to be sold at death are part of family property.

You might therefore point out that existing arrangements which your husband has with his associates may be invalid or seriously flawed in the absence of a marriage contract. (If he doesn't know about this, he may say you don't know what you're talking about, but he'll probably contact his lawyer. This is the equivalent of hitting the donkey over the head with a board to get attention.)

In all likelihood, he'll come back and suggest that you sign some documents, which, whether he says so or not, will be the equivalent of a marital contract under which you give up some of your rights. At this juncture you now have bargaining power. If he wants something from you, you can get something from him. Perhaps you want an agreement in which he specifically says he'll pay for some additional education or training for you. Or an explicit agreement which says that he will not put any impediments in your way if you decide to return to work—and will pay for day care if necessary. Think of what you want and ask for it. You'll never have more power.

And remind him that any paper you sign isn't worth a thing unless you can testify that you've had independent legal advice. Tell him you'll pick your own lawyer and, if you haven't money of your own, that you expect him to pay the costs.

If your husband isn't in business, you may still have some bargaining chips. Don't forget that you probably have the right under your state law to a substantial portion of his assets on death. If he hoped to leave a substantial part of his estate to anybody else (a parent, sibling, charity, or child, for example), you can remind him that in the absence of an agreement to the contrary, you might get more than he intended. And you might be prepared to waive some of your rights under his will in return for some current concessions you might want.

He might want you to agree to getting a second mortgage on the house so that he can invest the money. (Financial advisers are always suggesting that canny investors "tap the equity in their houses" for investment purposes.) If he wants to take this step badly enough, tell him you want a share in the profits—and get it in writing. You might also point out that sharing the profits and having the deal in writing makes a lot of sense in terms of tax planning. But this may also be the opportunity for you to extract some other "concessions" from him, either of a financial or nonfinancial nature. (And don't forget to tell him that if he reneges on the agreement after you sign what he wants, the effect will be to nullify the validity of the deal. No court would enforce his end of a contract if he didn't fulfill his obligations under the agreement.)

The state of your own marriage may determine whether he'll agree grudgingly or whether he thinks a contract is a good idea. But what you're likely to find is that he recognizes that he is in a situation where if he wants to do something which is important for him in terms of business or financial planning, he has to be prepared to deal with you and give you something you want. After all, it's just good business sense. Just because you've accepted a particular role in your marriage up to now doesn't mean you have to accept it forever and the negotiating of a contract with your husband may offer the best means for changing your role within the relationship for the better.

In the past, the emblem of romantic love was "blindness." To have suggested that an engaged couple, for example, spell out on paper, in legalese, their financial holdings and responsibilities toward one another would, until recently, have suggested that the man and woman in question were utterly, lacking in the requisite trust and love on which to base a happy marriage. Precisely the opposite of what the opinion might be if a business arrangement were sealed with a kiss and an embrace! Business partners are typically told that they are fools to have any arrangement based on trust. Yet, until now, marriage partners were encouraged to build complicated financial structures on trust alone.

Today, the laws of several states almost require that women deal with their husbands and boyfriends as business associates. In many cases prudence will require the negotiation of contracts dealing with the separate and mutual assets, negotiations which will also require that each party retain a lawyer to advise them. If you don't each have a separate lawyer, in most states the signed documents will be subject to attack when you want to enforce them.

Many women who are active in the feminist movement, both married and cohabiting, told us that they did not have contracts. However, in almost every case they indicated that if there were a major change anticipated in their circumstances (as for example, deciding to have a child or inheriting a substantial amount of money), they would consider using a contract to protect their positions.

A freely negotiated and mutually understood contract which provides for true equality of the parties can, however, be the basis of a happy relationship—or at least one with fewer unhappy surprises. This possibility alone makes the exercise worth the attempt.

Financing the Modern Family

All this leads to two important issues: how will family finances be handled on a day-to-day basis, and how does a wife get the information she needs to be a fully-informed economic partner? There are a number of possible scenarios:

You can pool all your income into one account, with each of you taking a prescribed monthly amount for personal expenses, or on an ad hoc basis. The disadvantage of allocating expense money ad hoc is that there's more room for resentments if one of you buys a new compact disc player when the other one wanted a new cashmere overcoat that month and there wasn't money for both. This highlights the disadvantage generally of a joint account—each of you can withdraw without the knowledge or approval of the other, which makes for some degree of financial chaos even if you are that heavenly couple who would never quarrel over the expenditures themselves. And in the case of a serious fight, he could just grab all your money and run.

You can keep all your accounts separate, with each of you responsible for paying certain bills as they arise. The advantage here is that there's little dispute over who spends what as long as the basics are covered. The disadvantage, in a situation such as that of our friend who was considering quitting her job to have a baby, is that when one partner is not earning, the whole process must be reevaluated.

Another major disadvantage is that nobody ever plans for the future of the family. Each partner has total discretion over her or his earnings and expenses, and unless there is also provision made for some kind of enforced savings on a regular basis there may be no lump sum of money available when you want to buy a house, take a vacation, or face unexpected large expenses—say, in caring for a sick relative, or as a cushion against unemployment. Often, with the complete separation of finances, neither partner remembers to save or to invest wisely, as each might if they were single or if they reviewed their joint holdings periodically. In addition, complete separation with each partner responsible for certain expenses invariably leaves loopholes.

One couple we know had lived together before marriage and kept separate accounts. Shortly after marriage and the birth of their first child, their jobs necessitated that they live in separate cities for a few years. They worked out a *modus vivendi* whereby she paid certain household expenses for the apartment she lived in with their child, and covered all child care. He paid for other expenses, and each was responsible for discretionary expenses, such as entertainment, etc.

When they finally merged their lives, moved to the same city and shared a house, it was clear that their system had some flaws. The kitchen sink was badly stopped up for months because neither of them would call the plumber, knowing that whoever arranged for the service call would have to pay for it. She always used his car because after the birth of their second child she had to cut back on her work hours and could no longer afford insurance on her own car. He balked at having to pay the community-center membership which was a prerequisite for their son's day-care center, because he claimed it was part of child-care expenses and therefore she was responsible. She counterclaimed that it was a family membership which would provide recreational facilities for all of them. And so it went, literally for years. An otherwise loving couple had never been able to make the leap from the total autonomy of their living-together arrangements to the greater intimacy and sharing that most marriages represent (and, in fact, demand).

The best solution for this couple, and in fact probably for all married couples, even those where the wife has no independent source of income, is the "hers, his and theirs" approach. That is, *a joint account into which each wage-earner contributes, and an account for each spouse which is totally independent of the other.* With a joint account for household expenses, and perhaps another for savings, our friends who wouldn't call the plumber would at least have been spared some of the constant strife that haunted them. They could still arrange for salary bonuses or gifts or other windfalls to be considered separate and discretionary, but the smooth functioning of their family unit wouldn't be impeded.

Remember that there is always room for financial negotiation in every relationship (business or family) if you know what your options are. Things need not stay fixed. You will almost always have some choices available to you, if you can see what they are.

A case in point: a librarian in her forties, without children, gave up a tenured position to relocate when her husband moved. She was offered a substantial lump-sum severance payment ($15,000) if she would give up her rights to her pension plan. She took the option, because she felt they needed the cash to purchase a condominium apartment, then realized that she was in an uncertain position if her husband should predecease her. She had no job, no pension, and felt that he didn't have enough life insurance to support her if he were to die young. She shared her anxieties with her husband, and they were set to rest when he arranged to take a slightly reduced pension himself while purchasing substantially more life insurance from his employer. (In this case they knew that he planned to continue working in another job past the relatively young age at which he was entitled to his pension from his primary employer.)

Fortunately, this woman's husband was sensible and caring, and wanted her to be comfortable—emotionally comfortable now, financially comfortable later. Presumably most husbands share these feelings, at least while the marriage is in progress. But even if they're married to the best-intentioned men, married women may fall prey to one or another of the following financial problems, which can be avoided with a little forewarning.

- Learn all you can about your husband's (and your own) financial structures while the two of you can talk to each other—that is, before acrimony, separation, divorce or death make conversation as we know it impossible. This sounds simple, but in marriages where men have traditionally managed the money by fiat it's not so easy. Many, many women have reported that when, with raised consciousness about the importance of understanding money matters, they query their husband about insurance, safety deposit boxes, bank accounts and the like, the man's first response is, "My god, she's thinking about leaving me." You can show him this chapter as evidence of the innocence of your intentions, or remind him of the plight of those widows who were left floundering because they didn't even know how to get their hands on grocery money after their husbands died.

By "knowing about money matters" we mean everything (or everything you can legitimately find out about). At the very least learn:

- ❑ The names of his insurance agent and/or stockbroker (they may be your brokers too). For all you know there may be resources in your own name you aren't aware of. The names and addresses of his banks (again, and yours).
- ❑ Does he have a will? Where is it kept?
- ❑ Does he own any property (or do you?) that you haven't known about until now?
- ❑ Does he expect to inherit money?
- ❑ Does he have a pension plan and what is your stake in it, if any?
- ❑ How much life insurance does he have?
- ❑ Where are his safety deposit boxes, and do you have access to them jointly? Where are the keys kept?
- ❑ Does his health care coverage extend to you for a period after his death or a divorce?

He should obviously have the same information from you.

Even in families where spouses pride themselves on how much information they share, it's surprising to find out how little they actually know about each other's financial arrangements until they sit down to write it all out. You should each have a sheet with all this information spelled out. This need not raise the specter of divorce action. It's important and useful to have for any situation which might require prompt action by one of you in the absence of the other—e.g. if one is away on business or vacation and unreachable, or is hospitalized or otherwise temporarily dysfunctional.

Remember that such lists need updating. With the advent of home computers you can have information updated and new lists printed up quite easily, making several copies, even a copy for each of your adult children. Actually planning for an updating discussion session—perhaps over a "business" lunch or breakfast every six months—isn't such a crazy idea. One couple has used any upcoming travel as the incentive to catch each other up; the impending separation from home base serves as the spur to set things in order; for another couple their wedding anniversary provides the structure. Just remember not to let dust gather on your family and individual "worth" and "emergency" statements.

Do not fall prey to the notion that you're being petty or unnecessarily demanding when you begin to work out methods for sharing information and financial responsibility. The spirit of equality in a marriage is often maintained by these apparently small adjustments.

• Get (and keep) credit in your own name. A smart woman told us her own scheme to do this, although she hadn't worked outside the home since her marriage and had no income of her own. She was the one who paid all the household bills and made the arrangements for all domestic matters. When the family moved to a new house, she put the utilities accounts in her own name—and made sure that these were all paid promptly. She then, after a few months, opened up an department store charge account, again in her own name, using her utilities accounts as references, and again made sure that these bills were never in arrears, even if it sometimes meant paying some of the accounts in her husband's name a few weeks late. She reasoned that, first, he'd never find out, since she paid the bills, and, second, that he had a steady job and a good credit rating himself, and lots of charge accounts in his own name, and that his credit reputation would never be damaged by occasional late payments, whereas hers was just being established.

• As a woman, especially if you have not worked for pay during your marriage, or have worked only part time, learn to ask for what you want—because you are *entitled* to it regardless of the amount you've contributed in actual earnings to the marriage pool. One woman, married for twenty years to a pharmacist, says that she finally recognized recently that she didn't have to ask his permission every time she wanted to make a charitable contribution or do something for herself. (He had never questioned her expenditures on clothes or the house—since they increased her value as an adornment to him, of course). She formulated her newfound determination as, "I finally realized that I've kept him sane all these years so he could make the money. Of course I'm entitled to it!" Take a lesson from this woman. Do not denigrate your non-remunerated work at home—especially that kind of psychological support work which often has no name, and certainly has no price, though it definitely has value.

• If either you or your husband has a stake in a business, there may be good reason for negotiating an agreement whereby the business is not counted as something you own jointly. You should also discuss what provisions should be made by the non-owning spouse in case the owning spouse dies and the remaining business partners want to buy out the surviving spouse who has, presumably, inherited the deceased's share. (See Chapter 10, "When a Wife Becomes a Widow.")

• If you and your husband are in business together, or even if he is in some way involved in your work and you in his, there are specific pluses and minuses you should be aware of. Overriding all other matters (such as the desire to leave business problems at the store or office) is the need to have the nature of the financial arrangements in writing.

This is important for two reasons. First, if you are a co-owner with your husband, you receive Social Security credit for part of the income the business produces, giving you benefits when you retire. Only one of you will receive credit for this income unless it is "split" between you. Income splitting may also permit you to pay less in taxes as a couple than if all the income were credited to one. Second, in the event that you ever divorce, you want evidence that one-half (or whatever) of the business is yours and that the ultimate financial arrangements reflect the fact that you own part of it, rather than possibly being entitled to some part of it just because you and he were married.

- Become a good trouble-shooter. Try to keep the future in mind in the present. Here's an example: You are in your forties, in what both you and your husband of 20 years would characterize as a stable marriage. You own your home jointly. He comes to you wanting your signature on a second mortgage on the house in order to finance a business expansion he really wants to make. How can you respond to show that while you appreciate his financial needs, and the fact that his business largely supports the family, you are not prepared to jeopardize your family dwelling? Banks often advertise "home equity" loans (really a second mortgage) and he's probably just in good faith following the common wisdom of the ad campaigns without projecting himself (and you) a few years into the future. What if he becomes disabled? How will you cover the expense of two mortgages on the house? What if he leaves you, and thus leaves you holding the debt on which he has realized all the benefit, since the business is in his name alone?

Some solutions. Insist that as a condition to your signing the papers refinancing the mortgage, he must make you a partner in his business. Or have as a precondition that he increase his disability insurance so that you'll be able to manage the extra debt load if he falls ill. Or make sure that you are otherwise indemnified against major financial crisis if for some reason he defaults on this bank loan (which is what a mortgage is). There may be more potential risk to you than at first seems apparent in a seemingly innocent situation. Not that your husband wishes you ill. He just may not immediately perceive all the financial ramifications of his proposed course of action.

In sharp contrast to their behavior on the road (men never, ever stop to ask advice or directions at a gas station, whereas women almost always ask for guidance when they think they may be lost or going astray), men are far more likely to heed professional assistance when they are contemplating a financial change of direction than women are. For example, many men now know that they should not sink their own money into a down payment, but should carry a bigger mortgage, which might even be shouldered jointly with their wives.

How do men learn? Not because of biological necessity, and not even because they have directly asked for the advice. Often they learn because they read the financial periodicals, or they read the newspapers' sports pages or car ads ("men's" news), into which the financial pages are cozily nestled on the assumption that only men care about these matters (while articles on politicians who happen to be female appear in the style section, alongside recipes and late-breaking news about hemlines). Columnists seem to care very much about protecting men against the ravages of divorce under the new laws, whereas precious little advice has been directed at women in places to which they have easy access.

Sometimes married women don't know enough about the risks they face to consider asking for advice; more often they trust that their husbands will be acting in their best interest at all times. Even if this were theoretically true (which we doubt), even the most nearly omniscient man cannot predict the future—which is why it might be a good idea to seek some trouble-shooting advice or gain these skills yourself. Some women think they don't have enough at stake (no million dollar portfolios) to warrant asking a bank officer or lawyer or accountant for advice. Perhaps the laws about who owns the family dwelling are so concrete that they will force women to take financial matters very seriously. They must now face the fact that their own home will not necessarily go to them and the kids outright if the marriage falls apart—which is why other kinds of financial security should be built in, starting right now.

Not all financial advice is intended to protect against the inevitability of a future divorce. It's as important to recognize and salute the fact that many marriages are built on a good deal of mutual trust and understanding—a good basis for building in equality in all spheres. What most married women reading this book want to find out is how to make themselves happier and more secure financially *within* their marriages. Legitimately, you want advice that will help you maintain peace and not encourage a perpetual state of a teeth-gritting cold war in the household. The key to this is to recognize—and help your husband recognize—that enlightened self-interest should dictate his making you a more nearly equal shareholder in the "corporation" that is your family. And sometimes if you understand what you'd be entitled to by law in a divorce settlement (see Chapter 9, "Divorce: Coaching in Battlefront Tactics and Strategies," for details), you can, even in your own mind, make a stronger case for what's yours while the marriage stays alive.

A woman's drive to inform herself financially may be based on feminist principles or on self-preservation (or both, since they are nicely aligned). But this can have a salutary effect on the whole household. Her husband can then come clean if he himself feels ignorant; he is freer to drop the macho/omniscient pose so many men adopt over matters financial. Her admission of lack of knowledge and her openness to asking advice can help him too. Also, her sharing of the burden of financial decisionmaking can "legitimize" (as if it needed it!) her desire to have him share in other labors traditionally distributed along gender lines—for example, in child care or household maintenance. Unless he guards his so-called expertise like a chieftain with secrets—afraid that he'll lose power if he shares them—her desire to participate in the family's financial planning could be a boon to them both, with the net result that their implicit contract changes its terms, shifting away from roles based on gender and coming closer to a full sharing of all the aspects of their life together.

On Being a Daughter-in-Law

Many women find that they've married not just a man but a whole extended family. Depending upon the desires and expectations of each partner, and on their own backgrounds, that family may draw close or stay distant. The complexities of the emotional connections in an extended family are legion—to which the myriad obnoxious, misogynistic mother-in-law jokes attest. Where emotions and money issues overlap, these relationships can get white-hot, or with a little forethought and consideration, they can remain pleasantly warm.

Financial relationships with in-laws usually fall into one of three categories: the older generation helping the younger, the younger one contributing to the support of the older, or a fair balance, with neither giving the other money directly, although there may be unresolved money issues hanging around anyway.

In the first category, in which the parents of the married couple contribute to their support, or help with buying a house, treating the grandchildren to vacations, covering some or all of the costs of camps, private schools or colleges, there can be friction between the wife and husband over whose parents contribute what. Since all this help is, of course, voluntary, the squabbles can't really have any concrete resolution, unless the spouse whose parents give less is willing to ask them to give more. The amount that the senior in-laws contribute may be as much affected by their feelings about children's independence as it is by their financial means. Since coercion is impossible, we will deal only with situations that arise when there is financial help offered by one or both sets of in-laws.

Gifts of money for casual purchases or for luxuries (or the gift of the items themselves) can be a windfall, especially for young couples. So can the relief of having the older generation help foot the bill for schooling, either for the husband or wife or for their children. The danger zone comes into view when the person(s) giving the money also want to exercise a degree of control over how it's spent. In the case of luxuries, having someone tell you what kind of microwave to buy may be irritating, but inconsequential. In the case of the choice of your child's school, you have three options: go along with the grandparents wishes, present your own choice with your reasons for it and the request that they pay for the school you want, or decline their generosity. Choosing one of these alternatives is up to you, and all are honorable ones, unless you fear that in choosing the first you'll make your child uncomfortable by putting him or her into a school environment you essentially disapprove of.

The catch with all these dealings is to be able to present your arguments and your decisions in as kindly a way as possible. Remember, their generosity is wholly voluntary, and you will stay connected to your in-laws for as long as your marriage lasts (and if you have children, your in-laws may be around for longer than your husband was), so remember that courtesy gets high marks in dealing with offers of financial help. You may have chosen to reject the offer this time, for whatever reasons, but if they have the means you may need or want to turn to them in the future, so do not close any doors because they sent you a pink cashmere sweater and they should know by now that you hate pink.

The most complicated financial dealings with in-laws usually have to do with one of two major purchases: education and buying a home. Parents who extend money to their children for university costs as a loan are, interestingly, not usually those in the lower-income brackets who need the loan money repaid (such parents don't have the cash for the loan, in the first place, and such students usually qualify for grants and scholarships). Rather, it is middle-class parents who want their children (sons, usually) to be independent and self-sufficient as soon as they turn 18.

If you are a woman whose husband is paying money back to his parents for education expenses, you may feel, as one young bride has said, "They should just forget it. They don't need the money, and we'd like to start planning for a family of our own, and it seems so chintzy of them." Maybe so, but if your husband took the money willingly and its repayment was part of the bargain, there's only one thing you can do about it (aside from persuading your husband to ask them to forgive the loan or reduce the periodic payments) if you are going to have to underwrite some of this repayment from your earnings.

The something you can do is this—and it can be important: if a portion of your salary is going to repay the education loan (whether to his parents or to a bank), don't just pay more than your share of household expenses and let him pay the full amount due on the loan each month (that's just subsidizing your husband). Instead, pay the in-laws or bank directly, with a check on your account or with your signature. That way, although his degree may have been obtained before you were married, you can rightly claim to have helped pay for it. Should you split, you might be entitled to a part of his future professional earnings based on this earlier investment in his degree.

And assuming your marriage lasts, it does no harm to be clear about the fact that early in the marriage you made a very real contribution to his present earnings if he should ever declare himself to be doing you a great favor by supporting you.

The other common in-law-related money problem—accepting their money as part of the purchase price of a home—is more complicated. You should make sure that, if they are giving you the money outright, it is in the form of a check made payable to the two of you, so that you can legitimately be the co-owner of the house. This will also make you feel like less of an appendage to an important decision you and your husband should be making jointly. Likewise, if your in-laws give you a mortgage so that you can buy the house, or make a loan to you for any such major purchase, make sure that you are named as co-owner. You may then be liable for half the payments (or more if your husband defaults), but your ownership claims will be substantiated.

In addition to the relationships between grown children and parents-in-law there are possible financial entanglements with other members of the extended family. Such "enmeshing" most commonly occurs over the caretaking for an elderly parent or other relative in need of financial support or direct care. Women often get the short end of the stick in these situations. (There's more on this in Chapter 14, "Parent Care: The Child as Adult.")

As daughters, daughters-in-law or sisters-in-law, women are assumed to be the family members most likely to provide (and "best at" providing) the care for the elderly or infirm. What so often happens is that the person taking care of the daily needs of the situation also ends up footing the bills—for medicine, unreimbursed medical payments, transportation, occasional relief help. If you are in this situation, some family mediation is in order. If you can't get everyone together for a powwow, or are shy about asking the others to contribute money (or time), call in a good friend or friend of the family to be the plant in the audience, and invite over the extended family and have your shill mention that "Janey is just worn down by all this responsibility. I hope the rest of you intend to help with your Mom's care too." This is manipulative, of course, and is a ploy of last resort. Anyway, it only works if you can get everyone together physically. If not, don't be afraid to state your needs. At the worst, you can just bill the other family members for their pro-rated contributions, with a note of explanation.

Remarriage—Yours or His

The women (and men) who are most likely to want "full disclosure," a blending of roles, and a marriage open to the financial realities of life have been married before. They've often been burned, and with the benefit of hindsight they perceive quite clearly the high cost—emotionally and financially—of ignorance (or at least lack of foresight). They no longer equate love and trust. This new pragmatism in approaching marriage is equally apparent in those who have come out of an acrimonious divorce and those who as grief-stricken widows have had to find their way alone through a tangle of financial matters that would have been much simpler to negotiate had there been more sharing of information while the husband was still alive. The difference is that the divorced woman is more likely to be the one who has learned that a once-loving spouse is capable of unexpected financial cruelties. (You've heard this joke. Q: "What's the difference between love and herpes?" A: "Herpes is forever.")

A specific sub-set of women likely to remarry are those between 25 and 45 years of age with 3 or more children. According to one study, more than 83% of these women remarry! The reasons for this tell us a lot about women's financial dependency on the men they marry, and underscores the feminist contention that every woman with children is only one man away from welfare. These young women with dependent children remarry in such great numbers because they cannot support themselves and their children, and they need the security of marriage because they are often living in poverty.

Divorced women who are more self-sufficient (usually those without children) remarry with less frequency, as do older women (past 45). The poorest, least-educated women are the most likely to remarry; highly educated and self-sufficient women are likely to stay single after a divorce or death of a husband. Interestingly, among men, those with the highest incomes (and therefore the greatest options) are likeliest to remarry.

Please do not, however, allow yourself to be fooled into thinking that remarriage is the cure-all for a divorced mother's woes. Plenty of second marriages have foundered on the shoals of financial difficulties, especially in those cases where there are children from previous marriages to support. Everyone is resentful of the demands of past lives, and problems arise both when there is not enough money to go around and also in those rarer cases where there's too much money coming from one side of the relationship. (For example, an ex-husband might give so generously to his kids, who live with his ex-wife and her new husband, that the new husband feels controlled by the shadow of the other man and resentful that he cannot provide as generously for his own children, now living with *his ex-wife but visiting him on weekends. You get the picture.*)

The ties can be so complicated that one woman, living with a man who pays alimony and child support to dependents from his first marriage, speaks of "our ex-wife."

For a remarriage to start off happy and healthy, it's necessary to make full disclosure of each person's assets and expectations, as well as each person's current lifestyle expenses and desires—e.g., the children must stay in private schools, etc. (See *Rewedded Bliss*, by Davidyne Mayleas, for very useful budget forms you can follow here.) Crucial to this process is for the woman remarrying to find out if her alimony and child-support payments will continue through her second marriage. Her new husband may be expecting this, and may get a nasty surprise to find out that he's taking on the support of her children in the new relationship.

Or take this example—an unhappy ending because neither party thought to clarify financial matters before the marriage. A man married a divorced woman with children, assuming that they would all continue to live in her comfortable house. It never occurred to him that the house belonged to her first husband and was hers to use, according to their divorce agreement, only until such time as she remarried. He'd never asked her outright about the ownership of the house, and she had never imagined that he was marrying her on the assumption that she'd be the one to provide the domicile. (He'd already arranged to turn over his house to his ex-wife and their kids.) A remarriage that, beforehand, looked like a match made in heaven, began to take on nightmarish qualities as he, she, and her three kids tried to find adequate housing without disrupting their lives completely. Had there been full disclosure earlier, they might never have gone ahead with the marriage, but decided instead to live together under her roof until the kids were grown, or created some other arrangement whereby they could continue the relationship without putting themselves into a financial danger zone.

Or consider the case of a woman with three young children who married a financially secure man who already had two grown kids. She assumed that in due course he would be paying for the education of her (which she now thought of as "their") children, since he made much more than she did. In fact, the stepfather had a fight with her eldest, a boy, and threw him out of the house when he turned 17. He got along well with the second, a girl, and tolerated the third, another boy. When the kids reached their late teens he made it clear that he'd pay only for the girl's education. "In retrospect," the woman says, "I should have gotten his obligations to my kids in writing before we got married, when he was begging me to marry him and I had my doubts. Now it's too late, and short of ending up a fiftyish divorcee, I have no choice."

Again we have evidence that women's financial inequality with men leads them into decisions they would have been able to avoid had they not been financially vulnerable, especially when faced with "rescue" in the form of a prosperous new husband and stepfather.

For women who have never before been married and who are marrying men who have, it's often very painful to get over feelings of anger and jealousy toward the "old" family, whose financial demands may cramp the new bride's lifestyle considerably, and may even put a halt to her dreams of starting a family of her own. It may not be financially feasible for her new husband to consider producing any more dependents. (See step- parenting in Chapter 15, "Modern Problems"). These are not insurmountable financial obstacles always, but they are certainly money-linked issues which are highly charged emotionally, and which must be discussed honestly before the re-marriage takes place. If not, the marriage may really be beginning under false pretenses, with assumptions of financial ability that may not be warranted by the situation.

Mayleas, in *Rewedded Bliss,* calls the new and complex system facing remarried couples a form of "economic polygamy." Describing her own marriage—her first—to a man with an ex-wife and a child, she says, "From a financial standpoint, our family structure was much less like that of my mother and father—100% pure monogamy—and much more like that of an East African Bantu chieftain. Of course, on a smaller scale."

Couples marrying for the second time (or couples in which at least one partner has been married before) are the likeliest candidates for writing prenuptial agreements or marriage contracts. Especially where there are children involved, the spouses may want to make sure that their own children inherit directly from them, and that their step-children won't unfairly take part of a legacy not intended for them; it's also true that some wives and husbands want to limit the amount they leave to each other, wanting most or all of their assets to go to their children instead.

Whatever the individual's wishes, the premarital contract is an effective way of making them manifest. Of course, some of the issues that arise in negotiating a prenuptial agreement are the very same ones that will cause conflict at every stage of marriage—including at its dissolution.

The caveat about marriage contracts that we would issue to women remarrying or marrying for the first time is the same: the person with the most assets is usually the person calling the shots, and this is likely to be the person of the male persuasion, for obvious reasons. Which is why it's absolutely necessary, if you are considering drawing up a marriage contract or if your prospective spouse has already had one drawn up, to have an independent lawyer look at it first—she or he may be able to foresee potential difficulties that no one else has.

Consider the situation of a woman whose first marriage is to a man who has been married before, and who is, as a result, far more wary than she. Such a woman is especially vulnerable to the possibility that her husband will set up any marriage contract exclusively in his favor. She may be making many sacrifices for this relationship—including taking on the duties of a step-parent—and yet may find herself closed out from some of the financial benefits of marriage—even, possibly what she will inherit.

It is imperative that a woman under these circumstances try to get independent financial advice before she signs any agreement that would waive the minimum automatic settlement in a will or after a divorce. Your feelings now, that you don't want to put added financial strain on the man you love, that you want to make his life easier, not harder, that no able-bodied woman should expect to be kept by a man or to receive alimony from him, are understandable, but naive and dangerous to your own fiscal well-being.

A particularly dangerous situation—which may not appear so at first—is that of the classic May-December marriage. A young woman marries a man considerably older than she, with children (often grown) from a previous marriage. The man may be worth a lot of money, but look out! Some unforeseen circumstances: If the couple have children themselves, the husband may die before they are grown. She may be left a single parent with fairly young children, and her husband's financial obligations from previous marriage(s) may mean that she is entitled to very little of his estate. This is particularly true if she has signed a marriage agreement pegging her inheritance (or support payments in the case of divorce) to the number of years of marriage. He could die after only a year or two—but if she's had a child by then she'll have lifelong expenses.

Make sure that if you are in this situation and thinking of such a prenuptial agreement (with escalating settlement or inheritance amounts for each year you are together), that there is a clause in there about children! You might not see children in your future when you're signing the contract, but protect yourself anyway! Even if they have no children together, a younger woman may find herself nursing an old man just as she reaches her own prime, and may find herself saddled with major expenses for an elderly spouse whose funds are running out.

For an older woman remarrying, vigilance is also not a bad idea. A widow with grown children and considerable assets left to her by her late husband is planning to marry a man whose children are also grown, whose financial worth appears to be less than hers. (She's a little embarrassed to get into the "full disclosure" routine with him, because she thinks he might be offended, think her money-hungry, or fear that she'll think less of him because he isn't "worth as much" as her first husband was.) She's heard horror stories of widows being taken advantage of in such remarriages. Even if she trusts that they won't apply to her situation, she wants to make sure that her children won't suffer financially if she dies before her second husband. She certainly doesn't want him to inherit her money—she feels guilty enough as it is, marrying after her first husband's death, but feels that it would be a simply intolerable betrayal for her to pass his money along to another man in addition. What to do?

One woman said to her fiance, "We aren't children; we can behave as the responsible adults we are and arrange things so that our children won't be upset by our marriage, thinking that each of us is somehow trying to take advantage of the other. Let's agree that we'll rewrite our wills, leaving something to each other but most of our money to our own children. The apartment is mine; let's leave it that way so that my children can inherit it after we're both gone. I'll put a provision in my will that you have the right to live here for absolutely as long as you want to, and the daily maintenance expenses of the house let's share. We'll each put into a household account the same amount of money each month, but we'll obviously keep our other expenses separate. I still want to be able to invest my own money, deal with it independently, and buy things for my children and grandchildren, and I'm sure you do too."

In this case her husband-to-be agreed happily with her conditions because he felt uncomfortable with the idea that her adult children might see him as an interloper, just after their mother's money. But the story is also instructive as another example of who wields power in setting forth the conditions of a marriage—the person with the most to lose if things don't go his or her way. (For further discussion of items to be included in such an agreement, see Chapter 10, "When a Wife Becomes a Widow.")

Remember, with or without a formal contract, every licensed marriage is a legally binding agreement with mutual obligations. You would investigate thoroughly, seek sage advice and think very carefully before you'd sign an apartment lease, a mortgage agreement, a summer sublet or a car loan. Make sure that you examine with at least as much care the financial consequences of a relationship that will, you hope, outlast the summer, the car, the apartment lease, and maybe even the house.

8

Myths About Taxation:
Their Impact on Women

Knowledge is power. Witch doctors in primitive societies, scribes in illiterate societies, and scientists in modern societies have exercised power because of what they know or, in many instances, because of what they are perceived to know. Expertise is not necessary for one to be accepted as knowledgeable. As the old saying goes, "In the land of the blind, the one-eyed man is king." The sexism is apt when we're talking about attitudes about personal income tax.

One of the most important and yet arcane features of contemporary economic life is income taxation. Nevertheless, hundreds of thousands of otherwise ordinary people use their alleged knowledge of the tax system as a source of power over others. The vast majority of these people are husbands trying to dictate their wives' economic actions by calling upon the purported impact of the tax system as justification. But there is a secondary aspect, whereby wives are not only trammeled themselves, but effectively encouraged to "rip off" other women.

The husbands' knowledge usually stems from the simple fact that, in many marriages, he is the one who actually prepares the tax returns. This may be because the husband is the only income earner, because he is "better at mathematics," because he "handles business" or because he is the one who willingly undertakes what is, for the vast majority of people, an onerous, time-consuming, and distasteful chore. But a couple of things flow from this "sacrifice" he makes. First and foremost, he becomes the one who "understands" the tax system, so that when he pronounces upon the wisdom or otherwise of a particular course of action "for tax reasons," his wife is often unable to argue with him effectively. Second, by doing the tax returns himself, he has available to him all the family financial data, both his and hers. She never knows, unless she asks and he tells her, what the figures are on which he is basing deductions he is claiming and so forth. On the other hand, if he is to do a proper job, she must disclose to him all her sources of income and expenditures which may have an impact on taxation. Consequently, he has the information and data, which means that he has the power.

Do men really use this power for their own purposes? Certainly many appear to. In fairness, however, it is likely that in many instances they simply do not understand the impact of the tax system and therefore make uninformed judgements, some of which may not even be to their advantage.

Let's look at a number of typical situations, after a short guided tour through tax law. By filing a joint return, married couples can claim a deduction for each spouse. Taxes are computed using the tables for married individuals filing jointly. Generally, the tax rates are lower if you use this table than they would be for married individuals filing separate returns.

Models from Real Life

In the event that Mary works only in the home, it is particularly advantageous for John to file jointly with her. *It will be obvious that even though Mary does not generate cash income, she produces a tax benefit for John.* While not having income, she may have deductions which he can claim on his tax return, for example, medical expenses, real estate and mortgage interest on residences owned by her, charitable contributions and the like. John benefits because any additional deductions available to him will reduce his tax liability for the year. It depends, of course, on the nature of their own arrangements about money whether she will personally get any benefit from the tax reduction John has received as a consequence of their being married.

Now consider this common scenario. John is earning about $24,000 a year. Mary stays at home and takes care of the children. Once her two children are in school, she finds significant time available and is offered a part-time job which will pay her a modest $5,000 a year. The job is in her neighborhood and will entail virtually no additional outlays. And the hours of the job are such that she won't need any day care or baby-sitting services for her children.

In the past it was not uncommon to hear that John told her not to take the job because it will "screw up my tax position." What John understands, from having done the tax returns, is that her additional income would result in his being in a higher tax bracket. This he translates as meaning that it doesn't pay to have Mary work. This has become less true with the current tax code but may change again as tax rates change. The question is whether her additional income changes the rate at which John is taxed.

But look at it from Mary's point of view. If she earns $5,000 she will pay little or no income tax if she files separately. John may not realize that they may now be entitled to a credit for child care and dependent care services because she is working.

If she takes the job, she is $5,000 ahead and he is behind. If they operate on a "whats his is his and what's hers is hers" philosophy, it becomes apparent why John doesn't want her to take the job. If they operate on the concept of pooling income, more analysis is necessary to calculate the net benefit and loss.

But Mary's taking the job should have additional attractions for her. For example, it is unlikely that a low-paying, part-time job such as this would offer a perk such as a pension plan. But if her husband cannot invest in an individual retirement account because he is covered by a pension plan where he works, or he refuses to invest in one in her name, if she so desires, the earned income would allow her to make a contribution to an individual retirement account in her own name. She would also start to build up Social Security benefits. In other words, *earning even modest amounts in her own name allows Mary to start building a retirement fund independent of anything her husband may have.*

Not all husbands will try to keep their wives at home because of tax considerations. Some will attempt to make their working wives into tax evaders, while at the same time taking advantage of other women. The situation typically is as follows. The wife, Sarah, is offered a job baby-sitting for a single mother, Alison, who lives in the neighborhood. Alison offers Sarah $120 for a five-day week to stay with a three-year-old and to be around when the eight- and ten-year-olds return from school. Under the child care credit, Alison can deduct up to $2,400 a year for each child under the age of thirteen, but no more than $4,800 a year. So on the basis of fifty weeks of work, if Alison's income is $30,000 per year, she would get a credit of 20% or $960.

Frank, Sarah's husband, doesn't object to Sarah taking the job, but tells her to get her pay in cash. That way, he says, they won't have to declare the income. The proposition might be presented to Alison as "Frank says that because of taxes, the job isn't worth taking unless I get paid in cash."

What follows from this?

First and foremost, Alison will be cheated of a deductible expense since she cannot claim the child-care deduction unless she can produce a receipt from Sarah with Sarah's Social Security number on it. Many working women are thus denied tax deductions they have a right to, not by the tax collector but by other working women who take advantage of them.

What is the overall effect if Sarah reported the $6,000 of income? Frank's tax liability might rise. Sarah might have tax liability of as much as $450 but would also get the opportunity to build up pension income. Alison would have additional deductions of $1,200. It is apparent that the big winner from Sarah's nonreporting is Frank, the big loser is Alison, while Sarah takes the legal risks and probably loses more than she gains—from not making Social Security contributions. Second, Sarah has become a tax evader by not declaring her income. If she is caught, she will be subject to penalties and interest even though, if she filed a tax return, she might have very little tax to pay. (In terms of the number of people involved, if not in terms of the dollar amount, the bulk of tax evasion is probably committed by women in household work and low paying jobs, such as waitresses. While you might argue that it is unlikely that Sarah would be caught, occasionally even low income earners are "targeted" for in-depth tax examinations.) Moreover, if Sarah and Frank are ever divorced, Frank can accuse her of tax evasion and hold it as threat over her head.

Third, by not declaring her income, Sarah is depriving herself of the opportunity to provide for her own retirement years, either through an Individual Retirement Account or the Social Security system other than by what Frank has contributed.

The irony of the situation should be apparent. Women who are in what we might call the "regular" work force who have taxes withheld at the source from their regular paychecks get both the benefits of the tax system and suffer its burdens. But at the lower-income levels, that of part-timers and household workers, there is strong argument that reporting income is a real plus. The tax payable is likely to be minimal while the tax-related benefits can be fairly substantial.

Yet in many, many cases, husbands (perhaps believing that their understanding of the tax system is correct) either coerce or convince women to avoid income-paying jobs which would be to their benefit, or "allow" them to take such jobs only if the women are prepared to break the law. In each case, the women stand to lose while the men are in a "no-lose" situation. The men, in turn, blame the tax system, and many women, faced with such authority, accept the rationale.

Let's now turn to a number of other myths about the tax system to see what impact they have on women on all points of the earning spectrum, and their approaches to personal economics.

Myth 1: The Tax System
Discriminates Against Women

Accountants and tax planners often report their clients' complaints that the tax system discriminates against women. Like most myths, there is a kernel of truth in this statement, but the statement itself is clearly wrong. The Internal Revenue Code has no section which makes specific reference by sex.

But because the Internal Revenue Code allows deductions and credits based on income, it's no surprise that it's only those people with income who are directly affected, and those with higher incomes are more significantly affected than those with lower income. Those who are investors have certain tax benefits that noninvestors do not. Those who run businesses get some significant tax breaks not available to nonbusiness people. As we know, men generally earn more money than women. Men are more likely to be investors than women. Men are more likely to run businesses than women. Thus, though the system is neutral, the economic facts of life are such that many more tax benefits accrue to men under the Internal Revenue Code than to women. But the Code itself does not discriminate. A woman who is in an identical economic situation as a man will be treated in exactly the same way as he will.

But there are some provisions which, because of the economic facts of life, tend to help women more than men. There is a limit to certain deductions (they are "capped"), which may, in percentage terms, give greater benefit to the lower-income earner. For example, the child care credit is equal to 30% of child care expenses for income of $10,000 or less but decreases by 1% for every $2,000 above $10,000 but not below 20%. This means that a woman earning $5,000 a year can deduct more of her child care expenses than a family earning $30,000. (Of course, given the availability of funds, the woman's deduction may be only $300 if she spends $1,000 in child care while the family earning $30,000 a year and spending $3,000 a year on child care can deduct $600.)

It is interesting to note that where discrimination was attempted in the Code, it was designed to favor those with lesser income.

Myth 2: Women Are Better Off With Joint Tax Returns

Many countries, including the United States, allow or require married couples to file joint tax returns, aggregating their incomes and deductions and filing a single document for wife and husband. Many people believe that, given the concept of marriage as an equal fiscal partnership, joint returns make sense. But the emotional attractions of the joint return may well be characterized as thin gruel when one examines the fiscal results.

If the couple consists of a working husband and a wife who stays at home to take care of the family, the effect of a joint return will normally be to reduce the tax liability of the family. But the question is whether the wife gets any direct benefit at all, since the husband is most likely simply to pocket the savings. Thus, while the married man with a non-income-producing wife is clearly ahead using a joint return, there is no evidence that the wife is ahead. And since the wife has to sign the return, if the husband underpays his taxes, she is equally liable for paying up the difference to the government. Many American women have discovered this little problem after having been abandoned by their husbands.

But the real difference comes in the situation where both husband and wife work. Typically, the husband will be making more money than the wife. Under the Canadian system, for example, each will file his or her own tax return, and each will pay tax or get a refund. Their incomes are not aggregated, so each gets the benefit of progressive tax rates, starting with a very low rate of tax and rising. If the wife is earning $20,000 and the husband is earning $45,000, the wife will pay tax on approximately $15,000 of taxable income (say $3,900) while the husband will pay tax on say, $40,000, about $13,000. More to the point, on the next dollar earned, because the wife's income is taxed at a rate of 20%, she will pay only 20 cents in taxes while the husband will pay 30 cents since he is in the 30% tax bracket because of his higher income. This system encourages the wife to increase her earnings. Indeed, the family unit will be better off from a tax point of view to have her earnings rise until they reach the level of his income. If each has an opportunity to earn the same amount of additional income, say by working overtime, it makes more sense for her to work and him to stay home.

Under a joint return, such as the one commonly used in the United States, their incomes would be aggregated to $65,000 and the tax rate would be somewhere between his and hers. In effect, under a joint return, she pays more tax on her income than would normally be the case while he pays less. Thus the joint tax return has the lower income spouse supporting the higher income spouse by assuming part of his taxes. This will be true even if they divide the tax liability on a pro-rata basis with her paying 20/65 and him paying 45/65 of the tax.

Myth 3: Tax Loopholes Only Benefit High-Income Males

It would seem apparent that given the fact that men predominate as higher-income earners and that tax planning tends to benefit high-income earners, the elimination of loopholes which allow high earners to reduce tax liability will primarily hurt men, not women. The usual argument is that if all loopholes were closed, more tax money would be available for social programs. Putting aside the question of how the government would use any extra money generated through loophole closing, it is not necessarily true that all or even most tax planning benefits men.

We have a somewhat progressive tax system, one which takes an increasing percentage of a taxpayer's income as it rises, but which is capped at 28% for federal income tax purposes. A person earning say, $100,000 a year can figure, depending on his or her state, on paying around 28 cents on every dollar earned. On the other hand, a person earning little income might pay no tax on the first $5,000 or $6,000 of income, depending on how the income was produced. But even if the lower-income person gets more money, the tax payable may still be under 20 cents on the dollar.

Further, given the limitations on itemized deductions, where the wife has a small business and has many deductions she may be better off filing "married filing separately" rather than losing those deductions because they are not more than 2% of her husband's income. It is important to calculate the overall family benefit of filing jointly or married filing separately, and examining whether that overall saving is shared with the family or enjoyed by only one of the partners.

Another form of tax planning occurs if the husband runs a business. He may employ his wife and pay her a salary. This may permit him to make contributions to a pension plan for her which saves on taxes and helps her. The business gets a deduction for this expense. Obviously, she must actually work there. Often, a wife is not compensated for her contribution to the husband's new business and a good tax-planning mechanism is missed.

An interesting consequence of this type of tax planning was reported in a matrimonial case a couple of years ago. A dentist had arranged for a company wholly owned by his wife to manage his business affairs. They subsequently got a divorce and he requested the court to force her to return the shares in the company since its work was completely linked to his professional practice. The court gave him back the shares, but only after he paid his wife more than $100,000 for them.

Myth 4: The Tax System Keeps Women Out of the Work Force

In the first part of this discussion, we looked at games men sometimes play when their wives first contemplate looking for a job. We indicated that, in many cases, male intransigence was said to be based upon the tax system, though arguably personal selfishness was the underlying cause. But does the tax system actually create a barrier for women who want or need to work outside the home?

The facts suggest it does not. The personal tax rate system is progressive, lower income earners paying relatively small amounts in tax. The taxes would be further reduced if she chose to make contributions to an individual retirement account, if she had deductible child care expenses, or had other deductions. And she would become eligible for certain benefits which might include Social Security benefits (although she is entitled to those benefits by reason of her husband's employment, if she is employed, her benefits may be higher than her benefits as a spouse), unemployment insurance and perhaps additional perks offered by her employer.

On the other hand, it may work out that the amount of net income she brings home may make income earning unattractive. For example, she might have to incur substantial child care expenses which exceed her income even after considering any tax benefits. She might have significant costs in getting to and from work, in paying for lunches and clothes beyond what would be necessary if she didn't work. Or she may find that the dollars earned are not worth the additional workload she has undertaken, particularly if she has little or no support from her husband in terms of household tasks. It might also be noted that in almost every country where researchers have studied household work, statistics show that notwithstanding the fact that both spouses are working outside the home, the bulk of work in the house continues to be done by the woman and that men think they do more than they actually do.

In other words, there may well be situations where it is not worthwhile for a woman to take on a salaried job, but given the nature of the tax system and the progressive rate schedule, it is not taxes which should deter a woman from entering or reentering the work force.

Myth 5: The Tax System Imposes a Tax on Marriage

Many people believe that a couple is better off from a tax point of view just living together rather than being married. This may occur if one spouse will lose deductions by virtue of filing a joint return. If they file "married filing separately," this will subject both spouses to higher rates than if they were not married. The tax system penalizes married couples for filing separately instead of jointly.

But there is another side to the coin. There are some tax benefits from being married. For example, property can be transferred from one spouse to another (which usually occurs on death) free of capital gains taxation. This tax-free transfer is postulated on the couple having been legally married. In the absence of such a tax-free transfer, significant income taxes might have to be paid when one spouse dies and leaves property to the surviving spouse.

Also keep in mind that a marital deduction also can be claimed only if the parties are legally married. And where the woman earns no income, an individual retirement account can only be maintained for her by a legal mate.

If both parties work and earn substantial income, for most tax purposes they will have the best of all possible worlds, maximum deductions plus the ability to transfer property between them without tax.

Recent tax changes have also eliminated most of the tax biases between a married couple and couples which are separated or divorced when it comes to shifting property from one spouse (or ex-spouse) to another. But there is a major difference if a couple has never married. If this is the case, there will normally have to be a court order requiring payments to be made or assets to be transferred in order to get the best tax results. People who are or were legally married can make these arrangements privately in a written agreement.

In sum, there may be situations where being married is a plus and others where maintaining single status may be better from a tax point of view—not that getting married or staying single are decisions to be made on the basis of tax advantage!

Myth 6: Tax Planning Is Not for Women

Tax planning generally involves taking particular courses of action with a view to minimize taxes. Such steps could involve setting up a company to carry on your business, using a tax-deferral plan to save for a child's education or any of a score of different ideas, all with a view of reducing the tax you pay.

As we have observed a number of times in this discussion, the tax system is neutral in terms of gender. Whatever planning opportunities are available to men are equally available to women, if they are prepared to take the same steps as men.

But it is true that the lower a person's income, the less leeway there is in tax planning. Further, tax planning is much more difficult for those who are employees as opposed to self-employed business people or investors. And since most women with income are both employees and low-salaried, many tend to ignore any tax planning which might be available.

In the case of single women, the planning is often one of consumption choices. Suppose she has $500 in the bank in January after her December bills are paid? Should she keep it for a short, sybaritic vacation, splurge on a VCR, contribute to a mutual fund or put the money into an individual retirement account? The latter choice, which is a tax deductible payment, is a "tax planning" choice. But she has to make up her mind as to whether the tax benefits are as valuable to her as the pleasures she might get from one of the other expenditures.

Or, if she has $500 in the bank, she can decide whether she is happier getting the interest paid on that money or whether she'd like to go into the stock market and try to make the money grow. (See the discussion on investment choices.) The stock market investment in the long run may be a better tax-oriented choice than leaving her money in the bank.

Consider the married woman. At the start of this discussion we looked at the common situation where the husband does the tax returns. We suggested that this was a mistake from a number of points of view, one of which was because it leaves the wife ignorant of the tax system. But also in terms of tax planning, spousal returns should be done in tandem. There are a number of common deductions, such as those for charitable or medical expenses, which can be claimed by either spouse. Doing the returns in tandem and discussing options will allow them to make the best choices. At the same time, if a charitable donation made by her is claimed as a deduction, then this is also her opportunity to point out to him the financial benefit her generosity has conferred.

General Observations

A lot of economic sins against women have been laid at the door of the tax system. Some of these are based on a misunderstanding of the system while others have been based on a deliberate perversion of the facts for selfish ends. It is undoubtedly true that, on the whole, women have benefitted from the tax system less than men but, as we have pointed out, this stems primarily from the fact that the system itself tends to benefit the economically successful. Most of the problems women have had with the tax system stem from their economic position in society rather than from the system itself. Earning less than 70 cents for each dollar earned by a man means that women have a long way to go before income parity can lead to genuine tax parity.

The tax system is far from perfect. Indeed, once again we are becoming involved in a debate as to how it can be improved. While women can and should have the same general concerns as men in any move to make the system better, there remain some aspects which have a greater impact on women than men.

Once women achieve economic parity with men they'll likely find that the perceived problems with the tax system will disappear, only to be reminded that, regardless of income or gender, almost nobody likes to pay taxes. Several decades ago, the distinguished American judge Oliver Wendell Holmes said, "I like to pay taxes. It is the price we pay for civilization." Holmes was probably the last person who made such an observation. (Of course when he said it, the top rate of tax was about 4% of income—today it is 28% and likely to rise.)

Getting The Tax Message

Myths aside, what do you do about taxation? Try following these rules:

1. Almost every decision has a tax component to it. All you have to do is identify it, and then factor the tax issue into your decision making.

2. Making a financial, business or employment decision without considering the tax ramifications is akin to planning a

vacation but not selecting the destination. The same is true if you're thinking of getting married, divorced, having a child or buying a house.

3. Learning about taxation in the abstract is both time-consuming and almost impossible. And tax laws change from year to year. Therefore, the logical approach is to find reliable sources of information about specific aspects of taxation. If you have an accountant, use her. Use a stock broker when considering taxation and investments. Use your lawyer when dealing with the tax aspects of separation, divorce or custody. Your husband, lover or friend is not normally the best source of information.

You can usually get pretty good advice on specific issues from surprising sources. For example, if you are trying to decide whether it is better to buy or lease a new car for business use, the chances are that the salesperson or manager knows the tax wrinkles. The same is true of insurance salespeople, mutual fund sellers and loan officers at your bank. It is generally true that everybody knows the tax angles which will allow him or her to make a sale.

You can never go wrong when dealing with financial matters if you ask, "Is this payment I'm making deductible for tax purposes?" Or "What tax liability will I have when I receive this money?"   Which doesn't mean that you needn't double-check with your accountant to see if the advice you got was accurate.

4. There are a lot of books available on the general subject of taxation and tax planning which may be useful. There are many specialized books, such as the ones dealing with retirement plans, which are excellent. Virtually every issue of any financial newspaper or magazine will have at least one article on taxation. The odds are that at least occasionally, the article will be relevant to something you're thinking about.

Yet in just about every industrialized nation on Earth, those who pay taxes say the reform of the tax system (whatever system they might have) is a priority item. Every reform heralded as being new, simpler, more equitable (i.e., lower my taxes) tax law rarely delivers what is promised. Under President Reagan we got massive reform and confusion, but for many of the middle class it meant more, not less taxes. The debate on this subject is likely to last forever, and in this chapter we'll look at what we think are the key issues which women should be considering as part of the ongoing debate.

There will always be tax issues which are of primary concern to women, though it tends to be men who make tax policy. As a woman who is striving to control her financial life, taxation generally should be of great concern to you and changes in tax policy should be included as a key "woman's" issue because they have so much potential impact on your private life and plans. Which brings us to the final point to bear in mind.

5. There are many tax issues which are of primary concern to women, though most women should also be concerned about general tax policy issues. Make your voice heard on those issues which affect women. Remember, since women are grossly underrepresented among the policymakers, somebody has to get the right message across.

If you don't like the tax rules, fight to change them. The Internal Revenue Code is modified regularly and sometimes two or three times a year. If enough people think like you, changes will be made.

Key Tax Issues For Women

In "Myths About Taxation," we point out that there is no explicit gender bias in the Internal Revenue Code. It is careful to use neutral language throughout. But the problem lies in the impact the Code has, which means that its benefits will be distributed unequally, ostensibly based on income. But since men have significantly more income than do women, more benefits accrue to them. There are, however, some benefits which apply primarily to lower income taxpayers, often women. In this part of this section we'll look at some of the key provisions in the Internal Revenue Code which have a significant impact upon women. As the public debate on tax changes unfolds, you should be considering what might happen to each of the provisions we discuss. After that, let your representative in Congress know just what you think of the reform proposals.

(And don't forget, in this context, "reform" doesn't necessarily mean improvement; all it means is change. If that change
isn't good for women, then speak out.) Two examples:

Child Care Expenses   Since child care expenses are usually claimable by the lower-income spouse and because it is the
woman who is usually thought of as the "second earner" whose
job triggers the need for child care, this is a major women's
issue. Watch out for any attempt to scale down this deduction.
And this may be an ideal time to put pressure on the government to increase the paltry limits.

Given the problem of day care space, women should be
encouraging the government to create incentives for employers
who do provide day care facilities to their employees.

Individual Retirement Account Contributions   Right
now, if you are covered by a pension plan at work, you cannot
deduct contributions made to an individual retirement account.
Many say that this is "unfair" because so many wealthy people
end up getting better pensions and so many poor people have
minimal pensions and must rely upon their own savings. And
don't forget that women who do get pensions (often as a consequence of being widowed) are more likely to have lower pensions than men and they live longer. The retirement planning is
important in providing for elderly women. Fight to get back the
deduction for IRA's, even people covered by a pension.

We think that until such time as women achieve true economic parity with men, they should be giving less consideration
to changes which improve the system for all, and more consideration to a system which gives women a leg up the economic
ladder. If, for example, the ability to shift income from a husband to a wife (usually done for purposes of retirement planning) gives a tax break to a rich male, isn't it at least as important
that the economic consequences of the scheme puts assets into
the wife's hands that she never had before?

And why should we do away with a deduction which
benefits 100 elderly women of modest income simply because
it also benefits five older men who have substantial income?

Of course, it can be argued that the system should be revised
to give the 100 elderly women the benefit but not the five older

men. But in practical terms, these kinds of targeted tax changes tend to be complex and the "solution" to the problem is simply to eliminate the deduction.

Therein lies the crux of the problem. Historically, tax reform has always been a "give and take" affair, with trade-offs being made between what might be the best system for that which is politically most acceptable. Many groups (including women) have strong vested interests which they fight for. The result is compromise.

The important point is that before a compromise is reached, it is crucial to know what you really want. In political situations such as this, women should be fighting for their own objectives, not wasting their considerable political clout in trying for a "fair" system if achieving that system entails sacrificing their own interests.

In the United States, the Reagan tax reform exercise consisted of a trade-off under which many more items became taxable or nondeductible while tax rates dropped. But women tended to be taxed at lower rates than did men under the old system because their incomes were lower. The net result of tax reform for many American women was that they got a modest reduction in tax rates (especially compared to men) but found many other provisions which were beneficial to them scaled down in the interests of equity.

We have often argued in this book that women should give more consideration to their own self-interest,—"head over heart,"—in a lot of situations they are faced with than has traditionally been the case. When looking at public policy proposals, particularly in the area of taxation, it is important to keep in mind women's objectives. The winners in tax reform have historically been those who kept their own interests front and center, not those who were prepared to sacrifice for some notion of the broader public good.

And bear in mind, those who attack provisions which are important to women will do so in the name of fairness and equity—words always associated with any tax proposal no matter how abhorrent it might be. The goal is to protect what women have and to push for more.

PART III

SUCCESSFULLY SURVIVING CRISIS

9

Divorce: Coaching in Battlefront Tactics and Strategies

In your mother's or grandmother's day, divorce was uncommon. Marriage was "till death do us part," and no matter how miserable the marriage it was unlikely that the parties would split. A divorced woman was often shunned by "polite" society and, self-consciousness aside, most women feared that the reward for cutting themselves off from the family's breadwinner might be a one-way ticket to poverty. Divorce statistics have changed, but some of the economic perils remain.

Today, about 50% of first marriages begun since the mid-70's and 60% of second marriages end in divorce. Widespread social disapprobation is rarely a consequence of divorce today, and a wise woman anticipating (if she can) the break-up of her marriage can prepare herself to control the financial damage divorce can still wreak on her.

The most significant, ongoing problem revolves around how she will support herself, assuming that her husband was at least partially responsible for her support while they were married. Our thesis in this book is that a woman must have the tools and knowledge to take care of herself, even if she is in a stable, long-term relationship, be it marriage or cohabitation. Even if the couple doesn't split up, the fact that the parties are reasonably self-sufficient helps to produce a happier relationship. If a woman suddenly finds herself on her own, knowing how to handle herself financially and in the world of business will help ensure that the dissolution of a relationship doesn't mean dropping into genteel (or in many cases, not-so-genteel) poverty.

In this chapter we'll look at several aspects of divorce. Usually, we are referring to the dissolution of a marriage; but if you are involved in a long-term cohabitation, most of the suggestions given here (other than those relating to some specific legal procedures and rights) will also apply to you.

More than in any other chapter of this book, here we emphasize "head" over "heart." In divorce there is no advantage in allowing tender feelings to affect your critical faculties. We recognize, of course, that the break-up of a marriage or long-term relationship is a profoundly emotional experience. But one of the main errors women make at such a time is to allow their emotions—anger, guilt, love, fear—to rule their heads when it comes to the economic issues. This is seldom the case with men, which perhaps is one reason why men come out of most marital break-ups in much better financial shape than do women. There is no room for the traditional female concerns for the welfare of others (except for your children) at this time. If there is ever a moment in your life when your interests come first, this is it.

The Psychological Aspect

Despite the relatively high ratio of divorces to marriage, many women remain in unhappy relationships with men and many divorced people remarry. Even when there has been a final separation, women are much more likely to try to patch it up than men are, even if it is the woman who leaves the family home. It is important to understand some of the reasons for this, because they have an impact on the whole divorce proceeding, especially insofar as property settlements are concerned.

First, even in today's society, most women have been raised to believe that a primary goal in life is to marry and have children. If a marriage breaks down, they have feelings of both guilt and failure which most men do not have. Such feelings are more likely to drive a woman, particularly an older woman who has been married for a long time, to try to patch up a relationship which any outsider would say is not only dead, but which deserved to die.

There are now groups in almost every community who give support to women who have left their husbands or lovers or who have been abandoned. If you are in that situation and find yourself thinking about returning, look around for a support group. (We might add here that you should distinguish between these types of support groups and organizations and individuals who are involved in marriage counseling and other attempts to save relationships. We believe strongly that some unhappy marriages—where there is goodwill on both sides—can be saved, and the effort is certainly worthwhile. But in this chapter we are looking at relationships which are ending.)

Second, in the vast majority of cases, the man has had control of the family finances, even if he has not been the only earner. A woman faced with the breakdown of her marriage, or who suspects the relationship is about to end, must almost immediately figure out where the money is going to come from to meet her immediate needs and those of her children, if any. This is one of the reasons why we have preached the importance for women, at every stage of their relationships, to keep some control of their own finances and to be informed about the family finances. (Many a woman has been astonished to find that right after her husband walks out the door, the next step he takes is to empty their joint bank accounts.) Financial dependency keeps many a marriage going when every other criterion suggests it should end.

Third, and in some ways most importantly, *men and women view conflict in very different ways.* Carol Gilligan has looked at this phenomenon in her book titled *In A Different Voice.* What Gilligan found was that, at all ages, females are more likely to attempt to mediate solutions than are males. Boys reading about "Jack and the Beanstalk" cheer when the giant is killed. Girls wonder why he had to die, since Jack had everything he wanted. Feminists are now looking more closely at the consequences of these differences between men and women.

In the context of a marriage break-up, *you must be aware of the possible presence of these gender differences.* For men, it becomes a battle which must be won. Women generally would prefer a negotiated settlement which is "fair" to all parties. People who advise women should be aware of this and guard against it. The law has been developed by men and is essentially adversarial, pitting one party against the other. While this is somewhat less true with the divorce, custody and property law reforms of the past decade, in essence the law still produces winners and losers. A woman, left to her own devices, will tend to try to patch things up, even in a hopeless case. A man will more likely be "out to win."

Social scientists who have studied rape resistance say that the rage reaction one might expect is sometimes missing even in women who are assault victims. So it should come as no surprise that so many women haven't learned to fight back when it's "only" their livelihood at stake. Accustomed to doing battle for others, women may fight like crazy in a custody action where they feel the welfare of their children is at stake. But they are much less likely to fight any less altruistic battles such as the struggle for their own economic well-being.

And there is a comparatively new wrinkle to be considered. In the wake of the women's liberation movement which helped so many see new truths about their lives (including, of course, their marriages), women began leaving their husbands, rather than vice versa. These women were not instigating divorce proceedings because they suspected their husbands of infidelity, nor were they usually leaving for another man. They wanted out because their experience of marriage had been awful. And women, as men had sometimes done before them, left married life with considerable guilt—if not guilt toward the man himself, then with guilty feelings about their own failings for having entered into a less-than-perfect union in the first place.

Guilt is not usually an emotion which allows people to act in their own best interests while under its influence. Many women who have left their marriages since the late 1960's have declared they want no support; some have even stated that they want no restitution payments for time and opportunities lost, no rehabilitation money either. Don't do this to yourself either because of misdirected ideology or (more likely) out of guilt at having left an institution that was supposed to provide eternal bliss. Make sure you can get all the support you can.

Your future and your own capacity to earn may both look bright if you're under 45 when you divorce. But the truth you must face, as you contemplate your middle years and beyond, is that you are unlikely to live in comfort without additional support if, like many women, you took some years out to raise children. You may have no pension or other retirement funding, or inadequate provision for the final third of your life. The only way you're likely to compensate yourself for the losses so many married women have undergone is through a divorce settlement in which you allow your self-interest to surface, for once. Don't let yourself be motivated by guilt or allow yourself to be manipulated by your spouse or his lawyer so that you have to give up the opportunity to be more nearly financially secure in the future.

Almost every study done in recent years shows that after a divorce men end up better off financially than they were before, while women's situations are worse—notwithstanding the propaganda about poor males who are faced with the awesome burden of alimony paid to indolent and grasping ex-wives. The only cases where men and women end up in almost the same financial situation is where the family had almost no assets at the time of the break-up and the woman is being substantially supported by some form of public assistance.

While there may be cases of wholly amicable marriage break-ups, these are actually few and far between. Generally speaking, a friendly break-up is more likely to come where the marriage has been of short duration, and where, soon after the ceremony, both parties realize it was a mistake. Since they haven't invested huge amounts of emotional capital, since they probably do not have children, and since significant financial sacrifices probably have not been made, the relationship can terminate with relatively little pain on either side.

But in most cases, the fallout from the ending of a relationship is akin to legalized warfare. In situations of this type, a woman does herself a distinct disservice if her primary goal is a treaty with the other side at any price, whether "for the sake of the children" or because of false pride and a reluctance to compete for the family's limited resources.

An Overview of the Law and the Process

In this section we'll take a quick look at the law relating to marriage breakdowns. We'll follow up later in this chapter with a more detailed discussion.

Separation

Most marriage breakdowns will follow a general pattern. First there will be a separation, with one or the other parties moving out of the family home. This raises the immediate question (usually for the woman) of support: how will the mortgage, rent, utilities be paid? At this stage, some couples enter into a formal separation agreement. (You'll need a lawyer; more on that later.) If one party (and we'll assume it is the husband) agrees to pay support for his wife and/or children, a formal agreement is very important, because it will allow him to deduct the payments he makes for income tax purposes. The agreement is important for the wife because it sets out in legally binding terms what the husband's obligations are, and she can take him to court to enforce them. Try to arrange to get as large an interim sum of money as you can from your husband when you are discussing formal support arrangements. Remember that he also is likely feeling guilt at this time and is more likely to come up with money to assuage his conscience now than in a few months when he has time to assess his financial situation closely and has hardened his attitude.

If there is no agreement, the wife can go to court and get an order requiring him to pay support for her and any children. (The problem, as tens of thousands of women have found, however, is that getting an order and having it enforced are two very different things.)

If there are children, you may want to get a formal custody order. At the early stages, this order may be temporary, with the issue of permanent custody being thrashed out later. You and your husband (probably through your lawyers) will start to work on the terms of a permanent arrangement. They will include the question of a financial settlement (which may be in the form of a lump-sum payment, regular support payments, or a combination of the two.) The regulation of such payments is governed by state law and varies significantly from state to state.

Eventually you will probably want to get a divorce, although some couples remain legally separated for many years—even permanently—without taking this final step.

Divorce legislation is governed by state law. The grounds for divorce range from "no fault" (irretrievable breakdown) to fault based (adultery, cruelty or abandonment), with many variations in between.

In those states having "no fault" divorce, the vast majority of actions will be brought on that basis. It should be noted that this *can* be unfair to a woman. If your husband walks out, and meets the local requirements for a no-fault divorce, *he* can divorce *you*. While many have applauded the notion that fault or guilt need not be a part of divorce proceedings, the provision tends to work against women. In the days when fault (usually adultery) was the key to divorce, a woman had substantial leverage to use on her straying husband in making a financial settlement, especially if he wanted to marry again. The current law, progressive as it may seem, eliminated that leverage. Many feel that women have been deprived of a significant chunk of power in the name of social change, without there being adequate legislation to take their circumstances into account. If the court is adjudicating your settlement, a judge might well say "okay, no fault. Let's just split the assets and we're done with it." The real problem underlying this legislation is that the property and support laws are not as progressive, and we continue to find divorced women becoming the newly poor.

Once the divorce case comes up, the other main issues you may have been dealing with earlier on a temporary basis—custody and support—will as a rule be dealt with in the final decree.

Choosing and Using a Lawyer

The choice of a lawyer to act for you will be one of the most important decisions you will make in the whole process of a marital break-up. Remember that your lawyer will be your "army" in the fight with your husband, just as his lawyer will be acting in the same capacity for him. The object is to "win," to get the best possible financial and (if applicable) custody arrangements.

Not every lawyer handles this type of law, which is extremely specialized. If you have a lawyer or friends who are lawyers, start by asking them who they would recommend. Ask friends who have gone through a divorce. You'll find that they have very strong feelings about the competence (or lack thereof) of their lawyers. If you have no contacts at all, check with women's support organizations in your town, legal aid (even if you can pay, legal aid may be able to act as a referral), or your local bar association, which keeps a list of lawyers who do "matrimonial" or "family law," which is the current euphemism for divorce lawyers.

While it may be absurd to mention it in this context, experience suggests that a warning is in order here. Do not ever assume that you can get by with using one lawyer to represent both of you in a divorce. If the end of your marriage is proceeding so amicably that this seems a reasonable possibility, look into the question of divorce arbitration or mediation instead. This is a procedure where both parties sit down with an experienced arbitrator or mediator, usually but not always a lawyer, and work out all the details among the three of them. Even with an arbitrator or mediator, it is important to seek advice from a lawyer who will tell you what you are giving up in the arbitration and mediation. You may find yourself making concessions that no court would ever require.

If there is a real (or even potential) area of conflict, make sure you have separate legal advisers. Some critics of lawyers claim this merely enriches lawyers and causes unnecessary litigation and strife. Perhaps. But in our present imperfect world, assuming the worst about your ex-partner may not be a bad idea. Even if he started out a gentleman, he'll probably receive enough goading from family and friends to end up being a real bastard *just in case.* (In one situation we know of, he was all sweetness, light and generosity in arranging for her support; two years later she found that he had pulled a fast one which allowed him to deduct support payments from his income taxes *and* claim the children, who were partially supported by her, as *his* dependents for tax purposes.)

Another instructive tale. A New Jersey woman assumed she and her husband of two years would end their childless marriage cordially. In fact, she'd told her friends they were splitting "without acrimony." Even when he informed her that he'd taken all the money out of their joint checking account on the advice of his father, she "understood his reasons—most of it had been his anyway." She also "understood" why he insisted they use the same lawyer—"a friend of his family. He'd do it nicely and cheaply." In the end, no surprise, the allegedly impartial lawyer sounded so reasonable and so calm and reassuring that she was "glad to have it over so peaceably" and followed his suggestions not to use the joint charge accounts until things were settled—forgetting that the spouse whose credit rating she agreed not to jeopardize was the same one who'd so "reasonably" left her with nothing in the bank.

She had agreed, she realized when the dust settled, never to ask for alimony, though she'd helped support him during their brief marriage, and had relocated for him and derailed her own career plans too. She'd also agreed to let him have more of their household goods than she really wanted to. What she did get was a guilt-free divorce (her choice) with penury for several years in the bargain. None of this would have happened if she'd known enough—or felt sturdy enough or "entitled" enough— to hire her own lawyer from the beginning. But like so many women, she believed that only her husband had assets worth protecting, and she even colluded with him to protect them.

You are looking for two things when you choose your lawyer. As usual, when you look for a professional, try to find somebody to whom you can relate personally. But this time around we'd advise hiring even a "cold fish" if that fish is going to be your shark. As one experienced lawyer said to us, "If I were a wife looking to protect my interests, I'd hire the most experienced and toughest lawyer I could afford who has a reputation for getting the job done. But, beware of a lawyer whose principal reputation is that of being a bastard; he or she needs to do the hard work that is the real secret of success in a matrimonial settlement." Tax and business sophistication give you more power than a lot of bluster and tough posturing. A lawyer who is known to be a bastard may be so busy being a bastard that he may create strife and miss a good deal. While this advice may offend your sensibilities, remember you are now fighting on male terrain and you should abandon any tendencies to avoid conflict. The fact that the terrain is male doesn't mean you need a male lawyer. But don't choose a woman lawyer because you might get along with her better if all advice you get points to retaining a man.

Once you've retained a lawyer, let him or her know what it is you're after. The lawyer will ask a lot of questions, many of them intimate. If you're asked whether you've gone to bed with other men while you were married, it isn't because your lawyer is interested in vicarious thrills, but because this relates to whether your husband can sue you for divorce, and it may relate to custody issues as well. We cannot overemphasize the importance of giving your lawyer all material information— and the lawyer is the best judge of what is material. For example, this information will be useful if your husband wants a divorce immediately; if you lawyer can determine that he has no legal grounds to get one, your bargaining position is immeasurably strengthened.

Your lawyer will want to know everything about your finances as well as everything you know about your partner's finances. The initial interviews may well be gruelling experiences, but the more your lawyer knows, the better you will be represented. Of course, you may want to be discreet about the information you give until you've decided on whether you're going to hire this lawyer. If you are still in the "looking around" stage, a general outline of the facts, not the gory details, should be sufficient.

You should also bear in mind that even if state law provides that you are entitled to (for example) one-half of the family property, this does not mean that the lawyer's role is easy. There usually remain some serious problems relating to valuation and what constitutes the property to be divided. For example, if he has a business, there is the issue of how much it is worth. If you (or he) brought property into the marriage or inherited property, the value of that property at the time you married or inherited it has to be determined. Stating the law and fixing a number are two very different things.

Once you've picked your lawyer, let him or her run your case and decide on strategy. That's why you made your selection. You're going to hear a lot from friends and acquaintances about what their lawyers did (right and wrong) and you'll be tempted to check out yours. If you're satisfied with your initial choice of a representative, don't interfere but do remain involved. Do not abandon your case and say call me when it's over. The result may not be what you want. Stay in touch, but remember that you'll be billed for this time. Even good lawyers are even better with the help of an involved but noninterfering client. Also, when getting advice from friends, remember that laws are amended, tactics differ, and circumstances change. What was right (or wrong) a couple of years ago may not be germane to what is happening now. But at the minimum, your lawyer should be keeping you abreast of all developments, letting you know when the case will be heard, ensuring that you get any interim payments to which you are entitled, and be remaining available at short notice if any emergencies arise relating to the separation (as, for example, if your husband hasn't returned the kids from a visit).

On the other hand, *if your husband or his lawyer contacts you about any substantive matter, call your lawyer.* If you are represented by counsel, your husband's counsel cannot talk to you directly without the presence of your lawyer. If your husband seeks to resolve material issues without the attorneys (who, he may say, are "just causing problems"), be very wary. You should never make even the most innocuous decision about money, custody or access without checking first with your attorney.

Giving ground or accepting an offer now may result in legal problems in the future. If you're hard up for money, or support which has been promised and has not been paid, call your lawyer at once.

The issue of contacting your lawyer leads into the issue of fees. Your lawyer gets paid on the basis of time or a flat fee. That is negotiated when you retain your attorney. In many cases, but by no means all, your legal fees may be paid by your husband as part of the final financial settlement. But operate on the assumption that you'll bear your own lawyer's fees.

This means that your lawyer should not be used as a substitute for a psychiatrist or even a close friend. His or her time is being charged each time you talk on the phone. Recently we spoke with a woman who was enraged with a lawyer she had consulted. She had been thinking about leaving her husband and had made contact with a female lawyer who had an office nearby. She had had one appointment and "spoken with her a few times on the phone." Ultimately, she decided to stay with her husband. But she was outraged when she got a bill from the lawyer for over $400, with each phone call documented. "I thought she was my friend." No. The truth is, she was her lawyer. (The husband, incidentally and perhaps not surprisingly, refused to pay the bill for his wife.)

Many lawyers advertise very low prices for "uncontested divorces." If you see one of these lawyers, remember that what is meant is a procedure in which there is no issue of custody or financial settlement. As soon as either of these are at issue, the fees start to escalate.

You may not see a bill until the whole process is at an end. Very often lawyers don't send out interim bills, because they know that women in matrimonial cases won't have any money until the matter is brought to a conclusion. The fee may be substantial. If you think it is out of line, you can challenge your bill. (Contact your local bar association to find out the procedures.)

The odds are not weighed against you in this proceeding, as many bills are reduced by at least a small amount. In a recent case an attorney attempted to get paid twice. As part of the settlement, the husband agreed to pay the wife's legal fees. The sum was set at $3,700 and the husband paid it. As part of the settlement, the wife was to receive sole title to a cooperative apartment. After the husband paid the wife's attorney's fees, the attorney then sought to charge the wife for the costs of transferring the cooperative apartment. The wife challenged the bill and after a fee arbitration at which the attorney was represented and the wife was not, the attorney's fee was disallowed.

Discuss fees with your lawyer at the start, not just in terms of how much the divorce is likely to cost (don't expect more than a general estimate) but how the fee will be paid. You can hope for (but don't count on) a final financial arrangement which will have your ex footing the costs. Where the husband is the main income earner, it is fairly common that he is called upon to pay your lawyer as part of the financial settlement. And a word of advice: some portions of your legal fees may be deductible to the extent the fees are attributable to tax advice or the production of income. You'll have to discuss this possibility with your accountant and attorney.

If your former husband fails to make payments to which you're entitled and you have to go to court to get your money, the legal expenses you incur may be deductible in computing your income taxes.

Financial Arrangements

In a marital break-up, you have to consider three main types of financial arrangement. The first is interim support to be paid for you and any children while the separation or divorce proceedings are underway. Second, there is the question of your entitlement to a share of the family assets. This entitlement is governed by state law. In some states a specific formula is set out while in others, the law is more vague. Finally, there is the question of continuing support for you and/or the children after the divorce.But let's look at the matter of taxation first. This is an area where a well-negotiated arrangement can work to your advantage if you know what you're doing—or can result in some unpleasant surprises if your husband is slicker than you.

If the payments are made pursuant to (following from) a written separation agreement or pursuant to a judicial decree, these payments are "periodic" (that is they continue for an extended period of time), and they terminate upon your death, unless the parties agree in writing to the contrary. The person who pays them can deduct them from taxes and the person who receives them pays tax on them. Most men will be anxious to meet the necessary criteria to allow tax-free payments. (If they aren't tax deductible to the husband because they do not meet the statutory criteria, however, the woman will not have to pay tax on what she receives. If he fouls up in this area, you'll get a bonus.) Assuming that there are to be regular, periodic payments made pursuant to a legal obligation, don't forget you'll have to pay tax on what you receive. (This is not applicable to money paid for the support of children of whom you have custody; child support of this sort is tax free.) Therefore, it is important to take into account potential tax liabilities when you or your lawyer are negotiating support payments, be they interim or permanent.

A word of caution. A great many extremely competent matrimonial lawyers are not fully aware of the tax issues involved. If you feel that your lawyer is not taking these into account, ask him or her to consult with a tax specialist. It may cost a few hundred extra dollars but this is money very well spent.

Lump sum payments are neither deductible to the person who pays the money or taxable to the person who receives it. While occasionally a tax case arises as to whether a payment is "periodic" and deductible or not, generally speaking, if your husband has an obligation to pay you a fixed amount in settlement of your rights, even the fact that he makes the payment in four or five installments does not make it periodic, and you will get the money tax free.

Certain other types of transfers if made pursuant to a qualified domestic relations order, such as from his pension plan or his individual retirement account to your IRA, have no immediate tax consequences to either of you. You'll pay tax on this money when you withdraw it.

The recent tendency in the United States when it comes to support payments is to try to limit support to a relatively short period of time. The conceptual argument is that the man should not have the burden of support around his neck forever and that the woman should be encouraged to earn her own livelihood. This theory may operate reasonably well if the divorced wife is 25 and has no children. It operates very poorly where she has young children, where she is too old to embark upon a career or where health problems mean she cannot work. And this theory doesn't take into account the most pervasive problem, the fact that the man may simply not pay what he owes. While more legal emphasis is being placed on steps to enforce support payments, the fact is that in most cases there is little which can be done to allow a woman to collect from a recalcitrant ex-husband who staunchly refuses to pay.

One woman prominent in the legal community told us that in her view it was not the law itself which was creating the problem, but rather male judges who remained completely insensitive to women's needs and rights.

Support payments are usually awarded where there are children who remain in the mother's custody or where the age or health of the wife makes her return to the work force almost impossible. In many situations, support will be awarded for a limited amount of time to allow the wife to retrain or educate herself with a view to returning to the workforce and becoming financially self-sufficient. But as often as not, the woman will end up in a very low-paying job after support ceases, which of course means that her postdivorce situation may remain one of financial desperation even after the law has given her what she is "due."

Every state has legislation which sets out a formula for splitting family assets, however the term (or its equivalent) may be defined. As is often the case, the theory and the practice don't jibe. The theory is that each of the two parties to the marriage get approximately one-half or an equitable share of the assets which they have acquired during the marriage—a fair split between two equal partners. Usually assets brought into the marriage are excluded from the calculation as are such things as inheritances received during the marriage. Special rules may apply with regard to the house you've lived in together—the "matrimonial" home. Conceptually, the result is a fair and equitable split, calculated according to a formula. It means that "she" is paid off at once and doesn't have to worry about regular support payments. "He" on the other hand has fulfilled his obligations and is free to get on with his life.

There are two main problems. The most difficult lies in determining the value of assets. In some states, business assets are excluded from the calculation. Are pension rights to be included, and how are they to be valued? Does the value of his professional degree fall into the pot? (New York says "yes" and New Jersey says "no.") If so, how do you value it? (Since the award is in the form of a lump sum, there is a legal obligation to pay it even if the husband abandons his profession or business. If he goes bankrupt, his assets will be "lost" in bankruptcy, whereas alimony and child support payments are not lost in bankruptcy—although collecting the money owed may present practical problems.) As difficult as these issues may be, eventually the courts or state legislatures will solve them.

The more serious problem is that most families have very little in the way of assets after debts are taken into account. The house is probably subject to a mortgage. The car is worth very little. There are a few hundred dollars in savings. The furniture is worth a couple of thousand dollars. Each spouse has some clothes and personal effects. There is money owing on the VISA card, to the furniture company and to the bank.

In her book, *The Divorce Revolution*, Lenore J. Weitzman shows that where the marriage was less than five years old, the net assets of divorced couples (including the family home) was $3,000; in marriages of five to nine years, it jumped to $14,200, from ten to seventeen years, the net value was $46,100 and for marriages eighteen years and over, the average was $49,900. Of course, there is a big difference depending on family income. But even for divorced couples with substantial family incomes, $50,000 a year or more, the average net value of assets was just

$85,600. (The figures were for 1978. Even allowing for inflation and so forth, we think the point is made. Most families have very little net wealth. $85,600 may sound like a lot, but when divided by two and considering that this is all a divorcing woman will receive from her husband, the amount is minuscule, especially if there are children.)

Now, given our "progressive legislation," we find that a woman married for fifteen years with a couple of kids to raise may end up on the split of assets with a lump-sum entitlement to, say, $20,000. (In California, usually the family home had to be sold and the woman and her kids were on the street.)

The point we're making is this: you may have read a lot about new legislation in your state which gives women a greater degree of financial equality when a marriage breaks down. It is not at all certain, however, that women are better off as a consequence of these legal changes. (Weitzman, who had initially supported no-fault divorce and equal splitting of assets in California looked at the system ten years later and pronounced it a disaster area for women.) Even if you are leaving a comparatively wealthy matrimonial household, you're going to have a struggle for financial survival. This is so even though we now have fairer laws dealing with property division than in the past. If the family assets were barely enough to support one household while you were married, they aren't going to support two households.

This means that you have to fight for everything you can when your marriage breaks up. *He* certainly will, because he (being male, and power-conscious) knows instinctively, or because of earlier conditioning, that this is a kind of warfare in which there will be a winner and a loser.

Custody

Marital break-ups are difficult enough under any circumstances, but the presence of children adds a dimension which produces a great deal of added tension and pain. If you have children, you should raise the issue of custody and support at the first meeting you have with your lawyer. Child custody is within each state's jurisdiction. Because of the problems created when a child is snatched from one state to another there is now federal legislation which governs which state has jurisdiction, if the parents live in separate states. This is very confusing legislation but basically provides that the proper state for any custody litigation is the state where a child resided for at least six consecutive months prior to the commencement of any proceeding involving custody. A temporary order for custody might be given by a court shortly after the marriage breaks up, with a permanent decision coming somewhat later, perhaps when the divorce decree becomes final.

The decisions of the courts on custody are supposedly based on what is in the best interests of the child or children of the marriage. Obviously, this is often a fairly subjective matter. Where both parties agree on custody, the courts are inclined to accept the agreement, but they are not bound to do so. The courts' obligation in custody matters is to see to the best interests of the children no matter what the parents may say they want. In general, the state retains an obligation to the child, and therefore any agreement between the parties as to custody (say, in a marriage agreement) will not be fully binding.

Note one key point: the courts have a strong tendency not to move a child from an environment which appears to be satisfactory. The feeling is that if a child has adjusted to life in one place, a move to someplace else may have an adverse effect. What this translates into is a strong tendency to leave the child with the parent who has physical custody. If you want custody of your children, the most important step to take is to ensure that you *take the children with you* if you leave your husband. If you leave them with him, you'll enter any later custody fight at a distinct disadvantage.

You should also be aware that anybody can ask for custody of a child, not just the parents. Thus, there have been cases where a grandparent has succeeded in getting custody in a fight with a parent. Obviously, the courts start with the presumption that a parent is the logical person to have custody. (The desires of young children seldom are a factor in a court's decision. But if an older child expresses a strong desire to be with one as opposed to another parent, this factor is a major consideration in determining who will get custody.)

Normally, if one parent gets custody, the other will have right of access to the child. These rights will normally be spelled out by the courts, and if a problem arises you can return to the court for clarification or an amendment to the original order. No matter how unhappy you are with your former spouse, it is unlikely that a court will deny access. If there has been a history of child abuse by your ex-husband, it is possible that an order will be granted forbidding all contact. But generally speaking, it is unrealistic to expect that if you get custody you can deny the children's father the right to see them.

Despite what you may have heard or read in the media, the tendency of courts is to give mothers custody, and this happens in most cases. This does not mean that a custody fight is to be taken lightly. Many emotional issues are raised in one and even if ultimately won, the scars remain for many years. We might observe that the fact that women generally win custody is not so much a judgment that mothers are better parents, but probably reflects the law's male orientation, which assumes that it is the mother's "job" to raise children.

But as a mother, beware. If a father wants to fight for custody, he has some things going for him. Because he is likely to have more money than the mother and is better able to support the children comfortably, the courts may take this into account in determining what is "best" for the children. Some states—New York among them—specifically recognize that this is not a proper factor to consider, yet mothers tend to be caught in a Catch-22 situation. If they have a job and can support the children themselves, some judges have observed that they won't be home much during working hours and this will count against them. If they don't have a job, the issue of money for support becomes a factor. (The fact that fathers work all day doesn't seem to arise as an issue as often.) And ironically, if the father remarries, the fact that there is a woman at his home to play stepmother may have a positive impact on his application for custody.

Custody battles are often unpleasant. For example, in one recent case, the father was successful in getting custody when he provided evidence that the mother was living in a lesbian relationship with another woman. If a custody battle looms, your lawyer will play a significant role in defending your interests. But bear in mind that such actions often mean repeated attendance at court and may turn out to be expensive. We're not for a moment suggesting that you not fight for custody, but you should be aware that a bare-knuckles fight over custody may be a dirty, expensive and time-consuming process.

A lot has been written in recent years about joint custody of children. Normally, a court will not on its own award joint custody, since its job is to make decisions one way or another, not to act as a mediator between disputing parties. However, if both parents agree to joint custody and can work out the mechanics, such agreements will be accepted by the courts. If you feel that, apart from his other failings, your husband is a good parent, this is one area where negotiation may be useful.

Nonmatrimonial Break-ups

If your nonmatrimonial relationship breaks up after an extended period of time it is obvious that there is no question of getting a divorce. However, as we pointed out earlier, a woman who has been in a long-term cohabitation arrangement with a man may well have financial rights. What those rights are and how long you have to have cohabited in order to receive them varies from state to state.

Of course, if the two of you can agree on splitting property, if there are no children, or if you want nothing other than to end the relationship, you won't need a lawyer. But if you want to ensure that you get everything you are legally entitled to, our first bit of advice is to get a lawyer. Indeed, given the relative vagueness of the law in this area, only a skilled attorney will be able to tell you whether you have any rights at all and what they might be.

For example, if you live in New York, if you have a child, you may obtain support based upon the father's gross income. On the other hand, you do not have the specific statutory protections of the married woman when it comes to the question of a division of matrimonial property. This does not, however, mean that you have no property right claims at all. This will depend upon what written arrangements have been made between you. But because these rights are not specified in the laws themselves, the courts will have to determine them on a case-by-case basis without the guidance of even a legislative formula. You *absolutely* need legal advice if your goal is a property split after the break-up of a nonmatrimonial relationship.

Custody issues are the same for an unmarried couple as for a married couple. Even though the child is not the offspring of a "legitimate" marriage (the status of illegitimacy was abolished years ago in many jurisdictions) the father does have the chance to apply for custody rights, and therefore everything we said earlier with regard to custody will apply.

Battlefield Strategies

What do you do when your husband comes in from work, starts packing his bag, and tells you he is moving out? Getting a lawyer is a very high priority, but there are a couple of things you might want to do even before that.

• If you have one or more joint bank accounts, at a minimum you should at least freeze the accounts so that he cannot empty them. This is usually easily done by contacting the bank and advising them that there are to be no withdrawals without both signatures. If he has virtually all of the assets of the family, and you are facing the next year or more without any other assets, take out the funds (preferably after consulting with an attorney) and put them in your sole name. Do not waste time transferring the funds to someone else's name because you will eventually have to account for your use of the funds. Don't waste the money just out of spite. Do use the funds to retain an attorney. No one will blame you for that. (You may find that he emptied the accounts even before coming home to pack.) You may be strapped for money in the weeks to come and you'd best lay your hands on every penny available and put it where he can't get at it.

- Immediately collect all financial records which you can find and remove them from the house, including tax returns, records for all checking accounts (checks, statements, deposit slips and check registers), brokerage accounts, safe deposit boxes, savings accounts, business records and anything else you can find. It is an even better idea to keep these records as a regular matter so that in the event of divorce you will know where all money and investments are located.

- If you use credit cards which are in his name, buy essentials that you need before he cancels them. If you run up extravagances and luxury items, the courts may penalize you later. If you can use them to get cash advances, do so if you have no other funds or will need funds to retain a lawyer. Liability for payment can be sorted out later. Meanwhile, you will need the money.

- If you have joint safety deposit boxes, get into them and pull out any documents that are there. If he has such things as share certificates in his name, take them too. You won't be able to turn them into money but it assure you of having a record of the assets that exist and help prevent disposition of the assets before they are sorted out.

- Once he moves out, talk to your lawyer about changing the locks on the doors, and if appropriate do so immediately. If you live in an apartment, tell the superintendent that he has left and is not to be allowed in when you are away. To the extent that you have stopped him from getting his clothes, golf clubs, fishing tackle, VCR, stuffed animals and other personal belongings, this can be dealt with by the lawyers while the dust settles. More importantly, you must have the right to privacy and not have to worry about his going through your possessions while you're away. If for any reason you cannot change the locks, remove from the home your personal diaries, letters, financial records, communications from your lawyer and anything else that would be particularly disturbing for him to get his hands on. If you have valuable jewelry that is not listed on a schedule of insurance, remove it from the home. There are far too many stories about the suddenly disappearing jewelry that your husband will deny all knowledge about. In one case, a husband had denied for over a year that he had removed the wife's jewelry. Then the jewelry suddenly materialized in the wife's attorney's office as a settlement was being worked out conditional upon return of the wife's jewelry from whatever source.

• If you are moving out, remove any personal property that you want. Do not assume that you can return later. Later may never come. Take your grandmother's silver and your mother's china. Don't tell your attorney that you have no place to store it. It is cheaper to pay a storage company than to have your attorney argue with his attorney about it later.

• You'll have to tell your children. This may be one of the most difficult aspects of all, and we cannot advise on the best method. However, avoid lying. That is, don't tell them that Daddy is away on a trip or anything like that. Aside from the questionable wisdom of starting off your new relationship to them with a lie, you want to get two key points across to them. First, if Daddy comes to the house or phones and wants to visit, he is not to be allowed in unless you (and perhaps your lawyer) are present. Changing the locks doesn't do much good if the kids will let him in when you're out and he can then pick up everything he wants—including, perhaps, *your* items.

Second, they should be told that if Daddy comes to the school or meets them on the street when you have not told them that he is visiting, they are not to go with him. Make sure that they always have enough money to call you and are taught how to do that. The attempt to seize the kids may be a kind of power struggle and bullying technique in a custody battle. Courts do not like child snatching, and if their father attempts it talk to your lawyer and seek the court's help. If you do nothing, he will tend to try it again. Remember, he is testing you to see what he can get away with. Tell the schools, the play groups, the sports clubs, the piano teachers, and anybody else who has charge of your children that they are not to release them to their father unless you give specific instructions.

Longer-Term Steps to Take

Once the relationship has broken down, there are a number of steps you should take, some of which have been discussed earlier in other contexts.

• You should have a new will prepared. The fact that a couple separates or even divorces does not nullify an earlier will. Even while you are still fighting the postmatrimonial battles, there is a possibility that something might happen to you. A new will is therefore a high priority. The last thing you want is for him to have a claim on your estate if you die.

• Especially if there are children for whom you are responsible, you should immediately consider buying life insurance so that there is a fund available to take care of the children if you should die. You may now be their sole support. (See "Life Insurance," Chapter 12.) If the children are young, you may want the insurance to be payable to your estate, and you can create a trust under your will (see Chapter 13, "Wills") to handle the insurance proceeds. If you already have life insurance (perhaps through work), check to see who the beneficiary is. If it's your husband, change it to name your children or your estate.

• You'll have to get new credit cards in your own name if you have been using cards under his name—*e.g.*, as "Mrs. John Smith."

• You'll have to decide whether to retain your ex-husband's name (if you ever adopted it) or whether you revert to your premarriage name. If you are in business or are a professional, you may find it better to use the name under which you are best known, or there may be a business cost to a change. Talk to your lawyer.

• If you were covered by his hospital and medical plan, you'll have to arrange new coverage in your own name. You might want to look at medical insurance in your own name. It may be that if you were working before the break-up, you opted not to take certain benefits offered by your employer because you were covered through his plan. Check with your personnel people about whether you should now make changes.

• If you've received a substantial lump-sum payment in settlement of your rights to matrimonial property, you'll have to give some thought to investing the funds wisely. Take another look at Chapter 3, "Investing," paying particular attention to the issue of setting investment objectives.

• If you haven't until now had a retirement plan, this is the time to consider opening one. Look into setting up an individual retirement account into which up to $2,000 can be contributed on a tax-deductible basis. You might want to review Chapter 5, "Funding Retirement."

• Perhaps up to now all your joint financial decisions were handled by your husband. As the new head of the house, you may well need a lawyer (other than the one who handled your matrimonial affairs), accountant (even if just to deal with the complexities of a tax return), insurance agent and maybe a stockbroker. You will probably want to find your own advisers, though if you got along well with the ones your husband had you could continue to use them. As new needs arise, you should be gathering together your own "team" of people to call on if necessary. (A formal or informal women's network of colleagues or friends can provide early leads.)

• When you file your tax return, remember that if your children are living with you and you have not given up the right in negotiations, you can claim them as dependents. (A deduction of $2,000 per dependent) as of 1990. Even if you cannot claim the children as dependents because of your agreement, if the children principally reside with you, you may be entitled to file "head of household" for tax purposes, which is a more favorable status than married filing separately or individually. It may make sense to get professional help from an accountant in filing your first income tax return after a separation or divorce to ensure that you have made all possible claims.

This list highlights a number of matters which you will have to deal with early on as you come to grips with your new status. In many cases the level of urgency will depend upon whether you have young children dependent upon you. Women without children should check back to the first chapter, "Single and Solvent." Older divorcees may find their situations more closely analogous to that of widows, discussed in Chapter 10.

Running through the items above may also be of some benefit in helping to determine how his financial obligations to you will be satisfied. For example, you might want a provision under which he undertakes to provide health insurance or even life insurance coverage in favor of (at least) the children. Under recent federal legislation, most employers must make available medical insurance coverage for a divorced spouse for up to three years at almost the same cost as that paid by the employed spouse. This option must be elected promptly after divorce and should be carefully considered. In addition, if you have any preexisting medical conditions, you will have the right to convert this prior coverage into a policy in your own name. This coverage is often expensive, but may be critical if you have such a preexisting condition. If you are concerned about your ability to save in the future, you might want to negotiate for a provision which binds him to pay for the education of the children through college. If he wants the children to visit his parents occasionally, it should be made clear that he will pay for the trips. In short, be alert to expenses which may arise in the future which he should pay for, or you may find yourself eroding your own income or savings providing for the children to whom you *both* have a continuing obligation.

Some Concluding Observations

Few women will enjoy taking the advice in this chapter. For most, the assertive, self-protective approach we have suggested goes against their instincts or conditioning. Yet, in our view, these tactics and approaches are necessary. While there may be some friendly marriage break-ups, most have an element of bitterness and vindictiveness, especially when it comes to financial matters. *He's* unlikely to fight the battle halfheartedly and end up in a financial position which is weaker than it might otherwise be. Why should you?

The statistics about the postdivorce financial status of women and men are indisputable. Men come out of divorces much better financially than do women. Largely this stems from the "system," but partly it stems from the fact that in the past women were not always aware of the urgent need to approach the divorce with the same toughness as men.

We're not arguing for these techniques in other life crises, but the time for a woman to be "more like a man" is when a long-term relationship breaks up. It is naive to think that anybody except you and your lawyer will be looking after your interests. As the Talmud asks in a different context, "If I am not for myself, who will be for me?" This should be your credo when burying a dead relationship.

10

When a Wife Becomes a Widow

If you are married and the marriage continues, the odds are great (seven to one) that you will become a widow. Women tend to marry men who are older than themselves, and they have a longer life expectancy than men—one of the few gender-based inequities which cannot be overcome through legislation or attitudinal changes.

The primary emotional and financial task of the older widow is to learn, finally, what's in her own best interest and then to act on what she's learned. Especially for women who have spent their adult lives meeting other people's needs (being "a sponge for small wants" as novelist Doris Lessing puts it), this first recognition of legitimate self-interest may be the hardest part of facing Life After Man.

A woman is likely to become a widow in her mid-sixties. Sylvia [a pseudonym, as are all names in this chapter] is a typical widow in America. She was 64 when Fred, her husband of forty years, died. She had worked as a teacher before she was married and continued to work when her husband was overseas in the Second World War. Once he returned, she quit her job and soon was running a household and raising children. She considers that their marriage was a successful partnership; she ran the house and Fred took care of "business." She never had a desire to learn "about money and things," and was bemused in the seventies when she read stories about successful, upwardly mobile businesswomen, doubting that they "could do everything." But when Fred died after a sudden stroke, Sylvia found that she had to take over both partnership roles. Her children had moved to other states, and, while they were supportive, she found that in practical terms, she couldn't rely upon them. This chapter will deal with issues that Sylvia had to work out for herself as well as problems which other women in similar situations have to cope with. The older widow's success story doesn't have the glamour of the Yuppie, but in many cases, the price of her failure to succeed will be more costly than in the case of a younger woman.

Sylvia was lucky, however, since she and Fred had accumulated substantial assets during their marriage. It is a shameful fact of American life that one of the biggest social problems—the plight of elderly women without money—is seldom discussed. Many of these unfortunate women were either married to men who did little to provide for their future or who were abandoned without funds. Women in this category constitute a large and growing subgroup of the impoverished. Indeed, one of the objects of this book is to try to alert women to what may well occur if they do not take hold of their financial affairs during their younger years with a view to protecting their well-being when they are older.

Part of the overall difficulty older women experience stems from two main sources. Almost by definition, an older widow has had a man around the house for many years, perhaps decades. In many such cases, her husband, in addition to counseling his wife on household management and zipping up the backs of her dresses, has handled finances, picked advisers, handled the paper work, made investments, and generally dealt with everything not directly affecting the house and children, usually with little consultation with his wife. As a consequence, the older widow suddenly may find that she must assume responsibilities and make informed decisions about subjects she may never have considered.

The situation is exacerbated because it may well have been that over the years the only person to whom she would turn with problems and with whom she would discuss family matters would be her husband. With his death, she has not only been deprived of her marriage partner but also of her only adviser. Her women friends are likely to be people similar in position to her own, having no expertise in the very areas in which she now needs help. Any male friends may come on as being knowledgeable about finances, but may be just as uninformed. And if she's even the acquaintance of her husband's lawyer, accountant or business associates, the association has probably been only social.

Very often, the older widow will turn to her grown children (more typically, her sons) for advice, or to her late husband's advisers, or to friends, but more likely to the husbands of her own friends. There is a certain logic in relying on such people and there is the advantage of ease of access in most cases. However, there may often be very good reasons for her to seek other sources of advice, since she is now dealing with complications—such as a major reduction in income—which her late husband never had to cope with.

Even in dealing with her children, she should be aware that the old relationships may have changed as a result of her husband's death. For example, her children may now have financial interests which are not necessarily compatible with hers.

A few years ago, a Jeanne LeFeavre arrived at a lawyer's office. She had recently been widowed and after the family home had been sold, she had at her disposal about $400,000. She was a spry eighty-year-old, both mentally and physically active. After her husband had died, she moved to Boston to be in the same city as her daughter, a woman in her late forties married to a successful businessman. Mrs. Lefeavre chose to move into a senior citizens' residence where the rent was $2,000 a month but which offered all the conveniences she wanted, including proximity to her daughter. She also had a son in his early fifties who was a highly paid executive.

Mrs. LeFeavre had originally come to the office to draw up her will, but she soon revealed concerns about her financial situation as a whole. Her son had pointed out that if she invested the $400,000 in "safe" securities," the money would produce enough income to pay her rent, her taxes, with a few thousand dollars a year left over for other expenses. While they were talking, Mrs. LeFeavre pointed out that while the budget she had worked out with her son seemed "more than adequate," it did not allow much for travel, which she really wanted to experience while she was still physically able to undertake it; her son seemed to think she should be content to be "warehoused" in the old-age facility.

The lawyer she consulted looked at her late husband's will and found that he had left everything to her outright. He then pointed out to her that the budget her son had proposed involved her living on the income generated by the $400,000 and dying with the full capital intact. Now there was nothing sinister about this. Most younger and middle-aged investors are concerned about the preservation of capital—that is, keeping the available funds intact and living on the interest or dividends it produces. Indeed, her husband probably was equally concerned about this, since he wanted to ensure that when he died, there would be enough capital to support her.

But, the lawyer asked, why should she be overly concerned about capital? She had no legal or moral obligations to support anybody. Her children appeared to be financially comfortable and her grandchildren well supported. This being the case and given her age, why she shouldn't she draw down on her capital to do things that she really wanted to do? After all, if she took, say, an extra five or ten thousand dollars a year to take the kind of trips she wanted, her basic living expenses were still quite comfortably covered. If, when she died, she left an estate of, say $250,000 rather than $400,000, who would be hurt?

There are two related points to be considered here. First, even though Mrs. LeFeavre's son may have been advising her without any thought to what he might ultimately inherit, he did have a financial stake in her keeping her spending to a minimum, since this would ultimately mean a larger inheritance for him. And this is not by any means the most blatant example of a situation where a widow's advisers stand to gain if she follows their advice.

Most lawyers find that almost every time their client is a widow asking for advice, there is a potential financial conflict of interest with her children. For example, her husband may have left a will that directs that all his assets be invested with his widow getting the annual income to live on for as long as she lives (known as a life interest) and upon her death, the assets are to be divided among their children. (They have a capital interest in this situation.) The potential conflict arises because there are two main ways in which the assets may be invested. They can be invested to produce a high rate of annual income which, of course, will benefit the widow. Or the investment may be made with a view to increasing value, which will ultimately benefit the children. The problem is that very few, if any, investments will produce both substantial annual income and substantial growth in value. Thus the simple decision which investments to make can produce a conflict of interest.

Conflict of interest may also arise between a mother and her children in situations where the widow may control the family business while one or more children are running it. In Omaha, Nebraska, recently, a 95-year-old widow quit a family business—amid much fanfare—because of a control dispute with her grandsons. In this situation adult children (or grandchildren) may often advise their mother to turn over total control of the business to them (including a transfer of the shares of the company) with a promise to ensure that Mother is "well taken care of" (note the assumption that Mother is less than competent) for the rest of her life. Such an arrangement could work out satisfactorily, but always bear in mind that your children are not necessarily objective advisers, even if they would like to be—reflecting the same principle which requires that a doctor not treat his own family members.

The second lesson which stems from Jeanne Lefeavre's case is what might be called the rule of enlightened self-interest. Most women are trained to care for others: husbands, children and parents, often placing their own interests a distant last. If this describes your own experience, the time to change is when you become a widow. This is not to suggest that you suddenly become self-centered and uninterested in family or friends. Rather you should recognize that your own financial well-being and the enjoyment of the balance of your life should receive priority.

In other words, to the extent you now have assets of your own, do what is best for you. For women who have never had much (if any) money of their own, the experience can be alarming or confusing; but it can also be very liberating. This is the time of your life when you can now do what you like, without worrying about the needs or demands of others. Of course, if you have children or others whom you care about and who need money which you have in excess, there is nothing wrong in helping them out. In some middle-class cultures where funds are available, parents with extra money may want to help finance such things as higher education or a new home for their children. Widows, especially if their late husbands had been generous fathers, might feel pressed to honor their husbands' memory or intentions by continuing this generosity without considering their own needs.

But conversely, as was suggested to Mrs. LeFeavre, where there is no pressing need, there is no legal, moral or ethical reason why she should deny herself the things she wants in her old age simply because she wants to leave an estate to two children who are not in financial need. You have every right, to invest your money so that it produces more for you to enjoy or dispose of in your lifetime even if eventually it means less for others.

Many would think that this is a form of selfishness—and indeed you will find children who will not be averse to trying to lay a "guilt trip" on their mother to prevent her "profligate" use of "their" money. No woman should allow this to happen. Having the burden of managing money carries with it the right to enjoy it and to spend it in such a way that it benefits you.

Friends As Advisers

A while ago at a family party, a friend's aunt voiced a not uncommon complaint. "We seem to know a lot of widows. We knew them as couples and saw them socially often. One by one, their husbands died and, given our circle, each left his widow quite well fixed. I suppose that I should consider myself fortunate that John [her husband] is still around. But these women are driving him to distraction.

"Even though they have their own families and lawyers and so forth, they're always calling John for advice. After all, he has been extremely successful and in many cases he was in deals with their husbands. Now, I suppose they are sort of partners. It isn't that they don't pay him. John wouldn't consider that for a minute. But he feels an obligation, and he finds that their requests are taking time and energy which he doesn't have. And quite often he feels put on the spot, because the advice he might give to a widow with respect to a particular investment may well be contrary to his own interests. And besides all that, he feels emotionally burdened giving advice to women who are his friends and whose standard of living might well depend upon that advice.

"For example, last week, a good friend who owns a share of a building along with John and a number of other investors called him to ask whether she should sell her share. He thinks that she should take the cash. But he also thinks the building will go up in value over the next few years. If he offers to buy her share for a fair price now, how will she feel five years from now if he sells and gets double? But if he advises her to keep her share, she ends up holding an investment which isn't generating very much cash. He actually lies awake at night worrying about her problems, when he has his own to deal with." While that story came from the wife of a reluctant adviser, it sums up the problems neatly from both points of view.

On the one hand, it may be terribly unfair to the friend who is now called upon to advise on decisions in matters where the risk is not his own, where he may or may not have all the background or expertise, or where he may actually have a conflict of interest. But beyond that, he will carry with him his own personal prejudices and financial philosophy.

Illustrating this is the example of a housewife who was widowed some twenty years ago and who was left an inheritance and few family obligations. On the advice of family friends, she invested all the money in very conservative long-term bonds (paying the then munificent rate of 6.50% annual interest) which appeared to offer her a safe, comfortable living for the rest of her life. And, they told her, you never have to worry about an investment as safe as this is. But nobody anticipated the years of double-digit inflation and soaring interest rates which followed. By the mid-1980's, the real value of her bonds had shrunk considerably, the interest earned did not even cover the annual ravages of inflation while her living expenses had escalated to the point where she was relying to a substantial extent on funds from her financially successful children—a situation neither she nor her husband would ever have envisioned.

With hindsight, we can assume that if she had taken her capital to a professional, it is likely that a portfolio would have been put together with an appropriate mixture of securities which would have provided both income and a hedge against inflation. Further, as conditions changed, the professional would have been changing the nature of the portfolio so that now she would be as financially secure as she was when her husband died.

And the irony, of course, is that she cannot even vent her anger on those who put her in this position because they were just doing her a friendly favor, though with the best of intentions they left her high and dry.

The general rule of thumb is that while friends are indispensable for emotional and social support after a spouse has died, in almost every case it makes sense to employ and pay objective professionals to deal with legal and financial matters. If nothing else, you can sue them if they foul up!

Your Husband's Advisers

When looking for professional advice, it is likely that a very significant percentage of widows will turn initially to their husband's lawyer, accountant, and stockbroker at least in the early days. Indeed, there probably is no real alternative as they will be the people who have most, if not all the information about the estate and its assets.

The real question is whether the widow should continue to use them herself. There are some excellent reasons for retaining the relationships. First, it is more likely that you will know one or more of these people personally, probably in a social context, especially if your husband has used them for many years. Second, they will undoubtedly be the professionals who are most familiar with his business and investment interests and thus need not be briefed on this basic information.

On the other hand, remember that now *you*, not your husband, are the client and you have a right to demand that they do what is best for you. While this may sound obvious, the ghost of the departed may, in fact, be coloring their advice, and don't discount the fact that his advisers may have their own interests to consider.

For example, your husband might have been an aggressive investor, more interested in increasing the value of his investments than in getting dividends or interest. As a consequence, his stockbroker, who gets paid a commission based on purchases and sales, might suggest that he could continue to advise you in the same way he did your husband. But a wholly different investment policy might be more appropriate to you, one which meant less buying and selling and thus, less in commissions for the broker.

Watch out too for the lawyer who says something like "Frank left everything outright to you for tax reasons but he really wanted to make sure that your sons get control of the business." Or comments that a particular course of action "is what Frank would have wanted." If Frank "wanted" something, he should have put it in his will. If he didn't, don't let the adviser's comments sway what you want to do.

Another consideration, especially where the people you are dealing with are older, is whether they are the appropriate people to be advising a widow. (You may hate this word, feeling that you should not be defined by present or past marital status, to say nothing of the emotional "status shock" associated with the term. But reality requires that in financial planning, you should see yourself as your adviser does.) Clearly there are two aspects to this. The advisers may be of an age or disposition which continues to view women as basically incompetent to deal with financial matters or to make intelligent decisions. Thus they will want to take over the running of your affairs, doing this as they see fit, in effect "taking care" of you. If this is what you want, all well and good, but as we pointed out, this may be the time for you to start taking care of yourself.

There is one other matter you should watch for, especially when dealing with lawyers. Many older lawyers know everything they have to know about their own practices, but if called upon to deal with different sorts of problems, they may be at sea (though precious few will admit it). Conversely, many newly minted lawyers, though up to date in current law, just don't know how things are handled. You should recognize that just because your husband's layer had the ability and knowledge to handle his affairs doesn't mean that he can handle yours, or that he'll even think to pass along your case to someone who can. If you have some doubts about whether he is the right person for you, it may be useful to say something along the lines of, "Jim, I know you're an expert in business law, but maybe at this stage I need somebody who can give me more general legal advice on simpler questions. Is there somebody in your firm who might do this or do you think that maybe you could set up an appointment with Joanne Smith down the hall who seems to have much more time available?"

Is he up to date with regard to the tax system, in a position to offer the best advice on issues ranging from the consequences of selling your home and moving to an apartment to the taxation of investment income? Can he offer you advice about your Social Security entitlement? He should be able to draw up your will, of course. If you are to retain him, satisfy yourself about two things. First, that he recognizes that his duty is to you, and second, that he has knowledge or can get information quickly which will allow him to give you the information you need and want. If he fails on either point, start looking for somebody else.

Earlier in this chapter we talked about the possibility of a child trying to get you to transfer assets to him or her right now. Remember that if your husband's lawyer was also an adviser to his business, he or she may now, in effect, be acting for one or more of your children who may be in the business. If the lawyer joins with your children and starts advising you to take steps which would, in effect, transfer all or part of the property you inherited, for whatever plausible reason they may give, protect yourself by retaining another attorney to examine the proposal. Do not be deterred by suggestions that it is undesirable to discuss family affairs with outsiders (lawyers are ethically bound to respect professional confidences) or by the suggestion that you might "insult" an older friend of your late husband.

And where do you find the alternative adviser? The steps are no different from those we referred to earlier when we discussed how to find professional advice. In the end, probably the best source will be friends who have had similar experiences, good, bad, or indifferent.

If you're fully satisfied with those who advised your husband, try them. But if you have any doubts at all about a course of action they recommend, be it in law, accounting or investments, by all means hire your own people. With no emotional baggage from the old days, they know they'll be paid for performance, and you'll be the judge of how well they do. Why, you might ask, has so much time been spent discussing the whole question of advisers? The reason is that you have two main tasks to perform. First, you must determine what your assets now consist of and second, you will have to start to arrange your own affairs to ensure that the lifestyle you want can be maintained or attained. It is almost certain that, in each area, help will be desirable or necessary.

What Assets Do You Now Have?

The most important first financial step you must undertake is a determination of what you are left with upon which to build your financial security. This data will come in part from your husband's will (if he had one) but more likely from his advisers. Thus, if his will left everything to you, it is still crucial that you determine what "everything" is. And unless your husband was extraordinarily well organized and left detailed instructions, you will have to turn to his lawyer, accountant, business partner, insurance broker, stockbroker, and banker to get this information.

But let's suppose first that he died without a will. (In this case you can assume that his lawyer, if he had one, wasn't doing a proper job.) In such a case, the division of his property will be determined by the laws of your state. In some cases, the widow will get a preferential part of the estate (*e.g.*, a fixed percentage

or value of the property before anybody else becomes entitled
to something) with the balance of the property being divided
among the widow and other heirs. Others divide property
somewhat differently. If you live in a community of property
state, you will automatically get your half upon the death of
your husband, and may be entitled to more. If you have homes
in two or more states, one of the first things you'll have to do is
find out which state's laws (and there may be more than one)
apply to your situation.

But the important thing to remember is that since there is no
will, there has been nobody appointed to handle the estate. So
one of the first things which should be done is to consult a
lawyer to determine how, under the laws of your state, you can
be appointed administrator (feminine: administratrix), the term
most often used for the person who has to deal with the estate
of an individual who dies *intestate,* without leaving a will.

You should also remember that you may, as a result of his
death, "own" a number of assets directly whether or not your
husband had a will and notwithstanding what the will might
say. For example, assets owned jointly (and these would most
commonly be the family home or a joint bank account) automatically become yours alone as a consequence of his death. You
will want to arrange to transfer title to your own name immediately. And if he was insured and you were the named
beneficiary, the insurance proceeds will be payable directly to
you and will not form part of his estate.

Now let's assume that your husband did have a valid will
when he died. This will should be located (it would most likely
be in his safety deposit box or in the care of his lawyer) and its
contents examined. A number of items should be of particular
interest.

First, who is or are the executors? You may find you are the
sole executrix or you may be one of several executors, or the
executors may be other people such as children, the lawyer, or
business associates.

Second, what was left to you and in what form? Did he leave
everything to you or did he split the estate in some fashion? Did
he make a number of specific bequests prior to leaving assets to

you, say to charities or to other individuals? (Perhaps he has made a number of specific bequests with the residue, as the balance is known, to you. The size of the overall estate and the size of the specific gifts will then determine what you will get.) Did he leave the assets to you outright or are you to get only the income for so long as you live? (You might like to review Chapter 13, "Wills.") Here the property is technically transferred to a trust and the person in charge of it (the trustee) has a legal obligation to see that the terms of the trust are carried out. If he left property to you subject to a trust, what are its terms? In many cases, while the widow is entitled only to the income, a power to encroach upon capital, that is, to use it, may be given. If this is the case, under what circumstances are you allowed to encroach? Are you the sole judge of your need to use capital or do you have to meet some objective test or ask some other parties such as the trustees for permission to use this money?

The basic thing in all of this is to find out and absorb exactly what you are entitled to under the will, what limitations are imposed, if any, and what your duties may be. From a practical viewpoint, it's a good idea to keep dated notes on every business conversation you have at the time. It's hard to keep all details straight at the best of times, but especially so when you're under emotional strain. Your husband's lawyer should be able to help you in all of this, but if you are not satisfied, you have every right to find your own attorney and to discuss the issues with him or her. You as heir have the right to a copy of the will and there is nothing to stop you from going to some other lawyer if you have any doubt about your rights.

Some widows may find that the wills contain restrictions which appear narrow. You should bear in mind that, in many cases, these clauses have been inserted for tax purposes. Don't forget that there are a number of federal and state taxes which may be imposed on death, and many people draft wills which are designed in part to minimize taxes. If you wonder why a particular provision is present, ask the lawyer who drafted the will.

What happens if your husband did not leave you adequately provided for in the will, even though he had plenty of assets? If you think this has happened, whether deliberately or by accident, talk to a lawyer. Every state has laws which are designed to ensure that dependent spouses and children receive adequate support from the estate of a deceased person who legally owes them support. While procedures and questions of how the level of support is calculated vary from state to state, usually you can apply to a court which has the power to "rewrite" the will to provide you with the minimum legal level of support. If you find yourself in this position, use an attorney other than the one who drew the will. Normally, the costs of going through this procedure will be charged to the estate, which means you won't have to pay them yourself.

If the will contains conditions which must be fulfilled in order to get a bequest and the conditions are repugnant to you, you should again check with a lawyer. Courts in most states will strike down, for example, conditions on gifts to children provided they do (or do not) marry a person of a particular religious faith. This is contrary to public policy. Again, the approach to such questions will vary from state to state and what might be acceptable in one state may not be acceptable in another. If you don't like a condition contained in the will, find out whether it is valid where you live. You may be able to get a court to remove it from the will.

The overall objective of this first set of tasks is to help you determine just exactly where you stand regarding the assets you received as a consequence of your husband's death. But normally, the will will not reveal the extent of the assets. The executor (or you as executrix), will have to "marshall the assets"—that is, track down all the assets of the estate, pay the debts and then distribute the bequests. To do this, just what there is will first have to be determined. The lawyer should be able to give some help here, a considerable amount if he has had a longtime connection with your husband. The stockbroker should be able to tell you about the investments and reregister them into the name of the estate or the beneficiaries. The banker should be able to give you information about cash and investments in the bank. And your husband's insurance broker should be able to give you needed data on insurance and help you make the claims, either on behalf of the estate (if it is the beneficiary) or on your behalf if the money is to come to you. After these steps have been taken, the income from the property as it stood when your husband died should be flowing to the right people, preferably with all or most of it coming to you.

You will also have to touch base with your husband's accountant or find one for yourself because there will be a number of tax returns to be filled out as a consequence of his death. These are particularly important returns as there are a number of choices and elections you can make which can result in significant tax savings. Your husband's accountant, if he had one, would be the best person for the job, given his likely familiarity with the past tax returns and general financial picture.

If you are emotionally able to turn on your radar (also known as female intuition), this is a good time to assess whether you wish to keep the same person as your accountant. You should get a feel for whether you feel comfortable with him or her. There are a number of tax options available to you personally in filing your own tax return in the year of your husband's death and you will have to decide whether to continue with his accountant or find your own. If your husband's accountant is to be your choice, he or she should be treating you as a valuable client right from the start, even though he or she is preparing returns for your husband's year of death and/or his estate.

You should be trying to unearth other sources of income. Was your husband receiving a pension when he died? If so, contact the payor and find out what your entitlement will be. If he was not receiving a pension but was covered by a pension plan, check with the administrator of the plan to find out what you are entitled to. If he worked for any length of time for other employers before joining his last one, check with these companies to find out if there is any pension entitlement. Or, if he was a member of a union (and remember, many white-collar workers today are members) there may be a union pension plan. If he served with the armed forces, there may be pension or other rights due to you as his widow. And, of course, as a matter of priority, check with Social Security to find out about the benefits to which you may have become entitled as a consequence of his death.

When talking to your husband's advisers, also find out whether he had any private pension plan such as an IRA or Keogh Plan. His banker will probably be aware of this, and if not, the person who has done his past tax returns should know. Steps should be taken to transfer the benefit of these plans to you if you are entitled to them.

When you contact employers, you should be particularly careful to find out if you are entitled to any "death benefits," since up to $5,000 of such benefits may be received by you free of tax. The term death benefit has a technical meaning under the Internal Revenue Code, but generally it means payments made by an employer as a consequence of the death of an employee. Such a payment might be a lump sum out of the employer's pension plan or a payment from a stock purchase plan. The company personnel department should be able to identify what qualifies, and if not, your accountant certainly will be able to tell you.

When you contact the various people mentioned, bear in mind that you may have a real problem right now. Especially if your husband had been working when he died, bringing home a paycheck, you might find yourself quickly running out of cash. When you talk with these people, find out how quickly you can get the money you need for immediate and short term expenses. If need be, on the basis of the assets you are inheriting, you may need to take out a loan at the bank. Even if you have never asked for a loan, don't be afraid. You are now a woman of substance with assets of your own, and bankers make a living lending to those who already have property. They should be glad to lend. If they're not, remember there are other banks who will want your business in the future and will be prepared to help out now.

The Family Home

In just about every American family, the most valuable single asset is the family home. And in the vast majority of families, the family home represents more than half of the assets. It is no wonder, therefore, that making decisions about the family home requires some serious calculations by a widow. The various concerns of Deborah Moody, a sixty-nine-year-old widow, are not unique, and it is worth looking at her situation in some detail.

"George and I lived in the big house on First Avenue for more than thirty years. Imagine, we paid $20,000 for the house, and a few weeks after George died, a real estate agent came around and said she could get me at least $175,000 for it. I said no then because the thought of selling the home we had shared was too painful, but now I'm wondering.

"There's no mortgage, but heating, taxes, and repairs cost about $300 a month. I could rent an awfully nice apartment not too far from here for $750 a month. Or I could buy a smaller house, for about $100,000 and still have some extra room for the grandchildren when they visit. Right now, I can manage quite nicely on what I get from our investments, pensions, and the like—about $25,000—but if I decided to move into the apartment I'd be looking at a big additional monthly cost, even though I'd have a lot more money as a result of the sale.

Mrs. Moody had to come to grips with two separate issues. The first was whether it made sense to keep up a house which was much too big for her just for the memories and the options it offered to entertain family a couple of times a year. The second question has to do with money, which, as it turned out in her case, was not a serious problem.

She then sat down with her adviser and considered the various options. Right now, her accommodation costs amounted to about $3,600 a year. A home which you live in is a terrific investment because you get your "return" in the form of tax-free accommodation.

What happens if she sells the house for $175,000? Unlike some countries, such as Canada, the U.S. government will tax the gains on your house when you sell it, but there are a number of special rules which give relief.

The profit on the house, in this case $155,000 ($175,000 less its original cost) would be treated as a "long-term capital gain" provided you lived in it for at least six months. (If the Moodys had put money into improvements in the house, though not just routine repairs, the cost of the improvements would be added to the original cost to reduce the gain, as will the costs of selling the house.) Mrs. Moody would then bring into income only 40% of the gain or $62,000 and the tax bite might amount to about $18,000.

But because she is over 55, she can claim a special exclusion of profits up to $125,000. This is available only once in a lifetime and cannot be used up piecemeal. Mrs. Moody meets a second test because she has lived in the house as her principal residence for at least three of the preceding five years.) This law is, in fact, designed to allow older people to dispose of their homes with minimal tax cost preparatory to moving into other accommodations. Given this exclusion, Mrs. Moody's potential gain drops to a maximum of $30,000, with only $12,000 being added to her income and the tax bite probably being on the order of $3,000.

There are other, different rules which might apply for those selling a home and buying a larger, more expensive one. These rules will not normally be applicable in the case of a widow. The bottom line is that after sales costs and so forth, Mrs. Moody will probably net at least $165,000 after taxes.

Now suppose she chooses to move into the apartment at $750 a month. It will cost her $9,000 a year for accommodation, an increase of $5,400 from what she is now paying to live in her house. She can invest her $165,000 at, say, 8% and get an additional $13,200. But this income will be taxable. Still, the tax bite should leave her with over $9,000 a year. In other words, she can get the apartment she wants and pay for it using just the after-tax income earned by the net amount she received from her old house, and actually still have available the money she was spending on the old house.

In addition, she has converted a major asset of the estate into a liquid investment. She then is in a position to use all or part of that capital for other things she might want—travel, a late-in-life academic degree, major contribution to a favorite charity—or the money will be available as part of her estate.

Of course, Mrs. Moody had other options. She could have sold the house and bought a more modest one for $100,000. Had she done this, she still would have an additional $65,000 available to invest. A smaller house would have obvious benefits with regard to care and so forth. The major question would be the amount of the annual upkeep; is it more or less expensive than the older house? If it is more expensive, then the extra $65,000 will be available to help generate the extra income needed for upkeep and maintenance.

A third option she might have looked at, but did not, would be to rent out her old house and to use the rental income to pay for rent on the apartment. (Since she would not realize capital as from a sale, the purchase of a smaller house probably would not be feasible if she rented out her old home.) There are problems here. For example, as we noted earlier, the $125,000 capital gain exemption for those 55 and over only applies when they have lived in the home for three of the previous five years. If the house were rented out and then subsequently sold, Mrs. Moody might lose the opportunity to use this exemption in the future.

If she rents the house out, she would also have the responsibilities of a landlord, finding appropriate tenants, keeping the house in shape, collecting rent and so forth. Furthermore, except in very unusual circumstances, the net cash return she could get from renting the old house would not be nearly as much as the return she could get from investing the capital received when it was sold. Finally, she would find that she would be taxable on the net income she received from the old house (rent minus expenses) but would get no deduction for the rent she paid for her apartment. While there may be situations where renting out the family home has some particular attractions, this will not normally be the case. (Some women do this in hopes that, ultimately, a child will return to the family home a few years down the line; others because they want to postpone selling the family home but still cannot bear to live in it.)

Mrs. Moody had enough other sources of support that she did not need to sell the house to get her hands on cash to help her live. Others, not so fortunate, may be forced by financial practicalities to sell the family home to produce cash for investment purposes, or to pay off a late husband's debts. (Not all wills contain happy surprises.) The situation may also be exacerbated if the house is subject to a mortgage and the death of the wage-earning husband has eliminated the major source of payment. In such a case, the mortgage company may be in a position to force a sale.

But if the house is being sold, for whatever reason, the key factors to consider are how to minimize the tax consequences of the sale, how the proceeds are to be used or invested and what accommodation options are open to the widow. Once again, it probably is well worthwhile to spend the time and the money to find out just where you will stand after a sale before you take a step which is irrevocable.

The Family Business

In some situations, the major asset of a deceased husband will be the family business, most commonly in the form of shares of the company. In all likelihood, this business will have produced the bulk of the family income over many years and its value may be substantial. The main question facing a widow is whether the business will continue to produce that income after the death of her husband or whether the business should be sold.

In a large percentage of cases, the widow may not have much choice as to what will happen. Her husband may, for example, have left the shares in the company directly to one or more children or other relatives whom he feels will continue to run the operation. Normally, of course, if this has been done, steps will also have been taken to ensure that his widow will be provided for, either out of other assets or by requiring the children or the business to make payments during the lifetime of the widow. If control of the business has passed to others in this way, make certain that you understand how you will be "paid" and what the level of income will be. If your husband did leave the shares to somebody else, you will have no control over the future, other than a possible challenge to the will if you feel that you have not been adequately provided for.

An equally common situation will be where the business is controlled not by your husband alone, but by two or more shareholders or partners, who may be family members (siblings, children) or, in a legal sense, "strangers." In such cases, there will often be what is known as a shareholders agreement. This is a contract which contains the terms under which the business is to be run and, most importantly from your point of view, probably a provision which deals with the eventuality of death of the shareholders. Typically, the agreement will say that when one shareholder dies, the surviving shareholders can or must buy his shares from the estate. The agreement should set out a formula for valuing the shares and the method for payment. The payment typically will come either from insurance which will have been taken out by each shareholder on the other(s) or will follow a formula whereby the purchase price will be paid over a number of years.

In most cases, these agreements are to everybody's advantage. The surviving shareholder(s) can then "eliminate" the family of the deceased from any interest in the company. This is particularly important if no member of the family can step into the deceased's shoes and do the work he did for the company. In the absence of a buy-out arrangement, the surviving shareholder may find himself working to support two families, his own and that of his deceased partner.

But from the widow's point of view, a buy-out may also be an attractive proposition, particularly where she cannot or will not take an active role in the company. The effect of the shareholder's agreement will be that she (or the estate) is relieved of a major asset which might not otherwise generate sufficient income and which can deteriorate if the surviving shareholder cannot run the business efficiently. Instead of potentially unproductive shares, you will find yourself with cash, either immediately or over the next few years, which you can then invest or spend.

Being bought out, therefore, is not necessarily a bad thing and may turn out to be the best of all possible worlds.

If your husband was the sole owner of the business, his death may create significantly more problems. The single most important question is whether the business can continue to function without him. There are a number of possibilities here.

The first is that *you can take over the business.* We all know of a number of situations where widows have taken over their husband's businesses and have continued to run them successfully. In many cases, the wife has been closely involved in the business while her husband was alive and was thus familiar with it. In other cases, the widow took over cold and still managed to make a success of it.

Of course, if you are seventy-five years old, ailing, and have never worked a day outside the home, the desirability quotient of taking over and running the business may be zero. But if you do want to consider this course of action, you had best realize that the key to success likely lies in the loyalty and competence of the staff your husband has already hired. If the staff is good and if there is somebody you trust to manage the business while you learn it, the odds are favorable. On the other hand, it is possible for a venal staff to steal you blind while you are unaware of what is going on. If you're going to get involved, the business's advisers, primarily the accountant and the lawyer, should be able to give you invaluable help in assessing the viability of the business and the quality of staff upon whom you will have to rely, providing, of course, they are free of self-interest. (Their fees, of course, should be charged to the business.)

Another option may be to *retain the business but still not become actively involved.* You can only seriously contemplate this if you have super-competent staff whom you trust. You should then also consider the importance of some form of profit-sharing scheme for the key employees to ensure that they have a major incentive to continue to do their jobs. Holding out the possibility that they might acquire a share of the business could also be useful.

One or more of your children might enter the business. A woman we spoke with found herself the owner of a business when her husband died at the age of fifty-eight. Her four daughters were all living away from home, supporting themselves, but she had a seventeen year old son who was, even while his father was alive, being groomed to enter the firm. The widow then took charge and ran the business for ten years, during which time the son finished school and started working. A full fifteen years after her husband's death, she turned over effective control of the business to her son, though she continued to work on a part-time basis until she was almost ninety years old.

If you already have children in the business when your husband dies, a whole different set of considerations come into play. The main question is whether you have all, most, or just some of the shares of the business. It is unrealistic to expect that a child of the owner will work indefinitely just for a salary, however generous. The child should be given the same consideration that you would give a key employee: profit-sharing and/or the opportunity to get shares in the business. Obviously, if the child already has shares, this may not be a problem. However, there are pitfalls to avoid in this situation.

A few years ago, Martha Wainwright, recently widowed, required a lawyer's advice. The lawyer had acted for her husband in a number of matters, and had drawn up his will. The major asset consisted of a very successful retailing operation. Three sons were in the business and one was not, in fact had no interest in it. As a result of a complex bit of tax planning, each son owned 10% of the shares of the business and Martha, who had never been involved actively, had 60%.

The three sons in the business argued, with much validity, that since they were the ones who were working, the fourth son should not benefit beyond getting the value of his bequest and they requested that he sell his shares to them. Happily, he agreed and there was no problem once a formula was worked out to pay him off.

The three then suggested, again for tax planning reasons, that Martha transfer her shares to them as a gift. Martha was in the happy position of having more than enough other assets to live on. Further, her personal relationship with each son was excellent, and she felt sure that they would never see her in need of anything.

Her husband's attorney told her that she should see another lawyer! The point was that he had acted for her husband and was continuing to act for the business and for her sons. Thus, while he felt that there would be good reasons in this case for her to transfer the shares to her sons, he also felt that it was imperative that she get independent legal advice. This is an absolutely crucial point. No matter how good the reasons were for transferring her assets to her sons, it was important that an outsider with no knowledge of the business or the personalities assess whether it made sense for her to do so. After all, she had a range of options. She could just hold onto her shares, which she intended ultimately to leave to her sons anyway. (But, the lawyer asked, when he drew her will—to the three in the business or to all four? She wisely, in his view, divided up her estate so that the "outside" son got assets equal in value to what his brothers were to get, but the other three alone got the shares.) Or she could give the shares to the three sons in the business. Or she could sell the shares to them, giving them advantageous terms for payment. The important thing was that Martha Wainwright had to feel comfortable with her decision and had to feel that the advice she received was "untainted" by anybody's self-interest, except perhaps her own. In making her decision, she had to be satisfied that no matter what happened in the future, she was financially secure and independent.

There was one other point which the lawyer covered with Mrs. Wainwright. So long as she and the sons held shares in the business, it was important to have a shareholders' agreement. Make no mistake, it is as important a document when family members are involved as when there are strangers. In this instance, among the important elements of the agreement were provisions regarding the formula for the salaries to be paid to the sons, profit-sharing and a dividend policy. It was also necessary to create a legally enforceable balance ensuring that the profits of the business were not siphoned off through excessive salaries, while Mrs. Wainwright received adequate annual dividends, and the sons had incentive to continue with hard work. In just about every case, this sort of balance between the prerequisites of ownership and the reality that the person running the business must feel that it is worth his or her while to strive for success must be struck, whether the business is being run by a trusted outsider or by a child.

The hardest situation to deal with is one where your husband was, in fact, the heart and soul of the business, and it may not survive without him. Such a situation commonly occurs when the man was a professional, such as a doctor. Once he dies, the residual value of his practice, which might have been very valuable when he was alive, drops to almost nil. Usually, there are only two alternatives, neither of them terribly attractive. First, you can try to get somebody who has the same business qualities as your husband to keep it going. This may range from difficult to impossible, but if you do find such a person, you'll undoubtedly have to pay a high price.

The alternative is to sell the business as quickly as possible. The major problem here is that most potential buyers will be aware that your husband was the key and this may mean that the prices offered may not be attractive. Interestingly, in most such cases, the most likely candidate to buy will be a competitor, who may feel that by buying the business and using his or her own expertise, your business can be amalgamated into the existing business. If this is the route you are going to follow, then the advisers to your husband's business should be able to help in finding a potential buyer.

There is, we might note, a lesson to be learned here by anybody who is carrying on a successful business which depends on his or her own expertise or abilities. If you feel that nobody in your family will be able to carry it on, then you should contemplate one of two courses of action. One is to sell it while you are still alive and it can bring top dollar, even if the sale requires that you now work for the buyer. Alternatively, consider insurance. If the "money machine" stops when you die, then a replacement will have to be found to protect those dependent upon you. Insurance is, in most cases, the ideal. This advice, of course, applies equally to a widow who feels that she has obligations and who knows that the business she is running will not be continued by a family member.

The Next Steps

How do you manage to live on what you have available? The first thing you must do is make up a budget. There is no getting around this step and it is important that your budget be both accurate and realistic. You will need to bear in mind a number of factors. If you're in a house now, what does it cost to maintain it? Are you going to move, say, to an apartment and if so, what will it cost you, including moving expenses?

Second, you'll have to take income taxes into account. It may well be that up until now, your late husband handled "that sort of thing," but taxes are now your responsibility. You may need an accountant to help you approximate a figure for this item, and an accurate estimate might not be possible until you know what other steps you may be taking.

Some expenses, sadly, such as food, clothing, and other expenses incurred by your husband will drop. Will expenses for travel, for example, rise or fall? Only you know what your plans might be, but if you have children living in other parts of the country, you may now find it more convenient (albeit costly) for you to visit them more often rather than having them visiting you, since a change of scene may be refreshing.

Don't forget to allow for health insurance and medical expenses, especially if until his death you were covered under a plan provided by your husband's employer.

You'll want to budget for your food, clothing, gifts, charitable donations and the like. The key thing is to be realistic. Don't work out a budget that you could not exist on without discomfort. Once you see what your real needs and expectations are, you can *then* figure out how to augment income or pare expenses, if necessary, but you can't afford to delude yourself at this stage. Try to be as realistic as possible. Look at your (and your husband's) checkbooks for the past couple of years to estimate how much you *do* spend on each category of items. Try also to budget for your own *pleasure*, something most women forget to do. There may be ways to manage. And don't forget that there is still such a thing as inflation. This budget should take into account rising costs over time, and should recognize that, in all likelihood, there will not be significant increases in income.

And it is absolutely vital that you leave yourself some breathing room. It is probably prudent, after you have worked the budget out in detail to allow another 5 to 10 per cent for "miscellaneous" expenditures—they always arise in some form or other.

Once you have arrived at the "target figure" of annual financial requirements, you then have to work at the problem from the other end. How much money do you have available and what is the shortfall, if any?

The first thing to look at is the income which will be coming in automatically. This will include such items as Social Security, pension payments (from whatever sources), salary if you are working, and so forth. You would also look to see whether any of the expenses you allowed for are "covered." For example, you might be one of the fortunate few who, even having been widowed, are still covered by an employer's group medical plan. If so, this is like money in the bank and you can reduce the "budgetary" requirements to take it into account.

To this stage, we haven't looked at your "capital" position, the assets which have been left to you. If there are stocks and bonds, whether of public companies or of a family business, find out how much income these are generating annually. (This information should be readily available from past years' joint tax returns or from your husband's accountant or stockbroker.) For the time being at least, this income can be added to the first category of annual income. If there is a shortfall between your budgetary needs and the income, you will have to look further.

Was there insurance money? If so, this can be invested to produce additional annual income which will be used to close the gap between requirements and available income. Are there other assets which can be sold, with the proceeds invested? We already have looked at the possibilities of selling major assets such as the family home or family business. But don't forget that you no longer need two cars; one can be sold for cash. Also consider selling any hi-tech and recreational equipment you don't use yourself. You may also find that your husband had specialized collections—stamps, coins, antique toys or the like—which you don't want to retain and which may be quite valuable.

In the very short run, you may have to sell some assets just to get enough cash to meet immediate needs, but you should be thinking in terms of converting assets which do not produce income (such as the house) into income generating investments if you need the money. This is the time when you should make contact with an accountant and stockbroker. The accountant should be able to give you a good idea of how much additional income you need and whether you really do have to sell assets. The stockbroker is the one who can help you make the needed investments. They should, first of all, be able to explain their advice in a way you understand. Second, they should not be intimidating. You have to be able to deal with them on your terms—and you're the one who's paying. (In the case of the accountant, you'll pay on the basis of time spent, and do not *ever* hesitate to ask what the hourly rate is. In the case of the stockbroker, you'll pay a commission on each transaction you undertake.)

A point made earlier in this chapter is worth reiterating. Most professionals faced with a widow who needs cash will think in terms of preserving capital. Consider a situation where you need $25,000 a year to live comfortably. Pension and other income produce $18,000. Your "capital," say from the sale of the house, amounts to $100,000. The accountant or stockbroker would look for an investment which produces the needed $7,000, a 7% annual return on your $100,000. They will automatically look for an investment where the $100,000 is not at risk.

If the main object is to produce $7,000 a year, the value of the underlying asset is not important, so long as it is certain the money will be paid. For example, it should be quite easy to put the $100,000 into very secure bonds which will produce 7% or $7,000. The important thing from your point of view is that, come what may, the payor will in fact make the payments.

(Government bonds are, on the whole, safe.) But the broker might point out that if you buy a 7% bond and interest rates rise to say, 9%, the value of your bonds might decline from $100,000 to $80,000. That is, if you chose to sell them, you'd "lose" $20,000. But so what? If the preservation of capital is secondary and the key thing is safe income, what do you care? If, when you die the bonds are only worth $80,000, your heirs will just get that much less. Obviously, if you have somebody who is dependent upon you, say a developmentally handicapped child, preservation of capital could become much more important.

Thus, when you go to see the broker, you have to set out your own needs and goals. They will be what creates your investment philosophy. You might say that income is the paramount objective and you must receive at least $7,000 a year. Safety is also extremely important insofar as the income is concerned and you do not wish to invest in anything where there is a possibility that the dividends (if you're buying stock) might be missed or interest payments not made. Only after these two considerations have been taken into account do you rank safety of the capital and possible appreciation of the investment.

Now if you make an investment such as this, how does it differ from the case we discussed earlier of the widow who followed the advice of friends and found, as a result of inflation, she was caught with both insufficient income and seriously eroded capital? The key difference is that *you* should always be keeping on top of such matters as inflation and how it is affecting your personal needs. This may require that you start reading the business section of your local paper, *The Wall Street Journal* and/or various business publications. These may not be the most stimulating reading, but they are important if you want to know what is happening in the business world and how events may affect you and your investments. Secondly, you should instruct your broker to review your holdings regularly and to make recommendations which are consistent with your overall objectives. The more capital you have, the more likely you will be advised to diversify your investments so that while some might suffer in an inflationary period, others (notably common shares) might well help to compensate. Normally, you don't meet with a stockbroker on a regular, prearranged basis as you do with your dentist, but there is no reason why you cannot meet several times a year just to review matters.

We would say that if your broker suggests investments which do not produce income (say, gold coins) or which are tax shelters, make certain that he can explain the benefits of these in your situation. If you have doubts, avoid them.

And a final "investment" point. Generally speaking, leaving money in bank accounts will not produce nearly as good a return as other investments judiciously made. But our experience is that most older women feel much more comfortable where they have access to ready cash. Though your broker may advise otherwise, you probably can't go too far wrong keeping $5,000 to $10,000 dollars in a savings account or in short term deposits with the bank of your choice. It's nice to have funds available in an emergency and the foregone interest (the difference between what you get at the bank and what you might get from another investment) is likely a small price to pay for this convenience.

But there is one type of investment which could be useful in a situation where it is apparent that there may not be enough capital to generate the needed income. It is possible to buy an annuity from any of a number of financial institutions, most notably insurance companies. When you buy an annuity, you transfer the cash to the company and in return, you get a monthly payment which is a blend of income and capital. For more details on annuities, see Chapter 5, "Funding Retirement."

Property and Debts

One of the earliest steps you will have to take in the settlement of an estate is the payment of debts and the registration of property into the names of the new owners. If you are to retain ownership of such things as stocks and bonds, a broker will be able to register them in your name, which will ensure that dividends or interest will be payable to you. Otherwise, you will face a continuing problem of dealing with checks made payable to your husband. Private company shares should also be reregistered, and the stock register will probably be in the office of the company's lawyer or accountant. It is also prudent to put the title of real estate directly in your name. Even if the title of property (such as your house) automatically vests in you because the house was owned jointly, you should register the change legally. This will eliminate problems later on if you want to sell the house or leave it to somebody else in your will.

Cancel all credit cards in your husband's name at once. At the same time, if you do not already have credit cards in your name, you should apply for any which you might need. Given the ongoing problems of women getting such credit in their own names, do not be surprised (though you have every right to be infuriated) if the company is hesitant to issue such a card. You may find yourself in the humiliating position of having to get your lawyer or banker to write to the company to assure it that you do indeed have the financial wherewithal to meet the obligations you incur. Your choice, of course, is to refuse to deal with an antediluvian company or to swallow your pride.

We would like to mention a particularly sleazy scam to watch for. Shortly after the death of your husband, somebody might appear on your doorstep with something that he or she says your husband bought just before his death. This something now has to be paid for. Very often it will appear to be either a surprise gift for you or something of a religious nature, such as a bible. The price will always be highly inflated. The con artist is banking on the fact that you don't know anything about the item and that in the midst of emotional turmoil, you will pay for this "last gift" from your husband. Never pay for an item unless you are absolutely certain that it was ordered. If you have any doubts, turn the bill over to the estate's lawyer and have him or her look into the matter.

Your Will

A very high priority after the death of your husband should be to draw up a will for yourself, whether or not you already have one. If you do have one, it is probably now out of date, given the fact that your husband predeceased you. But in any event, it was also probably drawn at a time when your own property was minimal. This, of course, may not be the case now.

Many women are particularly anxious to insure that heirlooms and jewelry go to a particular person. Depending on the item, you might like to give it while you are alive, which of course ensures that your wishes are fulfilled. In the case of things such as furniture, paintings and so on, a move to new accommodations may make a gift before the move logical. A second alternative, albeit an often clumsy one, is to put in your will a detailed list of which items are to go to whom, with a detailed description of each item. A third and easier alternative is to put a clause in the will indicating that you are drawing up a separate list and directing your executors to distribute the items as per the list. Or you might, as one woman did, affix labels to various items of silver and jewelry indicating to whom they should be given. These alternatives may not be legally acceptable in your state and you should check with your attorney to see whether they can be used.

You might also wish to give consideration to one or more major gifts to charity. Again, in many families, the husband has dealt with giving to charities while the wife has "just" been a volunteer. Remember, that if you are now a woman of some substance, you are in a position to make meaningful cash bequests to charities you are interested in, or to give to them now, while you are alive.

The important point, of course, is not what you'll put into your will, which will be determined by your own specific circumstances, but rather the importance of having a will, and making it as soon as feasible after your husband has died. This should be high on your list of priorities.

Insurance

Another crucial item is insurance. There are three main categories which you should be considering.

First, as soon as you become the legal owner of any property, you should make certain that you have the basic types of property coverage dealing with fire, theft, and so forth, and that you, as owner, will be the beneficiary of the policies. It is also an appropriate time (since many assets will have to be valued as part of the settlement of the estate) to take steps to ensure that the coverage is adequate. One of the major errors in financial planning is that insurance coverage may not be sufficient to replace lost, damaged, or stolen goods because the coverage was taken out years before inflation drove prices higher.

Second, you should look at health insurance. We touched on this issue briefly earlier in the chapter but it is so important to older Americans that extra emphasis is in order. Unlike many countries such as Canada or Great Britain, the United States does not have automatic universal medical coverage. This means that citizens of these countries need not be concerned over the finances of being ill or injured, no matter what their ages. Since there is no universal coverage in the U.S., it is important to determine whether you have some form of private coverage, say from an employer's plan. If you do not have such coverage, it should be a matter of high priority to get insurance to cover medical expenses. This may well be expensive, especially as you get older, but it is one of the most important items in the budget for older people. Without such coverage, it is distinctly possible that a longish illness could wipe out everything you have. With this as a potential consequence, the importance of such insurance becomes obvious. You should also look into the question, if you are sixty-five or over, of whether you can be covered by Medicare.

Less important in most cases will be life insurance. As we have pointed out in earlier chapters of this book, life insurance should be bought with a particular purpose in mind. It may be to provide an estate for one's family if there are no other assets. It may be to pay off specific debts in the event of death. It may be to fund a buy-sell clause of a shareholder's agreement. Or it may be to produce funds to pay tax liabilities which can arise on death.

Before you buy life insurance (which for an older person will be very expensive) you must be satisfied that there is a legitimate financial purpose to do so. We would not, for example, recommend buying insurance just to increase the estate your heirs will get when you die. On the other hand, if you have direct responsibility for young or disabled children or aged parents, and you feel that your estate itself will not be sufficient to meet your obligations, life insurance may be an appropriate purchase. Some people have insurance programs under which the beneficiaries are charities. If you're inclined to help a charity in this fashion, it is certainly a legitimate method. And if your life is already insured, you may find that the cost of maintaining the existing policy is comparatively small, so that it becomes a good "investment."

The Second Time Around

It is not uncommon for older women to contemplate remarriage after the initial trauma of widowhood has passed. While one would hope that these second marriages have some degree of romance (we were once told that a second marriage is a compliment to the deceased spouse, testifying to the satisfaction of the first marriage), there is no doubt you should resolve certain financial issues before a march down the aisle.

One of the first should be whether a second marriage will have an impact on your financial situation. Did your husband leave the property to you only so long as you did not remarry? Are you getting a pension from his employer which will cease if you remarry? These are matters which should be understood before you take any precipitate steps.

While prenuptial agreements among young people are a relatively new phenomenon, such agreements between older couples have been common for decades if not generations. In essence, most of these agreements are designed to ensure that when both parties bring capital to the second marriage, upon death the original capital will revert back to the children of the first marriage.

In many cases, grandchildren oppose a second marriage. Often, this is because they fear that they may be deprived of "their" inheritance. There are two ways to deal with this. The first is to enter into a prenuptial agreement which will ensure that "your kids get your money and his kids get his money." The second is to tell your kids to go fly a kite. The money was left to you and you'll do what you want! The choice is yours.

Bear in mind that the type of contract which may be appropriate for two young professionals embarking on a first marriage may not be appropriate to you. Your focus should be on financial things, including who contributes to ongoing support of the household as well as the division of capital. But you may also want to look at some "little" things which can be a problem. Where are you to live? What do you do with the "extra" house if there is one? If he dies, can you continue to live in the house you share for the rest of your life or does it immediately go to his heirs? Where are you to be buried—beside your first or your second husband? Where are the various holidays to be spent—with his kids or yours? It is clear from even this abbreviated list that the issues to be settled by an older couple, whether by contract or otherwise, may be substantially different than the potential conflict issues of younger people.

It is crucial that these issues be ironed out in advance of a wedding. There are a surprisingly high number of marriages between "senior citizens" which don't last a year, not because death intervenes but because each has definite ideas about lifestyles which they did not discuss before.

Conclusion

A widow, of course, has many of the same problems as any single woman, be she unmarried or divorced. But in many cases, because of her early training (or lack of it), an older widow rarely feels adequately prepared to take on the burden of managing her financial life. Traditionally she has usually turned to her male children, her husband's (usually male) advisers or their mutual (usually male) friends for advice and support. Obviously an older woman *can* take on the same level of personal financial responsibility as a male. There is no question that she will need help along the way, both with many of the "mechanical" things which will have to be done and in evaluating general advice on the steps she should be considering. It will not be easy, given the myriad issues she must deal with, but it can be an experience which leads to personal growth and an expanded sense of self-worth. While there is no way in which every problem can be anticipated and discussed, we would hope that this chapter will act as a general guide to achieving the confidence necessary to take control of financial affairs and to handle them with at least the same degree of independence as would a man in similar circumstances.

PART IV

WHEN YOU'RE RESPONSIBLE
FOR OTHERS

11

Motherhood: Financial Strategies for Women with Children

Whether they are single mothers or happily partnered with their children's father, all women with children have to make financial provisions for their own and their children's futures; their money decisions have serious implications for their offspring. While parents have no guarantees that the latest ideas about childrearing psychology will have positive results, we can be pretty sure that predictions about the outcome of financial planning for children will be accurate.

Bearing and/or raising children is still a major economic (not to say emotional) factor in the lives of most women. Ninety percent of American women become mothers by age 40—although they have children later in life, often have fewer of them, and spend less time at home with them than previous generations.

The decline in fertility among married women (down to 1.9 children per woman in 1980 from 2.4 in 1970) can be explained by several factors. First, women are marrying later and, once married, are in no rush to have children; in 1982, the typical mother giving birth to her first child was 24-and-a-half years old—almost a year older than her counterpart in 1971. And family size has shrunk at least in part because of the increased access that women in their childbearing years have to birth control and legal abortion.

Two factors we have to recognize when we try to explain this dramatic demographic change in family size are the rising cost of bearing and raising children (including time out of the

work force) and the particular complexities and financial burdens of having children in a "blended" or remarried family.

In this chapter our concern is for the economic issues facing
women who are now parents, or who want to have or adopt
children, or who find themselves stepparents or legal guardians
of children not theirs by birth. More and more women working
for pay outside their homes, both before and after children
appear on the scene, make the issues around having children
far more complicated in the 1990's than at any time in this
century, with the possible exception of the Depression years.
Then many women (with no access to legal abortion) faced the
prospect of pregnancy and childbirth with the dread of the
destitute.

Children in the Two-Parent Family

Economic considerations may not be a factor in a couple's
decision to have a first child—although there are apocryphal
stories of couples trying to conceive in March so that a child will
be born at the end of the calendar year, thus ensuring them a
tax deduction for the full year in which he/she was born, but
"costing" the parents only at year's end. (Some women have
actually considered asking to be delivered by Caesarean section
if they aren't ready to give birth by late December.) As more
substantive financial realities make themselves known, financial considerations may well affect the choice to have two or
more children, especially when this may entail the loss of the
mother's income. And the financial responsibility for children
outlasts their infancy, of course.

Having children is a forever proposition. One can have
ex-spouses, but never ex-children. Recognizing that responsibility for your children may even last beyond their college
years, you can readily understand that it's in your interest to do
some advance planning.

First, if you don't already have one, *make a will*. You can wait
until after conception to do this, but do not, if you can help it,
postpone making a will until after the birth. You'll be very busy
then, and life will have complications of its own, with little
leisure time to contemplate legal matters. Don't let superstition

get in your way here. We all know people who won't put a crib into the house until the baby is there to sleep in it, in case the pregnancy fails or the baby doesn't survive. With all due respect to the crib postponers, there's no reason to carry these worries over into making a will, which can be phrased so that it speaks of "issue" (that is, any children you might have); thus, the will can be written conditionally, not naming this particular child at all, if you are doing it while you're still pregnant.

Now is also the time to think about naming a legal guardian for the baby, in case both parents die before she/he turns eighteen. (For more detail, see Chapter 13, "Wills," and the section in this chapter on Legal Guardians.) And if you already have children and still don't have a will, flip to that chapter immediately, find a lawyer, and do it!

Once the baby is born you can plan on the usual expenses for diapers, food, clothing, possibly expanded living space and, of crucial importance if both parents plan to return to work, child care. Before you budget for child care, find out what provisions your employer, or your husband's, will make for "parenthood" leave, so that the two of you can care for your own child, at least in the beginning, if you so choose. "Parental leave," if it is available to you, usually covers either birth or adoption of a child. Some insurance coverage may reimburse for time lost because of pregnancy and recovery from childbirth (although provisions such as these are hotly debated by concerned women because they suggest that pregnancy and childbirth are "disabilities" rather than the normal functions of a healthy woman).

Some companies offer paid or unpaid leave, the use of vacation or personal days, or a promise to hold the job open for a year or more. In the late 1980's, IBM announced employee benefit options that included up to three years unpaid leave for child care (or elder care), with health insurance coverage continuing and reemployment guaranteed. At about the same time, the government-owned Tennessee Valley Authority offered employees up to ten weeks of unpaid leave to care for a new baby (or a sick relative). More progressive employers recognize that a profamily workplace environment means that fathers as well as mothers need time to be with, and bond to, the new family member—but these recent policies probably have more to do with a corporation's need to attract and retain workers than they do with ideology. Paternity leave, while uncommon, may be one of the "cafeteria benefits" your employer(s) offer, or would offer if there were enough demand. Even just making the request may raise the consciousness of the personnel department!

Of course when you're thinking about family finances in the context of having a baby, you're subtracting from income the amount you won't be earning (if you're now at work and plan a long maternity leave). But try to keep some flexibility in the system. You may choose to go back to work while you're still in the hospital (assuming you give birth in a hospital) following the birth, as did a woman we know who worked for a clothing manufacturer. She was so anxious about the spring line that she began to do business from her hospital bed. But the press has now spotted a trend: women who were determined to return to work six weeks after the birth are finding themselves very reluctant to leave their babies, choosing (especially after the birth of a second child) to stay home for up to a year instead. Clearly, however, giving up a paycheck at the birth of a child is an option available to few working women. One solution might be to try to arrange for more flexible work hours, perhaps working part time or partly from home if you can.

Child Care: Family Policies and Social Policy

Most mothers no longer have the luxury of deciding to stay home full time with their children. More than half of all women in America who have children under the age of six are working for pay outside their homes. And the number rises with the age of the youngest child. Who cares for the children?

Only about one-fifth of children under six whose mothers and fathers work are cared for in day care or other regulated facilities. There are at least ten times more children who need care than there are daycare spaces available. These children are taken care of in their own homes or in the homes of other family members or babysitters.

While child-care workers are notoriously underpaid, nevertheless paying even these amounts can strain many a family's budget. Here is roughly what you can expect to pay for various kinds of child care. (The figures will vary depending on the city or town you live in, the number of hours you use the care, the availability of unpaid help to supplement the care, and whether or not you have space in your house to accommodate live-in help, thus defraying some of the cash cost by offering room and board.)

For children under six, family day care (that is, in another person's home) can cost between $1500 and $3000 per year, assuming regular daytime hours; more institutionalized or regulated care, in a day-care center of some sort, can cost between $2000 and $5000. The cost of having a housekeeper in your home to take care of your children can cost between $160-$350 per week, if the help lives in, and $200-$350 or more if the help commutes to you each working day. If both parents are employed, a percentage of your childcare costs will be tax-deductible (for children under age 14.)

This is also the time to remind you to add to the costs of child care the amount necessary to increase insurance coverage for anyone who is injured in your home—you're now likely to have more people (e.g., sitters) working in your home on a casual basis, and you do not want to be sued if one of them trips over a rattle. You must also remind yourself to be a fair and equitable employer; this means paying all relevant taxes, Social Security contributions, unemployment insurance costs, and filing appropriate papers. (Read over Chapter 2, "Women in the Workplace" and Chapter 14, "Parent Care: The Child as Adult" for more details on how to manage this role.)

In some ways it's ironic that at one end of the spectrum women are searching for the perfect nanny to tend their children so that they can return to professional jobs, while at the other end are women with children who have no access to adequate child care, and no money to pay for it, and who therefore can't go to work even though they desperately need the income to feed and house and clothe those children.

Nothing heightens our awareness of the plight of children in poverty as much as having children of our own and seeing just how dependent upon others they are. While the purpose of this book is to alert readers to the financial mechanisms appropriate to their own (largely middle-class) lives, it's important for us all to remember that not all children are born with equal advantages, and that as parents ourselves we have an obligation to press for social changes that would lessen the differential between comfort and destitution for so many children—and this includes pressing for the kind of governmental support for childcare and child welfare programs that are taken for granted in most other industrialized countries. In what she terms "paying the price of mythology," columnist Michele Landsberg points out the high cost to society as a whole and especially to its suffering victims—poor women and their children—that derives from the false assumption that women are cut out for wifehood and motherhood and that there will always be some well-heeled male around to support them. Not so, of course.

In *Women and Children First* (Penguin, 1983), she discusses the proposal to pay each parent at home with a pre-school-age child a monthly sum equivalent to the cost of an adequate day-care center. The mother could choose to spend it on day care and remain in (or enter) the work force, or she could choose to spend it on raising the child herself at home. Writing about Canada, but with obvious relevance to the United States also, Landsberg proposes that everyone in the country fall under the jurisdiction of a national pension plan, with the government paying the premiums for everyone who cares for a dependent at home, either a preschool child or a bedridden parent or other adult. (If a woman without small children chose to stay home to care for her household, her spouse or she herself would be responsible for paying into her pension plan.) "With one splendid move," says Landsberg, "we would at last acknowledge the dignity and worth of child care and housework as full-time occupations; we would remove child support and care from the gender wars; and we would ensure the dignity of older persons, male and female." The lack of affordable child care for so many families is one of several indications that society's institutions haven't yet caught up with the new realities in people's lives—among them the fact that women's presence in the work force is real and permanent, and that many women with young children will continue to work throughout their lives. In fact, so marked is the shift from previous generations, when a woman's work was very likely to stop with marriage if the family could afford it, and almost certainly would stop when children were born, that feminist leader Betty Friedan has predicted the big question for married women in the 1990's will not be whether or not to work, but whether or not to have children.

Financial Planning Strategies Involving Your Children

While it is urgent to support federal economic developments that affect women, we all need financial advice right now, before the wrinkles in the system are ironed out. So, until the revolution comes, here are some prerevolutionary tactics:

• In planning your children's activities as they get older, remember that certain of them may have a tax advantage for you. Summer camp and certain after-school playgroups or sports groups may be tax-deductible if they meet the criteria that both parents work and the activity provides the child care in that time slot for a child who has been under 14 for the whole year. You can deduct a maximum of $60 per week per child to a total of $2000 per year per child.

• If you are opening savings accounts or other accounts for your children, remember that their dividends or interest may be taxed at your tax rate. (Unearned income for a child under fourteen will be taxed at the parent's rate; for a child fourteen or over, it will be taxed at whatever rate the child's income would dictate.)

• To pass money along to your children—for college expenses, for example—you can pay your child for work (typing, babysitting, and so on). You deduct the wages as an expense and the child reports wages received. There is a tax savings by "payrolling" your children and having *them* write out the checks for college tuition rather than paying the bills yourself. Remember that the child must report the income and pay Social Security on it.

• Buying life insurance policies for your children may be a good idea, since they will be able to acquire them for premiums very much lower than they'll pay for the same policies as adults. And this may be a way of covertly filtering money to your children, or just investing it for them with some tax savings for your family. Just don't follow the example of one father who bought a policy for his young son but not for his daughter. Somehow he'd fixed in his mind that life insurance was for males only!

• Planning for your children's higher education can never begin too early. A small amount invested when they're young will pay off hugely when they're 18 or so. Remember—the best results come when you can put aside some money for your child's higher education at an early age—perhaps when he or she enters first grade would be a nice symbolic time to open up the educational saving plan, if you haven't done so already. But it's never too late to begin.

You might look at the educational savings plans offered by some banks. Under these plans, a parent or grandparent can put away funds for a child's education; once common, new tax laws have made these plans more complicated than before. You probably need to consult an accountant about how to do it best under your specific circumstances. Plans differ significantly in detail, and some comparison shopping is in order.

• If you have substantial wealth (a sum of $25,000 or more) you might want to consider setting up a trust fund for your children. Or you might want to make an interest-free "gift" loan to a child. But get professional tax advice before taking such steps; there are a number of tricky technicalities to deal with in order to avoid tax pitfalls if you would consider either of these options.

• It'll be much easier to budget for your children's ongoing (but not unusual) expenses if you decide when they are, for example, 12 or 13, to deposit a fixed sum into a checking account for each child each month to cover transportation, entertainment, and most nonmajor items of clothing. If the children want more money each month they have the option of working for it, either around the house or at outside jobs. They learn early to budget their own money, have the pleasure of deciding for themselves how they want to spend their allowance, and are spared (and spare their parents) the haggling that sometimes goes on if a child want to buy a costly item the parents cannot bring themselves to approve. An added benefit: they learn how to write checks, balance their accounts, and thus aren't intimidated by routine banking procedures. Aside from the psychological gain for all parties, parents really can budget for exactly how much they'll need to put aside annually for each child's spending money.

• Some state educational institutions are setting up programs whereby parents can contribute to a fund in their own state, locking in a certain tuition payment for their children at the state university in the future, and getting interest on their deposit in the meantime. These new plans are changing frequently; you might want to contact your state university system's finance office even when your children are young to explore what your options might be in this area.

Money and Family Dynamics

As your children get older, you may sense battle lines drawn between you and your husband with regard to children and money matters. Aside from the disputes engendered by feelings of economic helplessness on the part of a nonworking or lower-earning mother (dealt with in Chapter 7, "Women, Men and Marriage") there are a couple of specifics here to look out for.

When the parents themselves come from different backgrounds, conflicts may surface when children approach young adulthood (say, eighteen to twenty-one) and one parent believes that they should now be on their own financially while the other feels strongly that parental support should continue for as long as its needed. One woman describes the dilemma in her family: "When I started college I got a part-time job, lived at home and contributed to my room and board. My parents never insisted on this, but it was something I was proud to be able to do, part of my being independent. My husband believes this isn't right, that a child at college should spend all of his or her time studying if the parents can possibly afford it. He believes we should support our kids even if they re in school when they're ninety!"

In another family, one with considerable wealth, the father insisted on cutting off all support from the children as soon as they reached 21, regardless of their earning capacity; their mother was horrified, and it nearly caused the divorce of parents who had been married more than 30 years. There's plenty of time while the children are growing up to discuss and negotiate these matters of support vs. self-sufficiency, and the cultural differences probably appear along the way as distant early-warning signals when the children are younger, too. Try to recognize the underlying attitudinal differences while you're still flexible enough to negotiate around them.

Another problem creeping up more and more in allegedly egalitarian families in which mother and father have an equal stake in their work lives and have more or less comparable salaries, is the issue of who will stay home to look after a sick child, or whose schedule must give way to accommodate children's emergencies, school plays and the like. Some of this can be worked out by applying common sense and good will—which parent works closer to the child's school or to the home? Which parent took off last time? And so on.

Of course, for couples lucky enough (or sensitive enough) to be able to structure their family lives around child care that is genuinely shared—via alternating work force participation, flexible work hours, home-based jobs, job-sharing, workplace sick-child centers and the like—such dilemmas wouldn't occur.

For a glimpse of how shared parenting can work (and for checklists and quizzes you can try out before you have children, to see if it will work for you) see *Sharing Caring: The Art of Raising Kids in Two-Career Families,* by Margaret B. White. Also indispensable, even though we're into the 90's, is Letty Cottin Pogrebin's *Growing Up Free: Raising Your Child in the '80's.*

If two-paycheck couples have kept their personal finances quite separate until the advent of their first child, things may have to change. First, if one parent is taking unpaid leave to raise the baby, that parent should be compensated by the earning partner in some way (see Chapter 7, "Women, Men, and Marriage" for suggestions). And as the child grows, the parents must come to some agreement as to who will foot the new bills. Some parents begin to pool all their money after the child comes along, keeping only small personal accounts for discretionary expenditures.

Keep in mind that your old patterns of spending, even if you can still afford them, don't work when a child is on the scene. For example, in the old days if you wanted something and your husband didn't—a new lamp, say—chances are you bought it anyway, out of your own money, if you really wanted it in the house. What will happen if your child wants something, and you believe she or he doesn't need it or shouldn't have it. And your husband goes out and buys it anyway out of his personal account? Expenditures for a child are categorically different from expenditures you might have argued about in the past, because deeply-felt values come into play around your progeny which didn't surface (at least not as powerfully) before you had this shared responsibility for another human being.

Single Mothers: The Key Financial Steps

If you are a single mother, by chance or by choice, certain items should be of prime concern to you. (For women who deliberately choose motherhood without marriage, the issues are a little different, obviously. For a description of these, please also see Chapter 15, "Modern Problems.")

• *Support*   If you're single as a consequence of divorce, or if you have not married the father of your child, make certain that you establish your rights to child support—even if you believe that the father cannot or will not make payments. Once you have a court order requiring him to pay, you have established a legal right on behalf of your child and imposed an obligation on the father.

Even if you cannot collect a cent now, this may change in the future. And even if the order calls for just minimal support because the father has a very low current income, remember that it's easier to get child support payments increased under an existing order (especially if you have reason to believe that in years to come he'll have more money), than it would be to establish your right to support some years into the future, after you've asked for nothing at the start.

If you doubt that the father will ever make the regular payments he's been ordered to, you might try to get a lump sum of money from him or at least a contribution in the child's name for a bank's educational savings plan. However, do not sign away any future rights to support in return for a lump sum payment. (It's doubtful, incidentally, whether you could in any event, since a parent has an ongoing obligation to support a child, and that obligation cannot be transferred to somebody else or negotiated away.)

All of these suggestions about support are, unfortunately, meaningless unless the courts are prepared to enforce support orders energetically. Some jurisdictions have more convincing records than others, but everywhere one needs to make sure that no male judge will be overly sympathetic to an ex-husband's moans and groans about why he can't pay up, and that none will be reluctant to order garnishment of wages or even jail sentences if support payments are in default.

• *Your Will*   Just as in the two-parent household, writing a new will should be a first priority. And the most important part of your will may be the guardianship clause, particularly if you do not want the natural father to get custody of the child. You'll have to discuss with potential guardians whether they would be prepared to take custody and to assure them that there will be enough money available to support your children. (Later in this chapter we will discuss legal guardians.)

• *Insurance*   What you will be leaving to your children raises, in turn, the question of getting life insurance. Far fewer married women than married men have insurance coverage on their lives, but as a single mother, even if you're strapped for money, insurance should be at the top of your "must buy" list. Right now, as a single woman with children, you may be managing to support them because you are earning. What happens to the children if you die? If what you are looking for is basic protection for them while they're still dependent, you will need life insurance for a finite time—perhaps until the youngest reaches eighteen or twenty—which means you can buy term insurance, the cheapest coverage available. Remember that if you own a house and there's a mortgage on it, you'll want to carry sufficient insurance to pay off the mortgage while still leaving enough money for the kids to live on. Even if it means making some additional personal sacrifices, *you must have adequate insurance coverage at this stage in your life.*

If you can afford it and if you are not already covered by an employer's plan, you should look into acquiring disability insurance. If you are self-employed or do any freelance work, this insurance will ensure that you have some income if you fall ill and have to be away from your work or business for an extended period of time.

• *Savings and Employee Benefits*   You should also embark on a savings or investment program, providing of course that you can spare the money. Investing a small sum each month on behalf of the children is a natural for those who have some extra cash. And if you are on salary, buying government Savings Bonds on a payroll deduction basis is one of the safest and probably most painless ways to save.

You must also check on such matters as your employer's pension plan, health coverage and the like, and to see if you and/or the children still have any coverage or benefits under your ex-husband's plan if you are divorced or widowed. There are now regulations that protect the right of an ex-spouse to insurance coverage that was in place before the marriage dissolved. (For more on what you may be entitled to in this area, see Chapter 9, "Divorce: Coaching in Battlefront Tactics and Strategies.") If there seems to be a gap in coverage—say, for example, because the kids are not entitled to be the beneficiaries of your pension plan if you die—you can either try to negotiate extended coverage with your employer (pointing out that such pension plans routinely discriminate against singles), or you can add to the amount of life insurance you carry when your children are young.

Clearly, the obligations of motherhood require fiscal prudence both in the short term and in the long haul. If you alone are responsible for the financial well-being of your child(ren), the key determinant of their financial security will be how mature and well-informed you are in putting aside more immediate concerns in order to do some crucial long-term planning.

Custody Struggles and Related Headaches and Heartaches

Custody of children has been a particularly painful issue for all women, of course, and especially for lesbian mothers, whose sexual orientation has often been used to wrest their children from them in custody battles with the father.

Ironically, women receive little social support or recognition for their traditional role as mothers (or as the nurturing parent), yet this is the very role that men threaten to take away from them—the role that suddenly is made to appear very valuable in a custody suit or divorce action. Some women even sign away rights to adequate financial support in a divorce because their ex-husbands have threatened to challenge their custody of the children otherwise. The parent who wants most to keep the children is often the victim of a cruel kind of blackmail—"Press me for more money in this divorce settlement and I'll say you're an unfit mother and I'll take the kids away from you."

All married women run the risk of being caught in the Catch-22 situation: suffering economic constriction if they leave the workplace (or decide never to enter it in the first place) in order to raise their children; then, if they are awarded custody in the event of divorce, they're declared unfit parents because they haven't sufficient income to support the children adequately without a husband. Yet noncustodial fathers are notoriously unreliable about making child-support payments—if they can even be tracked down in the first place!

Remember too that all financial decisions regarding support after divorce will have tax implications for you. Even after you have received assurances of child support, beware—your child-support payments are generally not subject to income tax if they are designated not for your own use, but are held by you for your children. Be very cautious in how these arrangements are made under a divorce or separation decree—the technical wording may affect whether you or your ex-husband pays the income tax or takes the children as tax deductions. Often women in marital disputes are eager to get custody and eager to get assurances of support, but may be getting shabby treatment without even being aware of it, as the support amount gets eroded by tax liability thanks to creative footwork by the father's team of experts.

The same financial disabilities that plague women throughout their lives—often making them unequal partners in marriage, causing them to work longer hours for less pay than men—are particularly poignant and painful when we see that women who are the sole support of children are the new poor, the new underclass. A man's disposable income rises 42 percent in the first year after divorce, while the standard of living of the divorced woman and her children drops 73 percent in the same period, says Lenore J. Weitzman in *The Divorce Revolution: The Unexpected Social and Economic Consequences for Women and Children in America.* And she is usually the one with the dependent children to care for.

Joint custody, now being touted widely as the ideal solution for children and divorced parents, is a double-edged sword. Given extreme goodwill on the part of the father, it'll work, with the children dividing their time equally between the parents (a week with each, or a month, or whatever the parents agree to). One hassle is that the plan usually limits the parents' geographic mobility; another is that, in cases of serial marriages which have given rise to multiple custodial arrangements, family life can be almost unbearably complicated. Speaking about the progeny of his two previous marriages, one man describes his custody thus: "One week a month I have one child living with me; one week I have two children; one week I have three children, one week I have no children." On the plus side, the children need not become estranged from either parent, and neither parent has the full burden of raising the kids alone.

But the real financial risk to this arrangement, as feminists point out, is that the fathers must be prepared to pay two-thirds or so of the childrearing costs under this arrangement (keep this in mind if you're considering joint custody), because the mother usually makes much less than the father and cannot afford to shoulder fully one-half of the costs of the children's support.

Another pitfall to joint custody: if the father doesn't take the children for his full 50% of the time, there's nothing the courts can do. Visitation cannot be enforced, so the mother has the extra time with the kids and the extra expense for that time and loses the time from work if she has to stay home and care for the children when its his turn. Many women have pointed to joint custody under these circumstances as a ploy by fathers to get out of paying adequate child support by gradually eroding the amount of time they spend with the children while never increasing the support payments to the mother.

Sometimes fathers choose to be the custodial parent exclusively. According to Phyllis Chesler in *Mothers on Trial: The Battle for Children and Custody*, in the majority of cases when a father decides to fight for custody after a divorce, the courts grant it to him, sometimes on the basis that as the higher earner he could provide a more stable home or more advantages for the children. Money often sways the decision in the father's favor, and there have been cases reported of abusive fathers getting custody just because they could show more material advantages than the often impecunious mothers.

Battles over child custody can be the cruelest of all—for mother, father, and children alike. Many men seek custody, claims Chesler, not because they want to raise the children, but as a way of punishing the ex-wife, who really wants her children. Few situations are as coy and sweet as they re shown to be in the unrealistic movie "Kramer vs. Kramer," in which the father gets high praise for being a working parent—the sort of juggling acts that women have had to do forever, and without celluloid kudos, either!

If he does win custody, *you* can be forced to pay child support, even though your income may be substantially less than his. Both parents have support obligations to children, within their means. Here's one case history: A woman with two teenaged children was awarded custody of them in a separation agreement. She had worked part-time during her marriage, but had spent most of her nonchildrearing time doing volunteer work. After the separation, she began to work full time. "A confirmed feminist, I did not want alimony," she said. After a couple of years, her children, with their father's encouragement, decided to live with him and his new wife. He petitioned for child support payments from his ex-wife, and under the "gender-neutral" support laws, she was required to pay.

If you don't have custody and are asked to pay child support, and you think the custodial father can get along without it—or if it would be an excruciating hardship for you to pay—your only recourse is to fight it out in the courts, unless you take the traditional male route and simply disappear and default.

More common is the scenario where the mother has sole custody and the father, who has been ordered by the courts at the time of divorce to pay a certain amount in child support each month, defaults on his payments; or he moves away and can't be traced, or marries again and raises a new family and just doesn't have the money to meet this obligation, so he claims. (Just try this line on MasterCard or Macy's!)

There may indeed not be enough money for the man to support his "first" family and himself. The net worth of divorcing couples married five to nine years (the average number of years most divorcing couples have been together) is only about $15,000. There might not be enough to divide, even including a percentage of the ex-husband's current pay, to support two households. One study revealed that fewer than half of divorced mothers received the full amount of child support that was due them, although now such cases have the support of the courts. A 1988 Supreme Court decision says that in a civil suit if a parent claims that he cannot pay court-ordered child support, he must prove this inability.

Getting the ex-husbands to honor their agreements and pay their child support has been painful and frustrating to the thousands and thousands of women and children who wait every month for a check that might or might not arrive. There are a few procedures which might speed things up for you if you find yourself in this situation.

These payments are probably already low, since male judges are usually sympathetic to the hard-luck stories they're told when the amount is initially fixed. (And male judges continue to be too sympathetic to men, assert some critics.) It would clearly be better if, from the start, the courts could order automatic wage garnishment, and automatic withholding of income-tax refunds, government savings bond payments and other government monies to be used toward child support owed if the man is in arrears. Just "disappearing" shouldn't work either; motor vehicle registration records and phone directories have turned up 50% of recalcitrant and defaulting ex-spouses.

Adoption

One of the most expensive ways of bringing a child into your life can be through adoption, though current "alternative" reproductive techniques don't come cheap either. (See Chapter 15, "Modern Problems.") Prices in the "gray market" for indirect adoptions can often involve lawyers' and agents' fees in excess of $10,000. If you would like to adopt a child, either to add to your family or because you cannot or choose not to conceive yourself, there are reputable public agencies to start with that will explain the process to you and will likely charge considerably less for their services than privately arranged adoptions. Adoption of a school-age child, or even a preschooler, is often much easier to arrange than infant adoption, and does not involve the same initial financial outlay for finding the child through "gray-market" networks.

Some adoption of children takes place within the household, when a stepparent decides to adopt the child of his or her spouse, either quite by choice or because the biological father or mother has died. If the natural father or mother (who will now be replaced by the adoptive parent) is living, consent or a court order must be obtained before the adoption can proceed.

Since adoption is forever—unlike foster parenting or stepparenting—make sure as best you can that, if you are married, the marriage will last. We know of several cases in which one spouse adopted the children of the other spouse, only to find that, when the marriage dissolved, the biological parent did not want custody! Like the elephant in Dr. Seuss's *Horton Hatches the Egg*, these adopting parents find themselves sitting on the nest long after the biological parent has flown off. To avoid this and similar unexpected complications, postpone any discussion of adopting a stepchild until the new marriage has had a couple of years in which to work itself out, so that you do not unexpectedly find yourself with an adopted dependent child after a divorce from the child's biological parent.

Other financial issues in adoption have to do with inheritance; make sure that your wills are worded in such a way that your adopted child(ren) will inherit equally with any biological children you might have. You will want to protect the rights of all your children equally, we presume; this is another reason to keep your will scrupulously up-to-date and not rely on such words as "issue" to mean all your legal children, since "issue" might be interpreted to mean only those children who are your biological offspring.

From the birth mother's point of view, there are other concerns, of course—aside from the emotional complexities of the situation now being addressed in birth-mothers' self-help groups. Among the financial considerations are whether or not you want your child to have access to records in which you are identified as the birth mother. This may leave you open to claims for support at some later date, especially if the adoptive parents die or are unable to continue to provide this support. If you are putting the child up for adoption privately (that is, through lawyers or other go-betweens) remember that buying or selling human beings is explicitly against the law, and if your medical or other costs are being paid, make sure that you have a contract stipulating that these reimbursements are for personal anguish, expenses or whatever and do not implicate you in baby-selling for financial gain.

Legal Guardianship

Joanne, a single woman in her thirties, was asked by her younger brother and sister-in-law if she would consent to be named in their wills as the legal guardian of her niece and nephew should both the young parents die. They had rejected the idea of asking the grandparents, who were getting on in years and not terribly robust, and none of their friends was as close to the children as their aunt. (Note here that single, childless women are frequently asked to take on this responsibility for family or friends; men in the same position are almost never considered as potential legal guardians, unless as trustees or financial managers for a significant estate.) Joanne accepted, but with several reservations, which she didn't feel comfortable about airing. Her situation may have been unusual in that she didn't ever voice her concerns to the relatives she loved dearly, figuring that the chances of her actually having custody of the children were slim and not worth causing a family rift over.

Particularly if you are a single woman asked to take on major responsibilities like this, you must think very clearly about your own interests and how to deal with such a request, whether from a friend or a relative. Saying no would have been a terrible blow, Joanne felt, and might signify that she didn't love her niece and nephew enough. On the other hand, as a single woman, was she jeopardizing her chances of marrying if she did end up with the children? And how would she pay for raising them on her relatively modest teaching salary?

The answer to the first question, she decided after much thought, was that if any man she might consider marrying would see these children as an unwanted burden, she wouldn't want to marry him anyway. The answer to the second was resolved when her brother assured her that in their wills he and his wife had made provision for their life insurance policies and other assets to be available to her to cover any expenses she'd have in raising the children.

Nevertheless, the dilemma persists. Joanne marries, and the parents of her niece and nephew are, thank heaven, still alive. Until the children reach 18, it's a constant responsibility in the back of her mind; though both the parents are in good health, she knows an accident can fell anyone.

In some cultural, religious or ethnic groups, these discomforts may be resolved very early on, with the baby's godparents (who aren't necessarily married to each other) pledging at a christening or baby-naming ceremony that they will assume neoparental roles in the life of the child early on. These people acknowledge that they are taking on a near-religious responsibility for the child; built into the arrangement is the understanding among the adults that the godparents will take over in the event that both parents die. (If you are arranging guardianship this way, remember that you have an obligation, to the godparents and to your offspring, to inform them about how the children's finances are arranged in the event of your death.)

Here are some guidelines in choosing a guardian you want to name, keeping in mind that the courts do not always honor the choice of the parent(s) if they think it's inappropriate.

• If you and the father of your child(ren) are no longer together, make sure that you agree—and that your wills agree—about who should be named legal guardian. If you have joint custody, you'll have to decide together. If you have sole custody, you have to decide whether or not you want the father to be named as guardian.

• If you are a lesbian mother and you want your lover, who may have functioned as a co-parent, to be the child's legal guardian, you must make sure that all the documents are in place to convince the courts that she, rather than perhaps the father, should get custody.

• If yours is a two-parent family, your wills obviously assume that if one of you dies the other will take over childrearing; the courts assume likewise. It's if you should die simultaneously that the issue of legal guardianship arises. The least painful arrangement, if you have a sibling or close friends with children, is to make the provision reciprocal, with each couple writing the other into their wills as legal guardians, with appropriate financial support systems for maintaining the additional children.

- If you have named friends as legal guardians, make sure to review this arrangement periodically, to keep both the agreement and the friendship up-to-date. You don't want your children, traumatized already by the deaths of two parents, to go into the home of some family they haven't laid eyes on for ten years, even if they were your best college buddies.

- And if you, like Joanne, are asked to take on this responsibility, a perfectly appropriate reply would be. "Let me think about it for a few days. It's a big responsibility, and one you wouldn't want me to take on lightly." Either in this conversation or the next, it's appropriate to say forthrightly, "You know that my salary is quite comfortable for me to live on, but I don't know how I'd manage with more dependents, especially because I know you'd want your children to have whatever you would have been able to give them." This opens the door for the asking parent(s) to announce the financial provisions they have made for the children in their wills.

12

Life Insurance

You've seen the ad or a variation of it a thousand times, on television, in magazines and newspapers. It pictures the happy family (husband, wife, small child, and adorable pet). And it asks, always with the greatest of taste and delicacy, what will happen if husband/father is removed from the picture. The answer is that his financial role within the family can be replaced with funds provided by an appropriate life insurance policy.

What the ad never seems to address is that in the 1990's most married couples need two incomes in order to get by. Why don't the ads raise the question of what happens to the family financially if the wife/mother disappears from the picture? And we all know that even if the wife/mother is not out in the work force, her contribution to the family in terms of her work within the home is worth tens of thousands of dollars a year. If she dies, where does the money to pay for the housekeeper/cook/babysitter/chauffeur/nurse/psychologist come from? (Interestingly enough, even though insurance companies do not seem to grasp the economic value of a wife or mother, the courts do. If the woman dies or is severely injured through the negligence of a third person, her economic value is assessed by the courts, and a monetary award will be made—often paid for, incidentally, by the defendant's insurance company.) And why do the ads never portray that increasingly common family—the single mother and her children? This type of family is one where insurance is likely to be an extremely important part of financial planning.

While many of the ads are sexist, strangely enough, perhaps the only planning area where women have a distinct financial advantage over men is in the purchase of life insurance. Because insurance rates are based on the purchaser's life expectancy, and because women have longer life expectancies than men (that is, at any given age, the odds are that a woman will live longer than a man), the cost of life insurance for a woman will be lower than for a man.

Almost every woman will be asked to buy life insurance at some stage of her life. The approach may be from an insurance agent, may be as an offer through an organization she belongs to, or may be an optional or mandatory purchase through an employer. Not every woman needs insurance, but it is fair to say that there are many women who should have it who remain uninsured, either because of the cost or because they don't yet understand the role which life insurance could play in their financial planning. Because insurance companies and their agents usually are unable to appreciate the needs of a woman, the burden of deciding whether or not to buy life insurance may well fall on you. The purpose of this chapter is to give you some idea of the undoubted benefits of life insurance, the types of insurance available and, perhaps most importantly, the surprising uses to which you can put your life insurance.

Life insurance offers two very important financial features. The first is that it provides funds on death in the form of cash. Second, the payments made on death (referred to as "death benefits") are free of tax. Thus, when the insured person dies, a fund of tax-free cash becomes available to the beneficiary almost immediately. In the case of most other assets, a transfer to the inheritors cannot take place until the will is probated and the executors take the necessary legal steps to change their ownership.

But aside from these obvious advantages, the key thing to remember is that there must be a purpose behind the purchase of a policy. Buying insurance without looking at the particular purpose for which the money will be used is akin to buying an expensive and sophisticated computer for no other reason than to type notes to the gardener. And you'll have to evaluate your own needs because usually life insurance peddlers (the vast majority of them male, though women are now making inroads) haven't honed their pitch to women yet.

Here are the most common situations in which insurance may be important to you:

• **The Support of Dependents**   Many women are the sole or primary support of others. The most common such situation is the single mother who has children still living at home or needing college tuition. Or a woman may be contributing to the support of parents or other relatives. It may well be that so long as she continues to work the burden of such support is not a major financial strain. But this woman should be giving some thought to what would happen if she were to die while those she is supporting live on. If she doesn't have money available from other assets to help those who are dependent upon her, life insurance offers a method of guaranteeing that the necessary funds will be available when she dies.

• *Liquidity*   Many women will die with substantial assets which cannot be sold quickly or which, while valuable, produce little or no cash income. Very often this will be the case if you've made major investments in real estate, art or jewelry. In such a case, you can take out insurance to ensure that there is enough cash available to take care of obligations which may arise at your death or which may continue after death; this will mean that valuable assets need not be sold in haste.

• *Taxes*   In many situations, a death may trigger a substantial tax bill. This often will arise where a woman's assets have been inherited from her husband on a "tax free" basis. This is a common occurrence because the provisions of the Internal Revenue Code encourage this type of transfer, but what you have to remember is that while there is no tax liability when the husband's assets are distributed to his widow, there may well be a substantial liability when the widow dies and leaves assets to the next generation. The potential tax liability can be calculated to some extent in advance and you can take out a policy to guarantee that the cash will be available for taxes. The ideal "estate planning" situation would be for the husband and wife to draw up their wills together so as to coordinate planning. At this stage of the game, insurance coverage for both of them should be considered as part of the plan. In many instances, it will make the most sense for the wife, not the husband, to be the party who is insured, both from the tax point of view and from the point of view of cost. This stems from the fact that taxes will probably have to be paid when the second of the two, likely the wife, die, and it is then that the insurance money is needed. And since insurance is usually cheaper for a woman than for a man, the cost of getting the needed coverage will be lower if the wife is insured.

• *Charitable Donations*   Many women take out insurance policies which they donate to their favorite charities. There are some tax benefits from doing this, *because the premiums are treated as charitable donations.* (Normally insurance premiums are not deductible expenses for tax purposes.) But the major attraction is that insurance allows a woman to make a major gift to charities with which she may have had a long involvement, even though she might not have substantial assets in her own name which would allow making a large gift while she is alive. In a world which tends to value money over the contribution of time, letting a charity know that it may be a major beneficiary when you die is a sure-shot way to get recognition which may otherwise go only to those who donate money. Many charities now honor those who donate insurance policies which will "mature" in the future in the same method as they recognize those who give cash now.

• *Business Related Insurance*   If you are in business with a partner, you may well have an agreement under which if one dies, the other has an obligation to purchase the interest of the deceased partner. (This is commonly called a buy-sell agreement.) In such a case, it is common for each partner to take out an insurance policy on the life of the other to guarantee that the funds will be available to fund the buy-out of the deceased's business assets. (The amount of insurance your husband has purchased for this purpose may be used in a divorce action as evidence of the value of your interest in the business enterprise.)

• *Debt Insurance*   If you have major current debts which could not be satisfied out of your assets, insurance may be an attractive solution. Let's say you have bought a house for $150,000 and have a $100,000 mortgage. You may want to take out an insurance policy for $100,000 so that if you die, the mortgage will be paid off. (Many financial institutions offer "mortgage insurance" which is nothing more than a term life insurance policy geared to the amount owing under a mortgage.) Such insurance may be useful no matter why you are indebted, whether you borrowed to buy a house, to invest, for education or whatever. Insurance to cover debts is particularly important if you may be survived by dependents and your assets will be substantially eroded if the debts must be paid off at your death.

While the foregoing represent the most common and important uses for life insurance, some women have a strong desire to have insurance for what we might term psychological reasons. Jeanine, a forty-five-year-old married woman, was bothered by the fact that she earned a relatively low income from the part-time job she held. Her husband was a physician earning significant amounts of money and had built up substantial assets. There was no real financial reason for Jeanine to buy life insurance since their children were beneficiaries of her husband's financial planning. But she did so in order that when she died, her children would get something directly from her. While, strictly speaking, her purchase of insurance was not necessary financially, it gave her a feeling of self-worth which made the annual expenditure of a few hundred dollars well worth the cost. Insurance types would call this "estate creation," the establishment of a fund of money at death even where the individual did not have substantial assets while alive.

Types of Life Insurance

Despite the hype which a potential insurance buyer may be exposed to, there are really only two types of life insurance, "term" and "whole life," which is sometimes referred to as permanent insurance.

Term insurance is cheaper at the start. The initial rate is based on your age (with sex, health, and smoking habits also being factors) and will be the same for a number of years, usually five but sometimes ten. At the end of this period, the insurance can normally be renewed but the price will increase for the next five or ten years. Thus, you might have one rate from the time you are 31 to the time you are 36, a higher rate from 36 to 41 and so forth. One main drawback with term insurance is that at some age, usually seventy, it will "expire" and you cannot buy more insurance. One agent we know refers to the purchase of term insurance as "renting" a policy.

But the fact that a policy may increase substantially in cost or may expire when you reach age seventy is not necessarily a major drawback in every situation. For example, if you are a thirtyish single parent who is buying insurance to make certain that there are funds available to support your children if you die, you can figure that by the time you are about 45, your support obligations will likely be over and you might not have any need to continue the insurance coverage.

When you buy term insurance, it is possible to get additional protection for a relatively small additional fee. For example, you can get a policy which guarantees the payment of the premiums in the event that you are disabled and cannot work. Or you can get a guarantee that even if your health deteriorates, the company will sell you the same policy again, setting the premiums at the same level as they would be if you were healthy. Some policies offer a convertability feature which will allow you to shift from term insurance to whole life at some point in the future.

Permanent insurance is substantially different from term insurance in a number of ways. The initial premium, though it is set on the basis of sex, health, and whether or not you are a smoker, depending upon the type of policy, can remain fixed throughout the life of the policy. But that initial premium will be substantially higher than a term premium under a policy taken out at the same age. Unlike term insurance, the policy will stay in effect so long as you pay the premiums and, depending upon the type of policy, the premiums will remain at exactly the same level for so long as the policy is in force.

Since permanent insurance contains an investment element, as you hold the policy it builds up values in addition to the insurance benefits payable at death. After just a couple of years, the policy will have a cash surrender value. At any time you can give up the policy and get the underlying cash surrender value paid to you. You can often arrange to borrow against the cash surrender value as well. Many policies, after they have been in place for some time, offer an option whereby you pay no further premiums, with the premiums being paid for out of the investment proceeds.

There is an ongoing and substantial debate (which will probably never be resolved) as to whether it makes more sense to buy term insurance and invest the difference in cost between it and whole life or to buy whole life insurance and have the insurance company do the investing. A lot clearly depends upon how adept you would be in investing the difference, and the role the insurance is to play in your planning.

As we pointed out earlier, there may be many situations where term insurance is more than adequate to meet your planning objectives. But there are also situations where whole life insurance is more desirable. For example, if the reason you are taking out insurance is to meet tax liabilities which may arise on your death, you don't want to buy a policy which will lapse when you are seventy. Permanent insurance is what is needed in such a case. You might live to be 120!

Where Do You Get Life Insurance?

There are three major sources of life insurance: employers, so-called fraternal organizations, and private agents. Many employers offer life insurance as part of their compensation packages. This form of insurance is group term and it is unlikely that you will have to take a physical examination or answer any more than the most cursory questions. Such insurance is particularly attractive to those who are not in the best of health, since they are assured coverage despite their illness or disability.

There is a tax advantage to this type of insurance as well, since the employer can pay for up to $25,000 of coverage per employee, deducting the cost, while the employee need not report the employer's cost as additional income (i.e., the value of the premiums on up to $25,000 of such insurance.) Remember, normally any benefit you receive from employment is taxable; so the government offers a significant tax concession here for this insurance. Many of these policies will be linked to salary, offering a death benefit which rises as your salary rises. On the other hand, coverage will disappear when you cease to be employed by the company.

A young, unmarried woman might not particularly need or want life insurance from an employer if she had to pay anything for it. If this is a perk which is offered, you can check to see whether your employer has something available as a trade-off, such as increased salary or more vacation. On the other hand, since the employer is subsidizing the cost, this may be the cheapest term insurance you'll be able to buy.

A second source of group term insurance is through organizations which you may belong to. Coverage may be offered by a professional association, a university alumni association, or any other legitimate organization with broad membership. Again, one of the advantages of this type of coverage is that it usually does not require a physical examination and thus, in some cases, people who might be otherwise uninsurable because of poor health can get coverage. Our experience has been, however, that often the cost is quite high compared to what you can get through buying a policy privately. The premiums often seem low because they are shown broken down as monthly or quarterly payments. But some calculations show that the overall annual cost is quite a bit higher than a private policy might be.

The bulk of insurance is sold by insurance agents who represent insurance companies. Some are linked to only one company while others are independent, offering policies from a variety of companies.

Independent insurance agents will get you a range of quotes on policies from many different companies to allow you to make the best buy. There are no charges for these services.

The most important single thing to remember in dealing with *any* insurance agent is that he or she gets paid on a commission basis. The higher *your* premium costs, the more the agent makes. This becomes an important factor in discussing insurance needs with an agent. Most of the time the agent will prefer to sell you whole life as opposed to term insurance. And the agent is most likely to want to add on as many "bells and whistles" as possible, such as convertability of term to whole life, guaranteed premium payments while you are disabled, and so on. The fact that an agent is trying to sell you a more expensive product does not necessarily mean that the agent is bad, greedy, or incompetent. The agent likely believes that the product is excellent and that you should have the most complete of all policies.

This is why it's important that you have a good idea of exactly what you want or need before talking to an insurance agent. If you think you need a $50,000 term policy to meet your goals and the agent is talking about a $100,000 whole life policy (at four times the cost), make him or her justify the case for a more expensive policy. The best agents we have dealt with will, once you have explained the objectives you have, go along with your choice of a policy or make a very convincing case for an alternative.

The other point to keep in mind is that notwithstanding the fact that all insurance premiums are based on the same basic fact, your life expectancy, prices vary radically for what appears to be the same coverage. *Shop around.* If one policy costs 25% more than another apparently identical one, find out why. Most good agents will take time to shop around for you and to explain differences between policies even if your potential purchase is modest. If the agent appears impatient, find somebody else. There is fierce competition among agents and among insurance companies. And unlike just about any other product you can name, life insurance premiums have been on a downward slide for a decade, becoming a real bargain in many instances.

You can also ask an agent to assess the quality of any insurance policy you currently have and to suggest whether it should be kept or canceled. For example, Jane, who is 35 now, had a whole life policy for $30,000 taken out by her father when she was ten years old. (An unusual case, we might add. Many fathers take out whole life insurance for sons when they are young to guarantee a low rate for a permanent policy for life: few take out such policies for daughters.) The agent told her that the cash surrender value of the policy was about $7,500. But she could get $100,000 of term insurance now for about $300 a year. The agent pointed out Jane could invest the $7,500, get about $675 a year, use $300 to buy $100,000 in coverage and have $375 left over. One of the reasons for the difference in cost is that insurance was much more expensive when Jane was ten than it is today and she was holding what amounted to a very expensive policy. In addition, the $30,000 was a much more significant sum when she was ten than it is 25 years later.

Because there are so many life insurance agents in the U.S., almost everybody knows somebody who is one or has a friend who can recommend somebody. The ideal person to recommend an agent, however, is somebody who has recently gone out and bought insurance. If you have contact with a lawyer or accountant, ask them about life insurance agents. They tend to have dealings with many agents and can often give some real insights into which ones they think will do a good job for you.

But be realistic. Life insurance agents tend to be among the most conservative people around. Don't be surprised if you run into some (or many) who don't understand a woman's point of view and who therefore will try to tell you what you need. Be firm and don't be afraid to walk out and look for somebody else. You're the customer; you have a right to the information you are seeking and a right to buy what you want. Times are changing in the industry; some agents have already figured this out and respond to female clients with understanding and cooperation.

Beneficiaries

When you decide to buy a policy of life insurance, you will be asked to name a beneficiary, the term applied to the person or entity which will receive the money when you die. This may be a particular individual or it can be your estate. If you choose the latter, the death benefit will be paid into your estate and will be distributed as your will directs.

Normally, if a spouse is to receive the major benefit of a life insurance policy, he or she is named as beneficiary. (Except in the most unusual cases, you can change the beneficiary whenever you want.) This will put the death benefit into your spouse's hands directly, to be used as he or she sees fit. You might name as a beneficiary under an insurance policy a person you don't want identified in your will, say a child born out of wedlock or a former lover. One benefit of naming a specific beneficiary is that the money will pass directly to that person; even if the validity of your will is challenged, the named person will get the money, since it does not pass under the will. It makes sense to inform somebody you trust, such as your lawyer, about the existence of the policy so that the named beneficiary will be able to make the claim when you die.

You may also want to name a specific person as a beneficiary precisely in order to keep the money out of your estate. If you are deeply in debt and the money is paid to your estate, the funds can be seized by creditors. If the money goes to a named person, the creditors have no right to it.

If you wish the funds be used to help support your children or aged parents, you may not want the money to be paid to them directly if they are not mentally capable of handling it. In such a case, if the money is paid to your estate or to a trust, you can put conditions on the use of the money. For example, the money might not be paid to your husband outright with only interest paid to him for some period with the trustees having the discretion whether to distribute principal. Therefore, if he remarries within five years, the trustee can hold the money for your children. Or the income from the insurance might be used to support your children until the youngest reaches, say, 25, at which time they get the capital. In such a situation, the person or people you name as executors will control the money and use it as you direct. (These topics are discussed in more detail in the chapter dealing with wills.) Again, the naming of the beneficiary will follow from your own objectives in buying insurance. Remember too that the naming of either an individual or your estate is not irrevocable, and as your circumstances change you may wish to change the beneficiary.

Conclusion

It is likely that many women who should be insured are not. They have not put their minds to their particular needs or the potential needs of those dependent upon them, perhaps because buying insurance (like making a will) conjures up thoughts which are unpleasant, or perhaps because the myriad types of life insurance has so confused them that they wash their hands of the subject. Certainly, the insurance industry itself must bear at least a part of the blame in that its pitch to the public has been almost totally male-oriented. The industry, however, professes to want to change and service women (after all, there is a new, potentially rich market there) and it may be that in the future insurance companies and their agents will pay more attention to women's needs.

But right now, women, like men, who have support obligations, debts, business arrangements, tax liabilities, and charitable intentions are all candidates for life insurance. Because of the timing of death benefits and the tax advantages associated with such payments, life insurance often offers the ideal solution to vexing financial conundrums. And so long as policies are offered based on life expectancy, women are offered a financial bonus over men in a like position through lower premiums.

Life insurance may not be appropriate for every woman, but you owe it to yourself to examine your own situation to see whether insurance might not play an important role.

13

Wills

Making a will is a traumatic experience for most people. They come face to face with their own mortality and are forced to make difficult decisions which they'd prefer not to think about. Who do I trust to distribute my assets and fulfill my final desires? Who would I appoint as guardians to my children? How would I distribute my property?

Everybody should have a will. But many women don't bother, usually because they believe that they don't have any property to leave. This is normally a fallacy. A woman may have pension rights, an interest in the family home, insurance, jewelry, prized possessions, or an expectation of a bequest from a parent, relative, or husband. Since one cannot normally foresee one's own death, a will should be drawn which will cover future contingencies, not just the situation as it exists today.

But even if your assets are minimal now, the making of a will is an assertion of one's value as a person—a step on the road to financial maturity. The will has the benefit of forcing a woman to come to grips with the nature of her economic situation, her values and her family. While the experience may be traumatic, it may also be extremely illuminating.

The Will Is a Living Document—Until You Die

We asked Sheila, a 26-year-old single parent working as a bookkeeper in an advertising agency, whether she had a will. She proceeded to run through the wills she had made over the years. When she was eighteen (the earliest age at which a person can validly make a will), her grandfather, a prominent lawyer, insisted that she make a will because he was leaving property to her in his, and if she died after him but without a will, her property would be distributed according to the state laws in a way which was not what either of them wanted.

Sheila married at twenty and made another will in response to her changed circumstances. This time she did it because her grandfather correctly informed her that her first will, which did not provide for her husband, would be "attackable" by her husband. In the second will, she left most of her property to her husband.

Eighteen months and one child later, she was separated from her husband and was on the way to a divorce. She made still another will, after she was informed by her grandfather that divorce does not invalidate a will made during the marriage (though in some states gifts made in the will to a spouse will be invalid if the couple divorces after the will is made.) In this third will she was at pains to name a guardian for her daughter since she did not want her ex-husband to have custody. She created a trust so that any property she might inherit would be held for the benefit of her daughter, with income available for support and the capital being transferred to the daughter when she reached age 25.

This woman had the benefit of excellent legal advice from within her own family. And her financial and family situation was perhaps more advantageous than that of many single parents. But the differences between her and other women lies only in degree, not in concept. Having accepted the fact that she should have a will, she took the steps to ensure that as her personal situation changed, the will was changed as well.

Dying Without a Will

Every state has legislation which deals with the distribution of property in the event that somebody dies intestate—that is, without a will. That legislation divides the property owned by the deceased according to a formula, always among relatives. In extreme cases where there are no relatives, the property may simply revert to the government. What this means is that the division is automatic and does not reflect your desires in any way. At times, it can raise some very serious difficulties.

Consider this case. A woman living in New York with her husband died without a will. It turned out that, aside from the relatively few assets most women who have never worked outside the home own (a few pieces of jewelry, some clothing and personal possessions), the title of the family home was in her name. Her husband assumed that he automatically would get the house. But when he tried to transfer title to his own name, he got a shock. In New York, the spouse of the deceased was entitled to one-third of the estate where there are surviving children and the children were entitled to the balance. The house was worth $150,000. Thus, the children had a right to $100,000 from their mother's estate.

There were four children of the marriage, one living in New York and two in New Jersey. The fourth, a married daughter who had lived in Vermont, had died, leaving three children. (The grandchildren of the deceased were entitled to their mother's portion of the inheritance.) The three living children agreed to waive their interest in the family home so their father could take title. But the Vermont grandchildren were minors, and it was necessary to get consent for the deal from those representing the minor children. That consent was not forthcoming. The time consumed and legal fees involved were extensive, yet all the problems could have been resolved had the deceased woman executed a will. In this case there were no soap-opera-style animosities among the family members to complicate the situation—the bare bones of the law itself impaled them.

The failure to make a will can result in problems such as this one or more simple, but personal problems. Who gets the heirloom jewelry? Did mother intend some prize pieces of furniture go to a particular child or grandchild? Had someone been promised family photographs or portraits? Were there charitable donations which the deceased woman would have wanted to make?

The disruptive potential of these "loaded" situations are more likely to arise with women than with men. Most men draw up their wills looking only at the financial implications of who gets what assets. Women, on the other hand, may have much stronger feelings about objects which they own and cherish and which they wish to go to particular people. This is not necessarily because they are more sentimental than men; it's rather that these objects may be their only possessions.

Sometimes you may want to divide personal assets equally among people you care about but don't want to do the job yourself. Suppose you have two daughters and a number of possessions to be distributed. You can get one daughter to divide them into two groups, giving the other daughter first choice—a variation of the "I cut, you choose" ritual of childhood. Or you can simply tell your executors to flip a coin to give first choice, and each chooses in turn. Or you can let each choose what she wants and let the executor decide who gets what in the event that both choose the same item. Details of how the distribution is to be made, if you don't leave specific items to specific heirs, should be spelled out in the will for the executor.

The point is that without a will there is no way to ensure that your assets will go where you want them to go. You may "trust" somebody to do as you desire, but if your wishes are not explicitly put down in writing, you'll not be certain what will happen. And as most lawyers will tell you, more bitter family arguments after the death of a parent are incited by the division of assets (where the division is not clearly provided for) than over any other issue. You should also remember that a fair division should take place if you want to leave a united family. However, the decision of what is fair doesn't always mean a split of equal monetary value. You may want to explain in your will why you left "more" to one child than to another, which may simply reflect your children's economic status.

The will is also a vehicle through which you can reduce taxes on your estate. Under the Internal Revenue Code there are many provisions which defer or occasionally eliminate taxes if property is left to a particular person (say a spouse) or organization (such as a charity). If no will is left, any tax benefits which result from the distribution will be purely accidental. So you can look at drawing a will as a major tax planning and tax minimization technique, unless, of course, you consider funding government activities as being a worthy charitable endeavor.

Making Your Will: It's An Exercise in Pleasing Yourself

Besides the division of assets, the will is designed to do a number of other things, all of which relate to the final wishes of the person making it. For many women who have lived in the shadow of men, this is the ultimate opportunity to make their wishes known without fear of challenge.

The will appoints executors or trustees to oversee the testator's final wishes. The appointed person(s) have an obligation to assemble all the assets, pay debts and distribute the property to the heirs. Your choice of an executor is extremely important, since the executor has significant obligations. Married people often choose their spouses, widows often turn to children, unmarried people turn to relatives or friends. Aside from personal connections, you can appoint a professional organization such as a trust company. From your point of view, the key is that you choose somebody you trust and who is able to do the job. You can "mix and match," using a relative perhaps, along with your lawyer or your accountant. You should consult anybody you are considering as an executor before you name them to be sure they will accept. (But they may change their minds later or they may predecease you, so you should also name alternative executors.)

The executors also have the legal obligation to make funeral arrangements. Contrary to popular belief, it makes little sense to put your desires about your funeral in your will. The will may be opened and read only after your have already been buried. You should, if you care, give burial or other instructions while you are alive.

Guardians For Children

If you have minor children, you should name a guardian for the children in your will. This is extremely important even if you are married, since you must provide for the possibility that both you and your husband might die together in an accident. It becomes absolutely crucial if you are a single parent. It should be noted, however, that the guardianship clause is not binding. That is, a court of law can override your wishes if it thinks the children will be better off with somebody other than whoever you name.

In one case we know of, a single parent named her sister as guardian of her daughter. She also placed a long clause in her will explaining why she chose her sister rather than the child's father who, in the normal course of events, would have a strong case for custody. As she explained to us, this was the only chance she would have to state unequivocally why she felt her child was better off not being with her natural father. This was an important fact, since she had information about the child's father which the sister did not have and which might be crucial to a court's decision if there were a fight over custody.

One of the most important features which you can provide for in your will is a trust. Basically, you can leave the property in trust for somebody but set out the terms under which they get the assets. The executors will likely be the trustees as well. Here are some examples of how useful a trust can be.

The most common, perhaps, is to leave all assets in trust for your husband (or anybody else you might wish to benefit). The terms might be that the annual income be distributed to him but upon his death, the assets go to your children. This would ensure that more money is available for his support while he lives but would still go to your children. Or you might say that while he has the income for life, if he remarries, the assets immediately are to be transferred to your children. This type of plan does not save taxes but does often offer peace of mind to the person making the will.

A single parent might create a trust which is designed to ensure that her children are financially secure in the event of her death. For example, you might set up a trust which holds all the assets you have at the time of your death. The trustees could be instructed to pay out the income of the trust to the guardian of the children to pay for their support. You'd then require that when the child or children reach a certain age, perhaps 25, the trust will be terminated and the remaining assets given directly to the children. You might also insert a clause which would allow the trustees to advance some of the capital of the trust to the children at an earlier age if in their (the trustees') view, additional funds are needed for the children's education. (Where a clause such as this is used, it becomes desirable that at least one of the trustees have a close relationship with the children to be able to assess whether transferring capital is desirable.) Realistically speaking, if you are going to appoint a friend or relative as guardian for your children, you really should take steps to ensure that the guardian has access to funds from the estate to support the children.

If you don't have sufficient assets, you might take out an insurance policy which would be payable to your estate, with the proceeds used to fund the trust you set up under your will. (See the previous chapter, "Life Insurance".)

You can also use trusts to ensure that older dependents will be cared for if you predecease them. A daughter who feels an obligation to support aged parents might, for example, set up a trust under her will which specifies that her parents receive income for so long as they live and only after they die will the assets of the estate be transferred to any other heirs.

The point of creating a trust under a will is that it can be used to set terms and conditions of a gift, can give benefits to one person for a fixed period of time and then benefits to another person or can be used to delay the transfer of assets to heirs until such time as they are able to handle the bequest on their own.

Assets Which Are Not Transferred by Will

While the will can be used to transfer most assets, it is subject to a number of limitations. For example, in all states, spouses have obligations which cannot be avoided by death. If your husband dies and leaves all his property to his brothers and nothing to you, you can apply to the courts to get a share of his assets, thus overriding his will. The same will be true if he does not leave *adequate* assets to you. The law as to what you are entitled to varies from state to state and may also be subject to the discretion of the court. But many statutes give the surviving spouse, generally speaking, a one-third to one-half interest in the estate after various expenses are paid when the other spouse dies.

Conversely, if you decide that you don't want to leave any property to your husband, perhaps because he is financially well-off, and wish to leave all you own to your children, speak to a lawyer. While you may not be able to do quite such a total exclusion, there may be ways under state law that you can limit what is left to your husband without a later challenge to your will by your husband.

If you own property *in joint ownership* with anybody (and that would normally be with a spouse) upon the death of one, the other automatically gets the whole property. For example, if your home is registered jointly and your husband dies, you automatically own the home. He cannot leave his interest in the house to somebody else. This form of ownership is often used with the family home, bank accounts, and vacation property. Joint ownership may raise problems in nonmatrimonial situations. The most common situation is where two people have been cohabiting for an extended period of time and where they have each contributed to the purchase of the property. You might want to consult a lawyer in a case like this since it is possible to dissolve unilaterally what is known as "joint tenancies" and substitute "tenancies in common." Where property is owned in this latter fashion, each of the owners has a right to leave his or her share to a third party in a will. Generally speaking, joint ownership with a spouse in a solid marriage is quite acceptable; joint ownership with nonspouses carries dangers. Suppose, for example, you and your live-in have bought a house, with each of you making an equal contribution. If the house is registered jointly and you die, *he* will get the house and you will not be able to transfer your interest under your will to somebody else. If the beneficiary under your will is your partner, this may not be a problem. But if the interest in the house is your main asset and you want to make a bequest to somebody other than your partner, holding the house in joint tenancy strips you of the opportunity.

As we saw in the chapter on insurance, if you name an individual as beneficiary under an insurance policy, the proceeds of the policy go directly to that individual. But you can name your estate as a beneficiary, which means that the proceeds of the policy will be distributed under your will. Many women who carry insurance to meet the needs of those dependent upon them, especially children, have the insurance payable to their estates and then, under their wills, set up trusts for the children using the insurance proceeds. In this way, they can ensure that the insurance money is used for the support of the children while they are young, with the balance going to them when they are old enough to handle it themselves. If you make a gift of property before your death, the property will not pass under your will. Many women, especially older ones, will give particular pieces of furniture or jewelry to children or others while they are alive to ensure their wishes are carried out, rather than relying on their executors. This offers the benefit of having the pleasure of seeing the enjoyment the recipient gets from the gift, and may allow you to cancel insurance policies which you have covering the gifted property. Gifts of under $10,000 may be made free of tax—that is, the recipient does not need to pay tax on the amount received.

If you have the right to a pension, you may find that when you started to be covered, you indicated who gets anything which might be available after you died. In such a situation, the pension would not be covered by your will. Many lawyers, however, suggest confirming the heir in a will, just to be on the safe side.

Differences in Wills

Wills normally will be very different, depending upon one's matrimonial and parental status, one's age and one's assets. A single woman, for example, who has few assets will likely have a relatively straightforward will making outright distributions of her assets to family members, friends or charities. If she is in a close relationship with another person, whether male or female, and wishes to leave assets to that person, great care should be taken to ensure that the gift is clearly spelled out. Many wills are challenged by family members who are "offended" by a gift to a close friend, especially if the gift suggests or confirms a lesbian relationship. Even in a heterosexual relationship, the idea that property (however modest in value) is to be left to "a stranger" may bring out the worst in familial greed. As we pointed out in the insurance chapter, if you want to provide for a "secret" gift to somebody, it may be better to make the person a beneficiary under an insurance policy rather than a beneficiary under your will.

When you want to benefit friends but have modest assets, you might consider unusual bequests. One single women we know drew a will which named her three best friends as executors. The instructions were that she was to be cremated and that as soon as was feasible, the three executors were to personally travel to the Greek Islands to scatter her ashes in the Aegean. The money from the estate paid for a "forced" vacation which none of the executors might otherwise have taken or could have afforded.

Married women in a secure relationship are likely to draw their wills "in tandem" with their husbands. These are often "reciprocal" wills, with each leaving everything to the other, with each of their assets going to the children (if any) should they die at the same time. Joint will-making is recommended and desirable from an estate planning point of view to help minimize taxes. But doing wills in this manner does not mean that the wills have to be identical. If you want to make a charitable contribution, leave specific pieces of property to friends or children, *don't be browbeaten into stifling your own desires.* You may even choose other executors, though normally such wills will name the other spouse as at least one of the executors. It is important that the spouses discuss and agree upon who is to be named guardian of any minor children. (Most good wills take into account the possibility of joint deaths and take steps to avoid passing property to a spouse who is already deceased.)

Even if you are making a will in tandem with your husband, remember that you too are the lawyer's client. Feel free to talk with him or her alone if you want to make certain that your express desires are carried out. It is bad practice for a lawyer to take will instructions without having spoken to the client (say where the husband tells his lawyer what his wife "wants" in her will) and you should not feel obliged to sign a will which does not specifically reflect your own wishes.

Single parents, of course, have significantly different problems. For them, issues relating to the support of their children will be paramount and almost every will should contain a trust dealing with the assets to be held for the children. Again, remember that a detailed guardianship clause may be important, especially if there are reasons why the other natural parent should not have custody.

Older women who are widows will have significantly different will problems than other women. Very often they will have substantial assets and children who are grown. They may have more involvements with charities which they wish to benefit, may be thinking in terms of benefitting grandchildren rather than children, and may have some hard decisions to make when it comes to dividing assets equally among children or taking into account each child's financial position before making a division.

How To Make A Will

A good will represents one of the best bargains available from any lawyer. This is because the fees charged for drawing a will seldom represent anywhere near the time involved in doing the work. (But the lawyers are not being charitable; they hope to recoup the foregone income by doing work for your estate after you have died.) A will is one of the cheapest legal documents you can get. The cost may be as low as $200 and only more complex wills should cost in excess of $1,000. (But if you are involved in significant tax or estate planning in addition to having a will drawn, the costs will escalate.) Almost any lawyer will be able to draw a will for you. If you are going to use a trust company as an executor, it will normally arrange for the will to be drawn, perhaps at only nominal or no cost. There are some very intricate technical rules necessary to execute a valid will (including such things as who the witnesses are and where on the paper the document is signed). But in addition, a good will covers all the loose ends. For example, if you plan to leave money to your daughter, what happens if she dies before you? Does it make any difference if she dies before you and is married? Does it make any difference if she dies before you and has a child?

Suppose you have three children. One has one child, one has two children and one has three children. If you leave property to your grandchildren, do you leave each of them one-sixth or do the children of each of your children get one-third, resulting in some grandchildren getting substantially more than others?

If you leave your prized tea service to an old friend, do you want her heirs to get it if she dies before you? If not, you'd best be sure that she gets it only if she is alive when you die; if she predeceases you, the will should direct it to go to somebody else or provide that it simply form part of your estate, to be dealt with in a similar way as other assets which are not specifically bequeathed.

These types of questions (along with dozens of others) are those which a good will deals with and which a lawyer should pose to you in getting your instructions. Hundreds of wills are contested by heirs (or would-be heirs) every year because poor drafting left the wishes of the testator unclear. Having a lawyer does not guarantee you get a great will, but not having one almost ensures you'll have an inadequate one.

You can, in some states, do a will in your own handwriting and it may end up being valid. This is known as a *holograph will*. Other people go to a stationery store and buy preprinted wills. Both these types of wills are almost always inadequate. (A famous law professor used to tell his students that lawyers made much more money litigating home-made wills than they could ever make drawing wills themselves.)

Most state bar associations will, if you ask, give you the names of local lawyers who have expressed an interest in drawing wills if you don't know a lawyer yourself. But it is almost certain that friends, professional advisers, your bank manager or insurance agent will be able to steer you to a competent person for a will.

Conclusion

As we said at the outset, every woman should have a will. The will is your last chance to speak out about what you want in this world without fear of contradiction. If you don't take the opportunity, anything you own will ultimately be distributed arbitrarily, either by order of the state, by family members, or by friends.

The will also is the tool to ensure that you meet your obligations as you interpret them, offering as much protection as possible to those you care about, and helping to ensure that acrimony does not follow your passing because of uncertainty as to what you wanted. (The most self-seeking justification for survivors doing what *they* want is that mother would have wanted it this way. If you spell it out in a will, there can be little doubt as to what you want.)

A lot of women try to rationalize away not having a will by arguing that they have nothing. The truth of the matter is that making a will can be a traumatic and difficult exercise, but it is one that forces a woman to carefully consider her position in the world and her relationships with her family and with society as a whole. Will-making requires the setting of priorities, the consideration of possible future developments, and a clear-headed assessment of economic status. If nothing else, a woman who makes a will comes out of the experience with her consciousness raised about where she stands in her world.

14

Parent Care: The Child as Adult

The last chapters focused on issues facing women as parents.
But whether or not we choose to have children of our own,
we were all children ourselves once, and for daughters especially the ties with our parents, our mothers in particular, seem
to strengthen, not weaken over time.

While today the extended family of a generation or two ago
has become the exception rather than the norm, people are
living longer today than ever before. And while their health and
finances are both likely to be better than in years gone by, it is
an inescapable fact of life that at some stage most children will
have to come to grips with taking care of their parents—either
directly or by proxy. According to a 1989 report from the Older
Women's League (OWL), women today, on average, spend
seventeen years of their lives caring for children and eighteen
years assisting aged parents. The problems of giving parental
care tend to be exacerbated because recent generations have
been so much more mobile and it is not uncommon for older
parents to have all or most of their children living in another
city or country.

Daughters and daughters-in-law have typically been the
caregivers for the elderly (who are usually women, and more
often than not women in need either of financial help or physical care, or both).

Providing Financial Support the Smart Way

Marlene, a Los Angeles woman, who is a successful jewelry
designer, declared that she could no longer foster the "myth"

that her parents were self-sufficient, and she spoke with some bitterness of the costs to her. "I just can't go on paying a bill for them here and another bill there. They're living in their own apartment now, but the rent is going up by nearly $150 a month, and I am always making 'loans' to them that they'll never be able to repay. I don't resent helping them-they've had hard lives and they're my parents after all-but I have been laying out about $500 a month for them over the last few years, and I can't even take it off my taxes. I'm thinking of trying to buy them an apartment in a senior citizens' community because I can't afford to care for them here. I don't want to move them away from their friends, but I can't manage the continual financial drain, frankly".

There are a lot of possible solutions for Marlene and for others like her who are faced with mounting costs for the care of, or the subsidization of, elderly parents. The applicability of any particular approach will depend to a great extent on how much income or property you have available, and on what your parents own. Their health is a major factor, since you may have to consider whether they need full-time care at home, residence in a nursing home or maybe merely a new place to live—an apartment perhaps—where the burden of day-to-day maintenance is less than it was in the old family residence. There are many different types of residential arrangements for the elderly, and finding the appropriate one for your parent will require time and energy. There is a range of facilities with some offering 24 hour-a-day supervision to those which are merely custodial with health care not necessarily needed. In general, coverage by Medicare and private health insurance is very limited. Coverage by Medicaid, the state health program, may be available but the extent of coverage and conditions for coverage are subject to the specific state laws where your parent resides.

• If your parents have very little income, make certain that they are receiving their full entitlement under the various government programs for elderly citizens. Usually county or other local offices for the aging can help you identify these benefits and programs.

• If your parents need extensive care, either help at home or care in a nursing home because of physical or mental disabilities, the costs of such care are deductible as medical expenses. If their income is so low that they cannot use these deductions, there are special rules under the Internal Revenue Code which would allow you to claim the expenses.

• If you are hiring somebody full-time to care for a parent, remember that you may be responsible for such things as withholding amounts for tax purposes, and making contributions to Unemployment Tax for the employee. Discuss the situation with the person you hire and, if you have any doubts, with an accountant. If you fail to make the required deductions, you may be liable to make the payments later on, with interest and even penalties. (But in some cases, especially if the person is a trained nurse, he or she may be an "independent contractor" for tax purposes, which means that you have no liabilities to withhold taxes or make statutory contributions.)

• If your parents own their own home, consider having them sell it and move into an apartment or nursing home. The amount received on the sale may be tax free. If one parent is over the age of 55, up to $125,000 in gain on sale may be excluded from taxation. As a part of estate planning it should be considered that if the home has appreciated substantially and represents your parents' principal asset, upon death there will be no taxes on the gain, and when the home is subsequently sold, more money will be realized than if sold during your parent's life. Therefore, other strategies for providing funds should be pursued, with reimbursement made from the estate.

• If, like Marlene in our example, you have been giving money to your parents on a regular basis, think about formalizing the arrangement. If you have some money on hand, you might consider setting up a trust for the benefit of your parents, with the money returning to you when they die. The benefit of proceeding this way is that the income is taxable to them, not to you.

Let's say that Marlene was a high-income earner, paying tax at the 28% marginal tax rate. If she was giving her mother $500 a month or $6,000 a year, she'd have to earn $8,333 just to meet this cost. But if she had $75,000 in investments earning 9%, this money is generating $6,750. If she put the $75,000 in trust for her mother, the $6,750 would be taxable to Mom, who presumably would pay little or no tax. Obviously, this option is only available to adult children who have substantial savings.

• A more reasonable option for most people is this; if you are giving money to a parent, think about making it a loan. You could, for example, arrange for your mother or father to sign a promissory note for the money you advance, requiring that the loan be paid on demand. (If you do not place a reasonable rate of interest on the loan, the Internal Revenue Service will deem it to bear interest anyway, and if in fact the interest is not paid, the Internal Revenue Service will deem that interest as income to you and a gift by you to your parents.) You would not, of course, ask that the loan be repaid while your parent is alive, but it would be a debt of the estate. Thus, your loans would be repaid out of any money in the estate before there is any division of the balance of the property among the heirs. (In many cases, parental pride would mean that this sort of "business-like" arrangement would be welcomed.)

• It may make financial sense to put a parent in a condominium. One woman we know was faced with this problem when the apartment her 90-year-old mother was living in went "condo." The mother was offered the chance to buy her apartment at what was an attractive price, but didn't have the money. Her daughter loaned her the money for the purchase. Her mother then rewrote her will leaving the apartment to her daughter. When Mom dies, the profit on the apartment will be tax free, and since the daughter will get title, she should end up with a tidy profit, while at the same time having ensured her mother a more comfortable old age.

• If you are the sole support of your parents, you can claim them as dependents for income tax purposes, though the deduction in 1990 is only $2,000. However, the income of the parent cannot exceed $2,000 in the year, exclusive of tax-exempt and Social Security income. (If more than one child is contributing to the financial support and a deduction is available, they can, by written agreement, allocate the exemption to one child in any given year.)

• If you have a business and your parent is physically able to help, consider putting him or her on the payroll. One success-ful woman writer had her mother retyping manuscripts and was able to pay her enough (and help her retain a sense of self-worth) to make her financially self-sufficient when her pension benefits were taken into account. If this option is of interest, remember that to deduct the payments from your business income, the payments must be "reasonable in the circumstances."

Generally speaking, smart strategies for parent care involve ensuring that a parent gets the maximum entitlement under any government plans, planning financial arrangements to allow you to claim deductions for income tax purposes, and making payments to a parent which are either deductible by you or which have been diverted from your own pretax income.

This is an area where good professional advice from an accountant is useful. There are often large sums at stake (espe-cially where continuing medical care is needed) and very often the costs you'll incur once to make the appropriate arrangement will produce savings for as long as you continue to have a financial obligation.

Negotiating Parent Care With Siblings or a Spouse

In addition to maximizing whatever tax advantages are open to you, you should consider, if you are married, working out an agreement with your husband about the care of elderly relatives. (This is an important, though often overlooked subject which can be dealt with in a premarital, marital or cohabitation agreement.) This is, in some ways, more painful than, though just as crucial as, your arrangements for child care, with two important differences. First, the children grow up and need less and less direct care; seniors become more dependent through time, and anticipating even more responsibilities on your part is neither pleasant nor easy. Second, the children usually belong to both of you jointly; with parents there are sometimes divided loyalties.

One woman wanted her husband to put aside some of his considerable savings so that they could present her parents with the downpayment on the small co-op apartment they'd wanted. She finally figured out, after some covert conversations with the bank manager, that they could buy the apartment as an investment, and her parents could have the use of it. She then felt better about asking this "favor" for her side of the family— she felt her husband would respond more to the motive of self-interest than to charity. Which brings us right back to an issue raised in Chapter 7, "Women, Men and Marriage": divorce court would likely find that the woman had a stake in the husband's savings, because she had been his support system while he was stashing the money away. After a divorce settlement, she could buy her parents whatever she wanted with the money. Sometimes seeing how the family assets would be split in a divorce settlement can help a woman understand what she's entitled to while she's married.

It's often in the care of parents that conflicts arise between siblings also, especially if those giving the direct care are not those making financial contributions. If you have a sibling with much more money than you, you can suggest the tax benefits of his or her contributing more toward the parent's care. If you are the primary caregiver for a parent or in-law, keep track of your expenses, including relief time during which you hire help, and try to sit down with your siblings or others who could share the care, and tell them, as one woman did, that "I am doing all the work here. It makes no sense for me to bankrupt myself in the bargain. I'm glad to have a chance to help Mama when she needs me, but all this takes a toll on my life, and even on my own family too. *I expect that, since I'm taking most of the emotional burden off your shoulders, you will take at least the financial one off mine.*" Do remember that from a tax point of view, the giving of financial support can benefit any family member who contributes, and that deductions can be shared if everybody agrees.

While the subject may be touchy, it is also fair to raise the issue of compensation from a parent's estate. In one case, the three siblings (two brothers and a sister) agreed that all of the modest assets of their elderly mother should go to the sister who was the only one living in the same city as the mother and who was shouldering almost all the responsibilities. Since none of them wanted to speak to their mother about her will (though such a discussion might have been appropriate) they entered into an agreement under which each of the brothers agreed to give to their sister any property or other assets which their mother left to them. That way she was certain to receive whatever financial benefits were available from the estate without her mother possibly thinking that the care she was receiving from her daughter was in return for potential financial gain.

Head and Heart, Especially Head

The idea of worrying about financial benefits when considering what is best for your parents may seem crass. But as with so many other areas we run into in our lives, there are smart ways to handle things and inept ways. *Making smart financial arrangements will never detract from the benefits which you may want to confer on a parent*; indeed, you may well find that doing things the savvy way will make more money available, both for you and your parent.

On the other hand, don't fall into the age-old trap of shouldering the full physical, emotional, and financial burden of parental care. And if you find a fair part of your financial resources are going to support your elderly mother, take that as a cautionary lesson. In the 1990's, there should be no impediments to your taking steps to ensure your own financial comfort when you get older. After all, that's a big part of what this whole book is about. Your mother may not have had the chance to prepare for her old age, which is why you have part of the care burden now. Your goal is to try to ensure that your children are not faced with the same problems a couple of decades hence that you have today.

15

Modern Problems

Not all the "modern problems" discussed in this chapter are brand new, of course. Step-families have been around since Biblical times at least, and babies have been around for even longer. What's new here—and what makes the area feel so uncharted even though the family dynamics may sound familiar in some cases—is that women are discovering that they must protect themselves, financially and emotionally, against a host of unexpected possibilities.

The problems here, where technology and new social values appear to have constructed a brave new world, require a kind of pioneer quality in the women who have few role models on which to base their choices, and fewer legal guidelines. This chapter may be read as a first lesson in the various self-defense techniques necessary if you're going to live happily ever after in a world that looks less and less like Camelot every day.

Motherhood Without Marriage

Although it's certainly not a new phenomenon, the number of women who are choosing to have and raise children alone (whether they become pregnant by chance and choose not to link their lives to the father of the child, or because they become pregnant deliberately, conceiving a child with a man they have no intention of marrying) has grown markedly since the 1960's. These situations present women with different sets of financial choices and decisions than the more typical two-parent family faces.

First, if the father is known, comes the question of whether or not he will assume some of the responsibility for the prenatal care of the mother and the future childrearing expenses. If the mother and father are both minors, the prospective grandparents may become involved in sharing the bills.

If you are an adult woman who has consciously decided to have a baby by yourself (we obviously don't mean parthenogenesis here), you also should consider having a contract with the father. At the very least, we suggest getting him to admit to legal parenthood (with his name on the birth certificate as father) for the sake of the child, who will want to know about him later in life in case there are hereditary medical problems or other issues. Additionally, this man could promise to assume some of the financial responsibility for the child (though you may not at any time live together) if you should die or become incapacitated. He might agree to this even though marriage is not in the future plans, and even though he may not be part of the day-to-day financial plan. Beware, however, that with such a contract in writing he might later have claims for custody.

If you are pregnant by your married lover, however, chances are he will not want to sign such a contract lest it be made public. You could arrange for him to take out a life insurance policy naming you or the child as beneficiaries. No one would know about it until he dies, and then only the insurance company would know of any connection.

If what you are seeking is not a pot of gold many years hence but some financial support in those difficult and costly years when your child is young, remember that you can always suggest to the father of the child at the beginning of the pregnancy (if both of you agree that you have a relationship you want to maintain and if you both view the child as a desired outcome of that relationship) that he make a lump-sum payment as a guarantee of sorts that, even if he should opt out of the relationship with you, the child will be provided for.

One woman insisted on such a payment (which the man made with the help of a bank loan) before she was out of the first trimester of her pregnancy—telling him that she had no intention of carrying the pregnancy to term if he was unwilling to make this commitment. She feared (with some justification) that his initial enthusiasm for parenthood might fade when faced with reality. While she was willing to be an unmarried parent raising the child alone, she was not willing to do it in poverty.

If you are pregnant by artificial insemination and unmarried, you will likely have no claim on the man who donated the sperm. In fact, in many cases the donor sperm in sperm banks is mixed, to prevent just such situations as claims of paternity. And usually the sperm donor will have no rights as a parent; many states presume that the sperm donor is anonymous, and have laws saying that if the sperm donor is not the mother's husband he has no "right, obligation or interest" in the child.

Lesbian Mothers

Some unmarried women who choose to become pregnant with donor sperm are lesbians in a long-term monogamous union who have decided to raise a child conceived thus by one of them. The financial issues here have to do with adoption and naming the nonbiological parent as one of the custodial parents of the baby. (Obviously, having a truly anonymous biological father eliminates the horrible custody battles many lesbian mothers have come to fear.)

Courts have become increasingly positive about permitting lesbian couples to adopt children who are not the offspring of either partner, so by extension the adoption of a child born to one's partner should in theory present little problem to the authorities. In theory. But with what one writer calls "malestream" thinking, some U.S. courts have tried to press a known sperm donor into service as the father of the child, assuming that a heterosexual pair of parents is "in the best interest of the child." If you find yourself in this situation, consider consulting women's lobbying groups such as the National Organization for Women to obtain listings of lawyers and others who are experienced in handling lesbian adoption or custody cases.

One lesbian mother, Ann, (whose child is the offspring of an earlier, heterosexual marriage) says that she is worried about leaving custody of her daughter to her ex-husband should she die, since he has never been a particularly responsible parent. Now in her teens, the daughter has, in fact, been raised by her mother and her mother's longtime lover, Beth. Ann wants to make Beth the girl's legal guardian, and has taken out a special insurance policy to make sure that Beth will have enough money to support the girl if Ann should die before her daughter turns 21. But since the girl's father is alive and well, Ann knows that she can't count on the courts to honor the provision in her will that Beth will be the girl's legal guardian until she reaches 18. What this woman has done is to ask her ex-husband to sign an agreement that he will not seek custody of their daughter if Ann (the custodial parent) dies, and stating that he approves of the way Ann and Beth have raised her.

Another financial concern for lesbians is whether or not a nontraditional family will be accepted as a social unit for the purposes of assigning benefits such as health insurance. In one case, a library worker who lives with her lover and the lover's two children has petitioned that the children should qualify as her dependents, just as stepchildren in a marriage would. The case suggests that redefining our intimate relationships will have economic implications nationwide.

Stepfamilies

The problems of stepfamilies aren't all so modern; for different reasons, these situations were common in the past. Women died young in childbirth, causing widowers with children to remarry quickly so that the children could be cared for. Enter the wicked stepmother, partly a creature of fiction and partly, no doubt, a genuine response to a remarriage that was likely a union of mutual economic advantage rather than a love match.

The situation may be familiar, but the ways in which stepfamilies deal with their problems (and in fact the nature of the problems themselves) have changed considerably in present-day life, largely because remarriages among people with dependent children nowadays usually take place in the wake of divorce, rather than after the death of a spouse; this means that there are far more characters in the cast than the fairy tales took account of. Today, one of the thorniest problems for remarried couples and their "blended" families is how to allocate resources fairly. The usual scenario is that the divorced woman keeps her own kids, whereas the divorced man, if he remarries, may find himself living with a woman who has custody of her children from her previous marriage.

The chances that a divorced man will remarry rise as he ages, whereas the chance of a divorced woman remarrying diminish as she gets older. And since men tend to marry women younger than themselves, a familiar set-up would have one man supporting (or contributing to the support of) two families—that of his first wife, who has not remarried, and a new family consisting of himself, a second wife, possibly her children from a previous marriage (who would tend to be younger than his from his previous marriage, and hence need support for longer) and any children they may have together.

Since alimony typically ends with remarriage, this man's second wife (who may or may not choose or need to stay home with her young children) likely has no support for herself, although her children from the first marriage may be receiving child support. Now: who gets what under a system that one author has called "economic polygamy"?

The fairest method or distribution in the blended family would be for all the parents involved to sit down and negotiate how much is available for what expenses, and to determine priorities: which child goes to camp? gets tennis lessons? can buy an expensive ski outfit? However, it's difficult enough to conduct these negotiations in a less complete family structure; with limited resources and hard feelings in abundance, it's the rare family that succeeds in conducting such a meeting without acrimony.

A more practical method would be for the family generating the money payments—in this case the remarried husband and his second wife—to draw up a budget that includes his support payments to his first wife and their children, and present the budget periodically to all the parties involved. This may help neutralize the perpetual suspicion that one family unit is living well at the expense of the other.

For the woman who is a stepparent in this situation, and who does not have children of her own but does have a job, there's plenty of room for resentment over the fact that she may be, as one woman put it, "supporting him so that he can support her and their kids." True. This is, for better or for worse, the nature of the implicit or explicit contract this remarried couple has entered into.

For more details on the internal workings of the blended family, turn to Chapter 7, "Women, Men and Marriage," and read over the section on remarriage. You can also take a look at Chapter 9, "Divorce: Coaching in Battlefront Tactics and Strategies."

Where real pain, and not just financial resentment, enters the scene is when the support obligations owed to children of a previous marriage make the possibility of having children in this marriage no more than a pipe dream. The new wife's income is often needed just to keep the operation afloat, and unless she is earning so much that she could afford to pay child care out of her own salary and still help with the family's expenses, it's unlikely that there would be enough surplus for the new family to be able to "afford" a child. This is to say nothing of the fact that many men in this situation feel so burdened by the financial obligations to the ex-wife and the first set of children (even if the feeling is unjustified) that the very thought of starting all over with babies makes them cringe.

Clearly, if you are considering entering a marriage which is not a first for your fiance, especially if he has support obligations which will continue for some time, make your desire to have a child very clear to him, along with an accurate picture of the financial realities the two of you will be sharing. Make sure that the positions are understood by both of you before the marriage. You may disagree but decide to marry anyway. And your feelings may change in the course of the marriage, just as they sometimes do with couples who don't have the added complications of stepparenting. But at least you will know what you're facing from the beginning.

Here's a warning based on the experiences of many women we've spoken to: it's unlikely that he will be able to force or coerce you into having a baby you don't want. But if you're the one who wants a child and he doesn't, don't labor under the misapprehension that you'll be able to change his mind. Not one woman we know has ever been able to persuade her husband to agree to more children than he wanted, and none went ahead on their own to have babies without their husband's full consent, realistically fearing the economic consequences within the family, or the dissolution of the marriage and the ensuing drop in economic status that single motherhood would bring.

In a remarriage with children involved, it's a very good idea to spell out financial responsibilities contractually in advance. Even if you only get to the discussion stage, with no formal lawyer-produced contract, just clarifying what you want is useful. (Even if the agreement is handwritten on the dinner napkin it's a help in reminding you later of what you once did agree to jointly.)

The New Reproductive Technologies

Some aspects of motherhood in the late 20th century are startlingly new. Women today are coping with new reproductive technologies that make the complexities of stepparenting seem simple by comparison. In theory, it's now possible for a child to have up to five parents—a sperm donor, an egg donor, a "surrogate" in whose womb the pregnancy gestates, and the couple who raise the child.

Artificial Insemination

Earlier, we mentioned artificial insemination by donor (sometimes called "alternative fertilization" by women justifiably concerned about the male focus of the procedure's more common name) in the context of single parenthood. This means of conception poses no particular financial or legal problems if both partners in a married couple are fertile and the husband's sperm is used to impregnate the wife because the couple has mechanical problems with conception. The complications set in with the term donor—someone whose sperm is used without there being a relationship between him and the woman being impregnated. This is a choice some women make because their sexual orientation makes intercourse with a male repugnant or inappropriate. Other women choose to become pregnant by this means because there is no suitable male in their lives with whom they want to conceive a child. Still others choose artificial insemination because they want no connection to or later claim on (or from) the father of their child—not always so simple to arrange, as we'll see in a moment. These choices are certainly not the norm today, but they do represent new frontiers in the relations of women and men, new definitions of parenthood, and new attitudes toward family and motherhood. They also present certain still-unresolved complications for the women who have children in these unconventional ways.

One question that women must face relates to support obligations between father and child. The identity of the biological mother is certain, according to all traditional legal interpretations. Establishing paternity—legally, if not biologically—becomes complicated. If the mother is married, and her husband has consented to the artificial insemination, the husband is presumed to be the father in every legal sense, and children thus conceived have the same legal standing as if the husband's sperm had impregnated the wife. Some jurisdictions are suggesting that the sperm donor be held liable as the child's legal father if the husband has not consented to the procedure, recommending that child-maintenance obligations and inheritance rights of a nonconsenting husband should be the same as if the child were the product of an adulterous relationship!

If the donor sperm is mixed, then obviously no one man is responsible for paternity. There may be papers or releases to sign when you use a sperm bank or anonymous donor sperm which release the donor from any claim you might later want to make against him. (Keep in mind that in this era of the AIDS epidemic, you and your child may run serious health risks if the sperm bank has not adequately screened for AIDS in its donors. You may not want to sign because of some future risk.) If you are single and the sperm donor is a man you know, and you are convinced that you do not want him involved in the life of the child, you should consider asking him to sign a contract which absolves him of all responsibility but also removes his right to visitation, custody, or even support from you at a later date.

Keep in mind here that artificial insemination by donor is usually considered a medical procedure, and as such is covered by many insurance schemes. But women's self-help groups all across the continent have tried since the early 1970's to deprofessionalize this process, believing that the relatively simple injection of sperm into the uterus should be a conception choice available to women who want to make their own decisions (outside of a medical or legal content) about who the father of their child will be, just as they would have this freedom of choice were they to conceive in the more usual fashion.

In some jurisdictions, having a child together can be considered proof of your being a cohabiting couple, which carries with it certain automatic obligations of mutual support by law. Check this with a competent local lawyer, so that any contract you sign acknowledging that the sperm of your friend, Harry, was used for insemination resulting in your pregnancy won't get you declared as legal "cohabitants" and entangle you even further with each other.

And what if your husband is a sperm donor? Some men, for reasons ranging from macho to charitable urges, donate their sperm to sperm banks. As we've mentioned, sperm in these banks may be mixed to dilute any genetic abnormalities and to prevent just the kind of emotional entanglements all parties usually wish to avoid. In other cases, sperm banks, with the donor's consent, will label the sperm, so that the child at age 18 can have access to the name of his or her biological father.

If this is the case when your husband donates his sperm, make sure that the sperm bank has agreed that they will not allow any claims against him (if, say, an abnormal child is born, or if the mother later in life needs child support). Remember that the laws are changing rapidly in this area, and what might be inconceivable now (no puns intended) might constitute a valid legal claim 18 or 20 years from now. Any claims of paternity could, of course, reduce the amount that you and/or your children by this man would receive from his estate upon his death, and could also cause him to have to pay child support while he's alive.

"Surrogate" Mothers

In its complexity and its wrenching away from biological and social roles most of us had thought were immutable, the practice of women bearing children for other people is a far cry from the "rented breasts" of the wet nurse. It's more akin to the role division envisaged in Margaret Atwood's futuristic novel, *The Handmaid's Tale.*

It is obviously beyond the scope of this book to examine the moral, ethical and psychological issues of what is shaping up to be a notable battle over women's (mothers') rights. Here we will touch only on the economic problems and consequences of the practice, which involves the artificial insemination of a woman with sperm from a man who is married to someone else, and who intends, with his wife, to take possession at birth of the baby thus conceived.

Even the nomenclature of this increasingly common reproductive method discriminates against the woman who will bear the child. In fact, she is not the "surrogate" mother, but the real, or biological mother. It is the woman who will raise the child with the biological father who is the surrogate here. But the nomenclature points up an important aspect of the issue— namely that the biological mother has been underrepresented in discussions of the matter. She is usually (if not always) a woman who has considerably less money than the couple for whom she is bearing the child; for many, the fee paid for services (approximately $10,000 in most cases) is at least part of the inducement.

The economic interests of the so-called surrogate mother are also rarely debated. Among the health risks in pregnancy are high blood pressure, diabetes, permanent weight gain, hair loss, back problems, complications from anesthesia, postpartum depression, to name only a few. Is $10,000 nearly enough compensation for a procedure that may have lifelong physical and psychological consequences for the woman and her family?

Hardly, when one considers the enormous damages awarded by the courts for other kinds of workplace-related injuries. Yet this disparity is rarely noticed. The surrogate mothers have been judged, in the press and in the popular mind.

The focus has been on her motivation; one newspaper headline states, "Surrogate mothers: legislators haven't decided whether they're humanitarians or prostitutes." There has never been much analysis of the narcissism of the male sperm donor who, with his wife, is not motivated to adopt a child, thereby giving an already living child a needed and presumably loving home. Instead he is driven by a need to recreate a part of himself in this child. With the focus of the debate on his needs and her motivation, rather than the reverse, even the economic needs of the biological mother are neglected.

The issue, by the way, has created some strange bedfellows (all puns intended). Right-wing women and feminists have both decried the practice; both factions see it as based on the surrogate mother's lower economic status. In response to a comment that "surrogate motherhood" was a "free arrangement among equals," a woman representing a Catholic Archdiocese replies, "Ah, but I doubt they will be equal. First of all, the fact that the woman needs the money, and the man who's giving it doesn't, means that already there is a class situation involved. In many cultures women became concubines because they were in a position of needing money . . ."

Those who support the practice defend it ideologically as women's ultimate control over their own bodies (thus unnecessarily tangling it up with abortion); they fail to notice the coercive power of financial need that has always led to women's selling their bodies. It's interesting to note in this regard that when interviewed, many of the women who have borne children for other couples specifically mention wanting to have the money to provide for their "own" children.

In the publicized surrogate situations, all of which have been arranged by lawyers (who have profited from being the go-betweens), there has been a legal contract drawn up before the insemination even begins stipulating that the mother will relinquish the baby after birth. It usually also states that she will make no further claims upon the father after her agreed-upon fee and expenses are paid. In the much-publicized New Jersey trial over custody of "Baby M," in which the surrogate mother decided that she wanted to keep the child, the courts decided that the sperm donor and his wife would have custody.

If you are considering becoming the mother of a baby you will ultimately give up, no one but you can know your emotions and those of the people around you. Any other children you already have, for instance, will have to be told what's going on with Mommy's pregnancy, and that there will be no new baby in the house when it's all over. This is not an insignificant consideration. Most of the women chosen as surrogates do have other children. Having already borne healthy children makes one more qualified as a potential surrogate—and several surrogate mothers interviewed in the spate of publicity that followed the Baby M case mentioned that their other children needed psychological treatment in the wake of this pregnancy. Many young children fear the loss of their parents, or fear that if they misbehave they'll be sent away. That at the end of this pregnancy Mommy gave away the baby is living proof that, in fact, a parent can send away a child forever. The consequences of surrogate motherhood, in emotional terms, may cost you—not just for the psychological help to deal with the children's and your own sense of loss (much of which is likely reimbursable under your medical plan) but in extra help at home, lost time from work, and so on. If you work, your co-workers will have to be informed about the pregnancy. Remember, too, when calculating the financial benefits to yourself, to subtract whatever unreimbursed time you will be away from work.

All the consequences of surrogacy cannot be predicted, naturally. What you can predict, however, is that your body will change, as it does with each pregnancy, and that this is a situation not without physical risk to you, even if you've had other, perfectly healthy pregnancies. You should be properly indemnified against such risks from the outset. A cash payment for your services, plus payment for the obstetrician and hospital where you deliver, may not be enough. You might try to have the family for whom you are having the child pay for health insurance for you and your other children (if any) for the rest of your life. At the moment you may be covered under an insurance plan, but while this coverage may someday cease, the physical consequences of the pregnancy may not.

In the contract you draw up with the couple, remember that everything is negotiable. You can legitimately ask for a term life insurance policy on both of them, with you as the beneficiary, in case either or both of them dies before the child is born or before they legally adopt it; if this were to happen, you might unexpectedly find yourself raising the child, and might not be in a financial position to do so. You can also stipulate that there be a period after the birth when you have the right to change your mind and keep the child, as is the case in many standard adoption agreements. In this case, the biological father would likely have no obligation to support you or the child, but you could try to make that a stipulation also. However, if you really do want to act only as the "surrogate" mother, pressing for a back-out clause might indicate to the couple or their lawyer that you aren't a strongly motivated candidate.

You might also want it in writing that neither of the "social" parents will ever be able to have any claim on you for support— so that, for instance, if the couple divorces or the mother dies the father cannot petition you to help maintain the child.

If you are the infertile mother contemplating asking another woman to bear your child with her genes and those of your husband, be aware of those cases in which the birth mother has been reluctant to give up the child, or has even tried to kidnap the child later. It's obviously very important to have adequate legal counsel in drawing up any contracts between you and your husband and the surrogate mother, but it's also important to consider some kind of contract between you and your husband establishing your rights as the potential adoptive mother of the baby in case he decides he wants sole custody and/or you divorce before the baby is born.

A further note of warning to all parties involved: genetic screening is a very important procedure to insist upon during pregnancy. Since this is an "optional" pregnancy, so to speak, and since there might be horrible legal battles if the couple decides not to accept a child who is disabled or suffering from a genetic disease, provisions for all such matters should be built into the initial contract. This must include a commitment on all sides for genetic screening, and either an agreement that the pregnancy will be terminated if the fetus is unhealthy or that the "social" parents will raise the child no matter what. Covering the costs of the screening and abortion, if necessary, should be the responsibility of the couple.

If much of what we have discussed in this chapter sounds like genetic engineering at its most frightening, remember that these birth technologies are already on the scene. Nobody is being forced to utilize them just because they are available. But if you are even remotely considering involving yourself in these alternative forms of conception and childrearing, you must be alert to some of the financial danger zones on the road ahead as women come face to face with modern problems which have no real precedents.

BIBLIOGRAPHY

The American Woman 1990-91: A Status Report, edited by Sara E. Ris for the Women's Research and Education Institute (New York: W.W. Norton, 1990).

Blumstein, Philip and Pepper Schwartz. *American Couples: Money, Work, Sex* (New York, William Morrow, 1983).

Cohen, Leah. *Small Expectations: Society's Betrayal of Older Women* (Toronto: McClelland and Stewart, 1984).

Corea, Gena. *The Mother Machine: Reproductive Technologies from Artificial Insemination to Artificial Wombs* (New York: Harper and Row, 1985).

Ehrenreich, Barbara. *The Hearts of Men: American Dreams and the Flight from Commitment* (Garden City: NY, Doubleday, 1983).

Gelpi, Barbara C., Nancy C.M. Hartsock, Clare C. Novak and Myrna H. Strober, eds. *Women and Poverty* (Chicago: University of Chicago Press, 1986).

Gilligan, Carol. *In a Different Voice: Psychological Theory and Women's Development* (Cambridge: Harvard University Press, 1982).

Harwood, Norma. *A Woman's Legal Guide to Separation and Divorce in All 50 States* (New York: Charles Scribner & Sons, 1985).

Lewin, Elizabeth S. *Financial Fitness Through Divorce: A Guide to the Financial Realities of Divorce* (New York: Facts on File, 1987).

Kressel, Kenneth. *The Process of Divorce: How Professionals and Couples Negotiate Settlements* (New York: Basic Books, 1985).

Landsberg, Michele. *Women and Children First* (Markham, Ontario: Penguin, 1982).

Mayleas, Davidyne. *Rewedded Bliss: Love, Alimony, Incest, ex-Spouses, and Other Domestic Blessings* (New York: Basic Books, 1977).

Matthaei, Julie A. *An Economic History of Women in America: Women's Work: The Sexual Division of Labor, and the Development of Capitalism* (New York: Schocken Books, 1982).

Pogrebin, Letty Cottin. *Getting Yours: How to Make the System Work for the Working Woman* (New York: Avon, 1975).

Rapoport, Robert and Rhona Rapoport, eds. *Working Couples* (New York: Harper & Row, 1978).

Scanzoni, John H. *Sex Roles, Life Styles, and Childbearing: Changing Patterns in Marriage and the Family* (New York: The Free Press, 1975).

Scanzoni, John. *Sex Roles, Women's Work, and Marital Conflict* (Toronto: Lexington Books, 1978).

Sheresky, Norman and Marya Mannes. *Uncoupling: The Art of Coming Apart. A Guide to Sane Divorce* (New York: Viking, 1972).

Thomas, Edwin J. *Marital Communication and Decision Making: Analysis, Assessment, and Change* (New York: The Free Press, 1977).

Weitzman, Lenore J. *The Divorce Revolution: The Unexpected Social and Economic Consequences for Women and Children in America* (New York: The Free Press, 1985).

——*The Marriage Contract: Spouses, Lovers and the Law* (New York: The Free Press, 1981).

Index